HOLY
ROOT
HOLY
BRANCHES

*Christian Preaching
from the Old Testament*

Ronald J. Allen &
John C. Holbert

ABINGDON PRESS
Nashville

HOLY ROOT, HOLY BRANCHES:
CHRISTIAN PREACHING FROM THE OLD TESTAMENT

Copyright © 1995 by Abingdon Press

This book is printed on recycled, acid-free paper.

Scripture translations are those of the author John C. Holbert.

Library of Congress Cataloging-in-Publication Data

Allen, Ronald J. (Ronald James), 1949-
  Holy root, holy branches: Christian preaching from the
Old Testament / Ronald J. Allen & John C. Holbert.
    p.   cm.
  Includes bibliographical references and index.
    ISBN 0-687-07470-3 (alk. paper)
    1. Bible. O.T.—Homiletical use. 2. Bible O.T. Criticism interpretation, etc. I. Holbert,
John C.   II. Title
BS1191.5.A44 1995   94-48376
251–dc20   CIP

95 96 97 98 99 00 01 02 03 04—10 9 8 7 6 5 4 3 2 1

MANUFACTURED IN THE UNITED STATES OF AMERICA

CONTENTS

To
William Joseph Ambrose Power
Teacher without Peer
Preacher of Grace
Colleague of Conviction
Great Lover of the First Testament
and
Charles L. Rice
Priest, Poet, Pioneer
Living Parable
Who has taught Generations
to Preach with a
Holy Eros

PREFACE

Reverend Pat reads the text for Christmas Eve.
The people walking in darkness
have seen a great light;
those living in a land of deep darkness—
light has shined on them.
You have multiplied the nation,
you have increased its joy;
they rejoice before you
with the joy of the harvest,
as people celebrate when they divide plunder.
Surely, the yoke of their burden,
and the bar across their shoulders,
you have broken as on the day of Midian.
Now all the shoes of the soldiers
and the garments caked in blood
shall be burned as fuel for the fire.
For a child shall be born for us,
a son given to us;
authority rests on his
shoulders;
and he is named
Wonderful Counselor, Mighty God,
Everlasting Father, Prince of Peace.
That authority shall grow,
that peace shall not end
for the throne of David and his kingdom
so that it will be established and upheld
with justice and righteousness
now and forevermore.
The zeal of the LORD of hosts
will do this. (Isa. 9:2-7)

...ac sighs with relief. Such a familiar text will yield an easy movement from text to sermon.

With the help of commentaries and Bible dictionaries, Pat remembers that Isaiah 1–39 was spoken a little more than one hundred years prior to the Exile. Isaiah warns Judah that injustice and unfaithfulness are bringing God's judgment upon the community. However, Isaiah 9:2-7 assures the people that, beyond punishment, God intends restoration. God will send an ideal ruler who will inaugurate a new age of peace with justice.

Pat clears up the meanings of words that are obscure to today's listeners. For example, Pat examines the phrase "bar across their shoulders." Pat interprets Christ as the ideal ruler who ends oppression and establishes justice.

But questions begin to haunt the developing sermon. Pat believes that God's love is unconditional and universal. Yet vv. 4-5 imply that God sanctions violence toward Judah's enemies (see Judg. 7:1–8:21). How can Pat reconcile this ruthlessness with unconditional, unreserved divine love?

One of the cardinal principles of biblical exegesis is respect for the integrity of the text. Isaiah did not envision Christ as the ideal ruler. Is it fair, then, to speak of Christ in that role?

Further, Jesus has not brought fullness of justice into every sphere of life. Injustice is as prevalent in our day as in Isaiah's. Does church tell the truth?

In any event, Christians speak of Christ returning a second time to complete redemption. But if the church is like the synagogue—still waiting for the world to be fully conformed to divine purposes—then what are the real differences between Judaism and Christianity?

Holy Root, Holy Branches takes up a few such questions. On the one hand, the church affirms that the Old Testament is part of our canon. On the other hand, the church is not Jewish. This handbook offers a perspective within which Christian preachers can relate to the Hebrew Bible so as to honor the integrity of the text and our Christian identity.

The issues enveloping this subject have long and complicated histories. The bibliography is immense. In a brief book, we cannot set each subject in the full body of discussion that would be optimum.

Our modest hope is to provide a hermeneutical model that will l. preachers make Christian sense of Old Testament passages. Along the way we hope to leave enough clues for research hounds to chase their way into the library shelves for a fuller range of conversation. Toward this end, a (slightly) annotated bibliography is the benediction on the book.

The book begins with a cursory review of how the Old Testament has been understood in the church (chapter 1). The chapter reveals that our judgment is for a hermeneutic of critical solidarity between the church and the Hebrew scriptures as the preferred pattern of relationship. Chapter 2 specifies the content of this relationship by presenting a general hermeneutical model for how the church might view the Old Testament today. We suggest that the Hebrew Bible contains paradigms of God's presence and purposes. These paradigms can alert the church to the presence and purposes of God today. In chapter 3, the book offers a step-by-step method for interpreting specific texts from this perspective for preaching. Chapter 4 demonstrates this interpretive process through the exegesis of several texts from representative parts of the Hebrew Bible. This chapter also models how the preacher might follow a theological theme across the Old Testament; we trace four themes through several authors and paradigms: creation, *hesed* (steadfast love), the deliverance of Israel, and justice. We offer exegeses of texts and draw out possible directions for sermons from the texts. In chapter 5, the book pauses over preaching on texts that raise vexing theological and moral issues. For instance, what does the preacher do with a text from the Old Testament that seems hopelessly out of date or that appears to sanction vindictiveness or violence? Chapter 6 extends the discussion to how the Old Testament appears in the New. As a part of this conversation, we turn to the relationship of the two testaments in the Revised Common Lectionary. Chapter 7 includes five sermons that provide examples of how the book's approach might make its way, fully developed, into the pulpit. The sermons illustrate several of the main topics of the book. The first sermon deals with a text (Exodus 1) that can straightforwardly inform the contemporary church. The second sermon focuses on a passage that appears to be antiquarian (levirate marriage) while the third takes up a text that raises a theological difficulty (Ecclesiastes). The fourth sermon is based on a text from the New Testament that cites Old Testament passages and that raises the difficult problem of early Christian criticism of Judaism (Acts 7, Stephen's last words). The final sermon develops around texts from each testament (Jeremiah and Luke) that come together in a lectionary. The book concludes with a representative bibliography.

We reserve the term *we* to refer to the authors. We avoid the generic, homiletical *we*. All translations of the Hebrew Bible were made by John Holbert.

Before turning to the body of the book itself, we remark on the titles Old and New Testament and on how we designate the two parts of the Bible in this book. Irenaeus (who wrote about 180 C.E.), Tertullian (who wrote about 200 C.E.) and Origen (who wrote about 220 C.E.) were among the first to use the designations testaments, New Testament and Old Testament.[1] These have been standard Christian designations for about eighteen hundred years.

However, a small but growing number of Christians today are uneasy with the terms *Old* and *New* Testaments. We are among them. In North American culture, old often denotes that which is archaic, devalued, and worn-out, while new implies freshness and vitality. (This contrasts with the people of antiquity who tended to honor and value that which was old).[2] Such associations distance the Christian community from the First Testament (and its people as well as their sacred texts, practices, and institutions) and contribute to anti-Judaism and ultimately to anti-Semitism. Consequently, we sometimes refer to the first thirty-nine books of the Bible as the Old Testament, the Hebrew Bible, the Hebrew Scriptures, the First Testament (with the last twenty-seven books being the Second Testament), or the older testament.

Yet, the revised vocabulary is problematic. The terms *Hebrew Bible* and *Hebrew Scriptures* are imprecise because these materials also existed in Greek (and some in Aramaic). The early church largely regarded the Septuagint—the translation of the Hebrew Bible into Greek—as authoritative.[3] Further, today's congregation could understand First Testament to mean first place as superior to runner-up second place. Some today speak of the First Testament as the Prime Testament, but this practice seems to stamp the literature to come from the quill of the early church as the Secondary Testament. Some Jewish people speak of their Bible as Tanakh (an acronym derived from the Hebrew words for law, prophets, and writings—*torah, nebeeim, ketubim*). But at this moment in history, Tanakh seems too distant for the typical Christian community.

Some Christians call the last twenty-seven books the Greek Bible or the Apostolic Writings or the Christian Bible. However, the Greek Bible includes the Septuagint. And the phrase Apostolic Writings could refer to other writings from the first century outside the canon, such as the Gospel of Peter. In any event, few biblical scholars trained in the historical-critical and literary-critical methods think that the twelve original apostles wrote documents that bear their names. Other modes of speech, such as Canonical Jewish Literature or Canonical Apostolic Literature, are too cumbersome.[4] Further, Catholics and Protestants have slightly different views on the contents of the First Testament; Roman Catholics include several books as sacred scripture that Protestants omit from the canon.[5] And the term Christian Bible should embrace not just the last twenty-seven books but the whole canon.

As an alternative, Christians can often speak simply of the Bible. After all, the whole Bible is canonical. Or, Christians can speak of the specific book or author under consideration.

In these respects, the language of the church is unsettled. None of these patterns of speaking is quite satisfactory. We continue to use the term Old Testament. After all, these words have been in the church's vocabulary for eighteen centuries. A part of the church's theological task is to come to a critical understanding of its speech. But we also use the new terms as a way of helping the church explore their adequacy. We hope to err on the side of love and justice with minimal loss to Christianity and Judaism.

John Holbert had primary responsibility for chapters 1, 2, and 4. Ronald Allen took the lead in developing chapters 3, 5, and 6. We have both contributed sermons to chapter 7. To be candid, the two authors do not agree on every detail of interpretation. But these

differences are quite minor. We are bound together in such common-
ality of spirit that we are glad to send forth this work under our
common names.

We thank our respective spouses, children, colleagues, deans, presi-
dents, and boards of trustees. J. Gerald Janzen and Marti Steussy were
particularly helpful. The book is strengthened considerably by the
trenchant but friendly comments of Paul Franklyn, an editor at
Abingdon Press, and by two readers of the manuscript—Paul Scott
Wilson and Gordon Matties. Joyce Krauser provided exemplary edi-
torial guidance. Although these readers and consultants do not endorse all the lines of thought developed in this book, they helped us
refine and articulate our viewpoints. All of these people helped create
an environment in which two authors, separated by an ocean during
this writing (John Holbert was on research leave in England), could
find communion of spirit, intellect, religious vision, and commitment.

CHAPTER ONE

Holbert

THE OLD TESTAMENT IN THE CHRISTIAN PULPIT

Westminster Abbey. A misty, cold London Sunday in February. As usual, a small congregation has gathered in the great Gothic structure, their number dwarfed by the vaulting stone arches. Three preachers schooled in the Old Testament sit snuggly in the choir stalls awaiting the sermon. The preacher of the day is a well-known professor of New Testament. His stated subject is the Ten Commandments, and he announces that he will this morning deal with all ten. A too audible groan escapes one of the three preachers in the choir stall. We know we may be in for a long morning. The preacher begins with an erudite gallop through the familiar ten, pausing here and there to call to our attention something that has special significance "as we approach the final years of the twentieth century."

But then the preacher announces that since the time of Jesus, the old ten commandments are largely superfluous anyway; one need hardly wrangle any longer over the subtleties of their meaning. "With the coming of Jesus, all things have become new, and all old law has been forever thrown in the shadow of his glory." Thus the preacher sweeps away from the congregation any reason to be interested in the First Testament.

But why does this preacher upset us? We have heard many similar comments from Christian preachers. Through the centuries, expositors of the Hebrew Bible have implied or stated a similar conviction: the Hebrew Bible, the Old Testament, was just that: old, antiquated, past its day, slightly (or greatly) embarrassing to Christians. Like some eccentric uncle, it was occasionally suffered and allowed to offer a story once in a while, however strange the story sometimes was. But the rest of the Bible family, namely the New Testament, smiled politely and sent the uncle packing for the greater part of the year. It remains true that the majority of sermons preached from Christian pulpits each Sunday have little or no interest in the First Testament.

But is this patronizing approach to the Christian Old Testament a problem at all? Should preachers be concerned about the silence or diminution or outright disparagement of the Hebrew Bible in Christian pulpits? We think there is indeed a problem to be addressed. The Hebrew Bible is the Holy Root from which grow the Holy Branches of the New Testament. We affirm that both testaments are holy, equally revelatory, equally expressive of the presence, purpose, and power of the God of Israel and Jesus of Nazareth. It is necessary to preach the Hebrew Bible in Christian pulpits if the fuller music of God is to be heard in the church.

There is little controversial about either of those claims. Nearly every Christian preacher would join the chorus of Amen for each. *Of course* the New Testament sprang from the Old. *Of course* one should preach from the First Testament. But if the Amen resounds, why is there such a relative silence of the First Testament from Christian pulpits?[1] And why is the First Testament heard by many clergy and laity as a mysterious and dangerous jumble of amoral or immoral stories, incomprehensible poems, meaningless genealogies, and legalistic demands? Just what is the place of the First Testament in the Christian pulpit?

In an essentially practical handbook such as this one, we cannot offer detailed theoretical analysis of the relationship between the two testaments.[2] In this first chapter, we present the four main approaches to the appropriation of the First Testament in the Christian pulpit. We can only suggest the main features of these different approaches and concisely illustrate how each might interpret actual texts.[3] It will become clear that we favor the general outline of one of these approaches (a hermeneutic of critical solidarity) over the others.

THE GHOST OF MARCION

Marcion is often vilified as one of the most dangerous heretics that the second-century church produced. Unfortunately we possess not a single original work from this astonishing and bold thinker; we have only quotations from two of his most ardent enemies, Tertullian and Epiphanius. But we can be certain that his teaching, offered primarily in Rome between 137 and 144 C.E., created a firestorm of controversy. The storm was so intense that more than one hundred years after he died, his furious opponents dug up his bones and burned them in an apparent attempt to annihilate him even beyond death itself.

In simple terms, Marcion rejected the First Testament as the work of a different and alien God who was not the God of the New Testament. The God of Jesus of Nazareth, and the God of Jesus' most sublime apostle Paul, could have had nothing to do with the monstrous collection of writings that the early church had looked to as its scriptural guide.

Hence, Marcion rejected the First Testament *en toto* from his emerging canon. For him, Paul represented the loftiest portrayal of the gospel of Christ, so he retained the four best-known letters of the apostle: Romans, Galatians, and First and Second Corinthians. In the light of his interpretation of the Pauline Gospel, Marcion kept a much edited Gospel of Luke alone among the four Gospels.

Ironically, Marcion's ideas led to the formation of the Christian canon as we know it. He forced the church to consider the question of what should be in the canon and what should not. The church ultimately and wisely voted against Marcion and said that it could not live without the First Testament. Nonetheless, Marcion's ghost still haunts the Christian pulpit.[4]

1. *Law and Gospel*.[5] Contemporary preachers sometimes characterize the First Testament as a book of law. These preachers speak of the whole of the First Testament as law. In this scheme, law is essentially negative and stands in contrast to the New Testament, which is gospel. At best, law functions to heighten the listeners' awareness of sin. The law brings us to our knees before God and causes us desperately to feel the need of the gospel. Alas, law can only condemn; it cannot release us from the iron grip of sin. Law can impose God's demands but it provides no empowerment to fulfill them. At worst, law functions in the fashion of works righteousness. One must obey the law in order to gain a place in God's favor. But a

person cannot fulfill the law's demands. Christians, then, pity the poor Jewish people who anxiously try to fulfill the impossible, legalistic demands of the law but who can never do enough to satisfy God or their own consciences.

By contrast, Christians are freed from the law and its stern legalisms. Indeed, law belongs to an old dispensation that has passed away. Christ graciously does for us what law cannot: Christ fulfills the law and renders law unnecessary. The era of law has been superseded by the era of grace.[6]

This way of thinking runs aground on several shoals. It misuses the term *law* from the point of view of the classification of the literature of the First Testament. The Hebrew Bible and later Jewish interpreters seldom speak of the whole of the First Testament as law. Typically, law describes the first five (or six) books of the Bible, with the designations prophets and writings applying to the other contents.

But this caricature is mistaken even when the notion of law is taken more expansively. The English *law* usually renders the Hebrew *torah*. This latter word does not mean law in a simple juridical sense. Its basic meaning is teaching or instruction or even revelation. When the traditions of Judaism speak of God's gift of the Torah to Moses, they mean far more than a code book of legal and illegal behavior. Torah is the full revelation of God and includes stories, sayings, events, and psalms. In parts of the contemporary Jewish world, the rabbi's sermon constitutes an extension of Torah. Torah is not locked in a book but is living instruction in the gifts and calls of God.

To be sure, the Bible does contain specific regulations. These, however, are not intended as rules that must be obeyed in order to earn God's favor. Quite the contrary, the heart of Judaism is God's unmerited favor toward Israel. God graciously called Abraham and Sarah, showed kindness toward their descendants, delivered the Israelites from bondage, gave them the promised land, and continued to shepherd them. God gave them the statutes, commandments, and ordinances (to use the deuteronomic formulation) in order to teach Israel how to live in the light of God's steadfast love.[7] Obedience is not for the purpose of earning divine love but is a way of responding to it. "The law becomes the instrument of a mutual relationship in which faith responds to love. This transforms the law into a form for expressing gratitude."[8] To obey is to say, "Thank you for your continuous love. I am going to do my best to live up to the identity that is bestowed on me through the covenant." The first thirty-nine books of the Protestant Bible are thus every bit as much gospel as the last twenty-seven. Indeed, both testaments contain law and gospel.[9]

Consider this analogy. When our children were small, we had a rule (a law) that they could play in the front yard only as far as a certain bush. To go any farther would be too close to the street. This law was born of love for the children. Their obedience did not earn our love, but insofar as their obedience contributed to the preservation of their lives, it enhanced the possibilities for a long and loving relationship.

At first glance, the denigration of the First Testament and its religion appears to be sanctioned by texts in the Second Testament. Many passages in the New Testament appear to portray Jewish people and Judaism (or aspects of them) in the negative, legalistic caricature that Marcion inspires. However, a growing body of scholarship on the Second Testament is coming to believe that this portrait is less pervasive than formerly believed.[10] For instance, many interpreters now conclude that Paul did not mean to disparage the law or Judaism as such.[11] While scholars have not reached a unified viewpoint on how, specifically, to interpret Paul's relationship to Judaism and the law, many scholars take the position that Paul objected not to law as such but to asking Gentiles to adopt Jewish customs. In this reconstruction, Paul regards law as the appropriate Jewish response to God's grace as revealed through the central texts and traditions of the Jewish tradition. The Gentile knowledge of God comes through Jesus Christ; hence, Gentiles do not follow the Jewish statutes, commandments, and ordinances. Nonetheless, the spirit and overarching concern of Judaism and Christianity are very similar. In the next chapters, we contend that specific texts of Judaism, including commandments, statutes, and ordinances, can be very instructive for Christians when handled with hermeneutical sensitivity.

Many scholars of the literature of the early church think that negative statements about Judaism and the law appearing in the

Gospels and other parts of the Second Testament are often caricatures. Rather than accurately portraying Judaism as a religion of deadly legalism, these messages are polemical.[12] This theory is particularly true of material in the four Gospels. By the time of the writing of these books, synagogue and church had come into tension and conflict. As the conflict intensified, the church criticized traditional Judaism in order to put down its opponents in the synagogue and justify its own faith and practice. Admittedly, some (perhaps even most) of this caustic controversy took place as an intra-Jewish debate between Jewish people who identified with the church (Christian Jews) and Jewish people who did not identify with the church. In the process, the church misrepresented the main body of Jewish theology and practice. In a technical sense, such literature may not be anti-Jewish but may be intramural controversy. Still it is important for Christian preachers today to recognize that caustic comments about Jewish people, practices, and institutions in the Gospels frequently result from the polemical relationship from within Judaism and between Judaism and the nascent church. The texts of the early church, written in the heat of debate, do not give the contemporary preacher license to dismiss the First Testament with a wave of the hand as outmoded law. The circumstances of the origins of these polemics ought to cause the contemporary congregation to reexamine the Hebrew Bible and its positive contributions to Christian faith and practice. The circumstances of origin could also urge the preacher to help the congregation to repent of the harm caused to Jewish people and to our own souls by these distortions.

2. *The External/Internal Dichotomy.* This way of misusing the First Testament is perhaps more subtle than the law/gospel approach but is no less common.[13] It occurs when a preacher states or implies that the Hebrew Bible deals only with external matters, with the flesh, with the things of this world. In contrast, the New Testament is concerned with things of the spirit, the ways of God, and internal spirituality.

In John 4:23, for instance, Jesus tells the woman at the well that the time is coming when "true worshipers will worship the Father in spirit and truth." According to popular Christian interpretation, he implies by this phrase that arguments about the place of worship,

20

whether Jerusalem or Samaria, are beside the point. Thus, when this phrase is quoted, it is made to sound as if the centuries-long discussion about the proper place for worship of God is foolish. Jesus has come to ask the right questions, the spiritual questions, as opposed to the earthly ones so common to the Hebrew Bible and the Jews.

To the contrary, the First Testament, centuries before Jesus, addressed the issue of the internal motivation for worship and the proper place for worship. Note, for instance, Solomon's dedicatory address and prayer at the opening of the Temple (1 Kings 8), or Isaiah's exploration of right worship in chapter 58, or Jeremiah's scathing temple sermon in his chapter 7. Each of these examples, spanning several centuries, addresses both internal and external concerns, both proper worship and the optimum location for it.

The dichotomy of an external Jewish view and internal Christian perspective is simply a false reductionism. To be sure, the prophets of Israel sometimes complained that the community departed from its internal spirituality and obedience and let its life become nothing more than cultic externals. This prophetic critique is possible precisely because the religion of Israel had a vital internal core. In any case, the early church suffered from similar troubles. First John, for example, calls the church to rediscover its true (internal) faith so that it may practice love for one another.

3. *Ethnic Israel vs. Universal Church.* This misappropriation may be the most blatant ideology of the three that we are discussing under the heading of Marcionism, and perhaps the most dangerous in its implications. It goes as follows: in the Hebrew Bible, one finds only concern for the fate and future of the chosen people of God, Israel, and its heirs, the Jewish people.[14] By contrast, in the New Testament, one finds God's clear concern for all people, not just for Israel. The Hebrew Bible is thus hopelessly ethnic in its interests, finally unconcerned with the Gentiles, all non-Jews, who are either suffered to live alongside the Jewish people or who are wantonly destroyed by the God of the Jews in order to make a special home for the chosen. But in the New Testament, Jesus addresses all people, Jew and Gentile, with the message of salvation. So does Paul, as the famous text Galatians 3:28 makes plain: "all of you are one in Christ Jesus."

21

Israel is regularly described in the First Testament as God's chosen people. Exodus 19:3-6 is a classic description. However, we emphasize that far more space is given in the Hebrew Bible to the purpose of the choice rather than to the fact of it. Let us mention only three important texts.

In Genesis 12:1-3, a crucial hinge pericope uniting the primeval history with the traditions of the patriarchs and matriarchs, Abram is chosen by God for a specific task: "in you all the families of the earth shall be blessed." At the heart of the call of Israel lies a missionary task. The choice of God is not for privilege at the expense of others; it is precisely for the blessing of others.[15]

This same dynamic may be discovered in Amos. The prophet speaks in a towering rage against the social and economic evils of eighth-century Israel. But his specific charges are based on the same theological foundations that underlay the call of Abram. "You only of all the families of the earth have I known, therefore, I will punish you for all your iniquities" (Amos 3:2). Israel has failed to live up to the responsibility of God's call and is thus reduced to the status of any other nation; its great experience of exodus from Egypt is one among many that God regularly performs—even for Israel's enemies (9:7)!

That great prophet of the Exile, the unknown Second Isaiah, pondered the role of Israel as it was about to return to the ancient land from its exile in Babylon. Echoing Abram and Amos, he announces, "I will give you as a light to the nations, that my salvation may reach the end of the earth" (49:6*b*).

These passages, among many others, announce with clarity that the Hebrew Bible is not characterized by a narrow ethnicity. Quite the contrary, its central theological concerns lie with Israel's unique responsibility to be a light and a blessing in the world.

Thus, the ghost of Marcion is alive and haunting contemporary Christian pulpits. But this ghost of rejection needs to be exorcised. His Sabbath wailings and howlings are far more than minor disturbances. They are profound misunderstandings of the First Testament with dangerous consequences for all those who claim allegiance to these books as sacred.

2 A HALFHEARTED OLD TESTAMENT

Not all contemporary Christians wish to reject the Old Testament in the neo-Marcionite ways we describe. Many damn it with the faintest of praise. We call this general approach the halfhearted First Testament. In this somewhat facetious metaphor, we indicate that many preachers see some positive values in it but basically still regard the Hebrew Bible as inferior to the New Testament and to Christianity. But unlike the neo-Marcionites, they wish to retain the Hebrew Bible as a sort of foil for the New Testament. For them, the First Testament at best foreshadows, prefigures, or prophesies the coming of Christ, the New Testament, and Christianity. The Hebrew Bible and its people, events, practices, and institutions are incomplete and unfulfilled. Three such schemes are especially prominent.

1. *Allegory.* Allegory is an ancient mode of interpretation. In fact, there are a few allegories in the First Testament itself (e.g., Ecclesiastes 12, Ezekiel 15–17, 23). Most simply stated, allegory is an interpretive mode in which a particular meaning is read into a text from outside the text itself. The surface meaning of a text is passed over in favor of a meaning assigned to the text from some external presupposition.[16] The elements of the text are often read as symbols of true meaning that can be discerned only when one has the key to the meaning of the symbols.

Early rabbinic interpreters often used allegory as they read sacred texts. For example, the sensuous love poetry of the Song of Songs was often allegorized, most simply as a story describing the love that God (the male lover) had for Israel (the female lover). A similar allegorical move with the Song was made in the early church, where the figures represented Christ and the church. Allegorical methods of interpretation were an exceedingly popular interpretive move in Judaism and Christianity for well over fifteen hundred years.

The use of allegory is based on a significant theological belief about the Scriptures. God had spoken in the Scripture. But God's truths were obscure in the text and must be brought to the surface by allegorical interpretation.

Recent scholarship has resurfaced the possibility of using allegorical interpretation of the Bible when the allegorical reading is restrained and controlled.[17] Nonetheless, there are obvious dangers in the allegorical interpretation of texts that are not true allegories. There is little check on the imagination of the interpreter. In the worst instances, anything goes. One is limited only by one's fantasy and ingenuity.

One can still hear traces of allegorical readings today. They tend to be more subtle than the cruder forms of allegory from the past. Two examples spring to mind. In Genesis 22, the harrowing story of Abraham's near sacrifice of his son Isaac is still allegorized into a hidden figure of the crucifixion. Abraham is God willing to sacrifice the beloved son; it is done on a hill; the son carries his own wood for the sacrifice. The reader will have no difficulty supplying the other details. In the Genesis account of the story of Joseph (Genesis 37–50), Joseph's life is allegorized into another account of the life of Jesus. Joseph has divine power (his dream interpretation). He rises to great power. He offers salvation to his family even though they had rejected him.

Each of these readings attempts to salvage the accounts for Christian use. But they effectively assume that the texts themselves have no intrinsic worth. The texts must be transformed into something else, if they are to be rescued for Christianity. Although these readings appear to interpret the Hebrew Bible, in fact they do not. They merely employ the Hebrew Bible to say something other than what it wants to say.

2. *Typology.* This way of thinking has far greater attraction for the contemporary preacher, and it can be genuinely useful to the Christian preacher. In the broad sense typology finds correspondences between past events, practices, institutions, or persons and present or future ones. Of course, the First Testament itself makes use of typology. For example, Second Isaiah regards the first exodus as a type of Israel's release from the Exile (e.g., Isaiah 52:7-12). Hosea views Israel's experience in the wilderness as a type of God's faithful relationship with the people. As God communed with Israel in the wilderness, so the two will be together again (Hosea 11).

The Second Testament also employs typology. A famous example is John 3:14: "And just as Moses lifted up the serpent in the wilderness, so must the Son of Man be lifted up." In this reference to a tiny incident recorded in Numbers 21:4-9, God becomes so angry with the people's constant complaining that God sends "fiery serpents" (sometimes the word *fiery* is translated *poisonous*) to bite them to death. To assuage the plague of serpents, God tells Moses to place a fiery serpent (or an image of one?) on a pole so that all those who have been bitten may "look at it and live." The serpent pole becomes a means of life against death. The evangelist John read the story typologically. Just as the serpent pole was placed so that the bitten ones could see it and live, so Jesus—raised up on the cross—will be "seen" by those who are dying (spiritually) and may therefore live ("have eternal life").

Probably all preachers have heard and used typological exegesis. In fact, we have already used a form of it in this very chapter. In our discussion of the dangers of caricaturing the First Testament as being concerned only with an ethnic exclusivism, we encountered that at the heart of Israel's chosenness was a demand for mission to all. This universal mission was then briefly traced through Genesis, Amos, and Second Isaiah. This mission is surely a type of the universal mission of Jesus Christ as described in the New Testament. Abraham is thus a type of Jesus in his call to bless all nations. This sort of analogical typology is a fully appropriate way to employ the First Testament in Christian preaching.[18]

Even given this positive form and use of typology, however, the approach has two dangers. The first is that typological exegesis can easily drift into allegorical interpretation. This drift is especially dangerous when the details of the type are said to be directly reiterated in its counterpart type. James Barr, in fact, has argued that there can be very little methodological difference between the two, either as they were employed by ancient interpreters or as they sometimes appear in contemporary use.[19] Preachers who employ typology need carefully to avoid inappropriate allegory.[20]

The other danger is that Christian interpreters can regard the First Testament as nothing more than a prefiguration of Christ, the church, and Christian existence.[21] The First Testament and its people have no real life of their own. They are but a dim mirror made plain in the Second Testament. The Hebrew Bible is a partial type made full only in Christ and the church. This type robs the life of ancient Israel of its integrity. From this perspective, Israel did not enjoy the full blessing of God (nor did it witness to the same) but existed as a murky and unfulfilled preview of Jesus and the church. In the end, this perspective does not regard the First Testament and its people, practices, and institutions as a *real* type, but only as a passing prefiguration whose purpose has ended. While this is not a mature Jewish or Christian understanding of typology, it is nonetheless present and dangerously arrogant.

3. *Promise and Fulfillment.* We come now to a popular way of relating the two testaments. God makes a promise that is (or will be) fulfilled. This motif is sometimes referred to as *prophecy and fulfillment.* In this frame of reference, the term prophecy is used in the sense of foretelling the future. We approach this mode cautiously because (like typology) it contains a significant core of truth, yet it is complicated and can be greatly distorted.[22]

Promise plays a prominent role in the First Testament. To return to an earlier example, God promises or foretells that Abram will become a great nation. The ancestral stories of Genesis and much of the rest of the First Testament show how God makes good on this pledge. Indeed, the preachers of Israel assure later generations that a good reason for the community to trust in God is the long history of the promises God made and kept (e.g., Psalm 105). Promise and fulfillment are thus staple categories of the First Testament.

In a deep sense, Christians believe that God's promise to Abram to bless all the families of the earth comes to expression in Jesus Christ. Of course, God was blessing the Gentile peoples through the light that Israel shined in the world of antiquity. God continues to bless the nations through the presence of Israel's God in the world (would that we Gentiles were more receptive to that light!). But the church, a largely Gentile community today, has found itself freshly blessed by the God of Israel through Jesus Christ. In the best sense, the church understands itself as a community of the blessed alongside the blessed community of Israel. Yet, God's blessing of the cosmos is still incomplete. The eschaton is yet to come; it is still promise.

Our difficulty with this scheme comes not with the categories of promise and fulfillment in themselves. Indeed, these are staples of the Christian interpretation of reality. Our difficulty comes with a common Christian use of them. Many preachers functionally reduce the First Testament to promise or prophecy. In the mouths of such interpreters, the First Testament is a book of anticipation. The Hebrew Bible is said specifically to foresee the coming of Christ and the church. Indeed, a listener can receive the impression from some preachers that the Hebrew writers had preview videotapes of Jesus Christ playing on the screens of their minds as they penned their foretellings. In the worst excesses of this approach, the First Testament is merely promise unfulfilled. When the First Testament ends, its people are empty, longing, yearning for fulfillment.

This simplistic notion violates the historical and literary integrity of passages in the First Testament by reading into them a prophecy about Jesus that they were not intended to make. The significance of passages for their own times is lost.[23] More important, this oversimplified use of promise and fulfillment does not account for the entire contents of each Testament. The whole of the First Testament cannot be classified as promise, nor can the whole of the Second Testament be said to be fulfillment. There are elements of fulfillment in the former. For instance, God promises to be faithful to Israel, and God fulfills that promise. And there are elements of promise in the latter. For instance, Jesus prays for the church to be one (John 17:20-24), but after twenty centuries Jesus' prayer is still unfulfilled.

At one crucial point, passages in both the First and Second Testaments speak with a common voice. They still await the eschatological fulfillment of all God's purposes. For instance, the cosmic vision in Daniel 12:1-3 has yet to come to pass. God's promises for ultimate justice in every realm have not come to full and complete manifestation through Jesus Christ or the church. In the most anguished and profound sense, both Judaism and Christianity continue to yearn for the coming of eschatological shalom. Each community knows something of the fulfillment of God's pledges, but both communities and their testaments are partners in awaiting the final fulfillment of divine promise.

3 THE WONDERFUL WORLD OF THE OLD TESTAMENT

This third approach to the interpretation of the Hebrew Bible for Christian preaching is a fairly recent phenomenon. As we have demonstrated, there have been more than a few ways to reject or to misuse the Hebrew Bible. But recently, well-meaning preachers have begun to correct this loss in what we call "romantic" ways.

These interpreters are simply overcome with the beauty and power of the Hebrew Bible and extol its great virtues. Far be it from us to pour too much cold water on such efforts. Indeed, we cry, "May their tribe increase!" But we sound notes of caution because there are overstatements in these romantics.

In the heady discoveries to be found in the Old Testament—superb stories, powerful poetry, brilliant calls for justice—the romantics sometime forget that Christians are not Jews or reborn Israelites. Furthermore, the Hebrew Bible contains materials that are problematic for contemporary Christians. Romantics tend to overlook these difficult materials. For instance, the hardening of Pharaoh's heart is in its tradition, as are Psalms 58 and 137, as is the prophetic-induced assault of the bears on the forty-two little children in 2 Kings 2, as is God's desire to kill Moses in Exodus 4:24. No reader of the Hebrew Bible can negate these texts by drowning them in a sea of rose-colored stories and effusion about the wonders in the Hebrew Scriptures. To neglect these admittedly difficult texts (and the many others they represent) is to do no better than those who allegorize or otherwise explain away such real difficulties.

Enthusiastic immersion in the narratives and poetry of the First Testament is to be encouraged. But the energy of enthusiasm serves the pulpit best if part of it is channeled into historical, literary, and theological criticisms. These can help preachers discern whether their perception is sidetracked by naïveté when encountering a text.

4 A RELATIONSHIP OF CRITICAL SOLIDARITY

An emerging trend in biblical scholarship and preaching is to emphasize continuities between the two parts of the Bible while acknowledging differences between them.[24] These scholars and pastors attempt to avoid the hyperstress on discontinuities that we noticed in several of the approaches that we described as Marcionite or halfhearted. They also seek to avoid romanticizing the Hebrew Bible. Our proposal, which we develop in the next chapter, is located within this stream. Before turning to our perspective, we briefly consider some basic elements of this fourth approach. As we do, we note that this phenomenon is not univocal but is more an identifiable strain of preachers and teachers who have a general, common concern but whose emphases differ.

An important theological premise underlies this viewpoint: the nature and purposes of the God of Israel are essentially the same as those of the God of Jesus Christ and the church, for the God of Israel and the God of Jesus Christ are the same God.[25] Clark M. Williamson, a systematic theologian, articulates this position. "God's love is not contingent, provisional, or partial, but unqualifiedly all-inclusive and unconditional."[26] Williamson continues:

> These things we avow because we confess that all that is given to us to know of this ultimate and circumambient mystery in which we live is disclosed to us in the history of the Israel of God with the God of Israel, which history includes Jesus and Paul who are, as Barth rightly said, nothing without Israel. What is there disclosed to us is that the boundless love at the ground and end of all our being and becoming is the Holy One of Israel, the God whose command that we love God and do justice to the neighbor is grounded in having graciously made a covenant with us, a covenant contingent upon and only upon God's freely offering it to us. God freely elected Israel, freely chose Abraham and Moses, freely liberated Israel from oppression, and it is not the place of the church to put God on notice that we require this decision to be changed. This God also acted freely in Jesus Christ, self-revealing the heart of the love who is God, "a light for revelation to the Gentiles and for glory to your [God's] people Israel" (Luke 2:32).[27]

The First Testament is thus not *ad hoc,* preliminary, or secondary. It is constitutive for Christian identity.

In Schubert Ogden's provocative image, Jesus Christ re-presents God for Gentiles. God's grace, and the call to responsibility known for centuries by the Jewish community, are now known among the Gentile churches.[28] Aspects of the forms of the two religions differ, but they share a common essence. And this essence is first articulated in the Hebrew Bible.

At the same time, Christianity is not lukewarm Judaism. The two households of the one living God share the First Testament as a fountainhead of their religious lives, but each household reads it in the light of its history (and particularly in the light of its modes of biblical interpretation) since the emergence of Judaism and Christianity as distinct religious bodies. Judaism interprets its sacred scriptures from the perspective begun by the Pharisees. This movement eventually became the guiding light in Judaism in the wake of the fall of the temple. Over the course of many years, the rabbis generated the Mishnah, the Talmud, and succeeding generations of Jewish interpretation.[29]

When we turn to a Christian mode of interpreting the First Testament, Walter Harrelson and Randall Falk (the former a Christian professor of Hebrew Bible and the latter a rabbi) posit an important negative criterion. "Any Christian reading of the Hebrew Bible that does not leave the message of the Hebrew Bible *for Israel* intact is inadequate or is plainly wrong. The Bible of the Jews cannot be claimed as applicable to the world *only* in the form of Christian interpretation."[30]

On the positive side, an increasing number of Christians seek to respect the particularity of the First Testament and its people. The minister can regard Judaism as a valid religion whose adherents have full standing before God.

Christian interpreters can try to hear the First Testament without the distortions chronicled in the earlier parts of this chapter. Elizabeth Achtemeier summarizes: "After all, goes the reasoning, the Old Testament is fully as much canonical revelation as is the New, and one can therefore allow the Old Testament to stand as word of God to the people in its own right."[31]

Preachers can employ the best exegetical methods to locate the First Testament in its own historical, literary, and theological contexts. Such studies may not always lead to results and practices that are directly prescriptive for the Christian community. But they will often reveal insights for understanding God and God's relationship with the world that are directly helpful for Christians. In the process, the interpreter can honor instances of typology, prophecy, and fulfillment and other forms of interpretation that are contained within the canon itself or that can be carefully used to explain the relationship of the two testaments. In the next chapter, we take up the notion of paradigm as a way of focusing these perspectives so that the preacher can make full use of the First Testament in the Christian pulpit.[32]

CHAPTER TWO

THE OLD TESTAMENT AS PARADIGM OF GOD'S PRESENCE, PURPOSE, AND POWER

In this second chapter, we offer our own theological approach to the First Testament as a basis for preaching from it. The foundation of our approach is that the Old Testament contains paradigms of God's presence, purpose, and power (as well as paradigms of human response to the divine presence and purpose). These paradigms can be instructive for the church in their own right. The First Testament does not always need the Second to give it meaning and importance for the Christian community. To clarify how this is so, we explore the concept of paradigm.

The historian of science, Thomas Kuhn, wrote a much-quoted book, *The Structure of Scientific Revolutions*.[1] He spoke of a paradigm as "an accepted model or pattern." Kuhn is in accord with the etymology of the word in classical Greek, from which paradigm is derived. That term meant to show side by side or to represent, and it referred to a "pattern, exemplar, or model."[2] In grammar, a paradigm (for example, for the declension of nouns) may be easily replicated. In the sciences, however, a paradigm "rarely is an object for replication. Instead, like an accepted judicial decision in the common law, it is an object for further articulation and specification under the new or more stringent conditions."[3]

A paradigm is a pattern of understanding that helps make sense of data in disparate situations. It does not automatically take account of every contingency or every detail. But it provides basic principles and images that interpreters can use in specific situations to help understand those situations. Communities are often based on shared paradigms, that is, on commonly held understandings of reality. Innovations in paradigms occur when people become aware of data that a paradigm cannot explain; the data require a different paradigm to explain them.

For example, in North American culture the paradigm of parent helps explain what should (and should not) take place in the relationship of parent and child. The parent provides food, clothing, shelter, security, love, and opportunities for the child to mature and to acquire knowledge. But the paradigm does not tell the parent how to apply this vision in specific to the bed-wetting seven year old or to the gifted twelve year old or to the promiscuous sixteen year old. The parent takes the insights of the paradigm and works out how best to be a parent in each particular situation.

Insights similar to Kuhn's have emerged in science, technology, business and in theological and biblical studies.[4] James Barr contends, "Christian faith is structured upon a certain basic *model* of God." The fundamental model was "first worked out and appropriated" in the First Testament. "That model was reaffirmed, restated, and reintegrated in Jesus. Christian faith is faith which relates itself to this classic model."[5] The whole Bible, then, can awaken the community to the salvation God is bringing among us. For the whole Bible functions as a paradigm of divine activity.[6]

James Sanders asserts that the Bible reveals the paradigm of God's presence and purposes in the world. "Since the Bible comes to us cloaked in the idioms, mores, and cultural givens of the five cultural eras through which it passed to get here, we must be careful not to generalize on or absolutize any of them but try to discern in and through all the mode or modes by which our ancestors in the faith affirmed God's oneness, or integrity in their day—then take that as an inspiration and energy for going and doing likewise in our day."[7] The First Testament demonstrates God's will to effect righteousness. In Sanders's colorful speech, God worked another righteousness in Christ. The same work that is represented in creation and redemption in the First Testament is continued in Christ.[8] The full Bible, which Sanders calls the Torah-Christ story, is a paradigm that allows us to "conjugate the verbs" of divine activity in the contemporary world and to know God's "participation in our lives now and recognize a righteousness when we see one."[9]

The Old Testament is premised on an overarching paradigm (summarized below).[10] This paradigm is appropriated with particular nuances in different streams of Israel's life and thought. In the central part of this chapter, we identify the four major theological streams or trajectories within the present form of the First Testament:[11] deuteronomic, priestly, wisdom, and apocalyptic.[12] Obviously, the concerns and emphases of these trajectories sometimes overlap, but we discuss them separately for heuristic purposes. Furthermore, some texts do not fit cleanly into only one paradigm. We suggest below that the deuteronomic paradigm—with its notions of covenant, obedience, disobedience, blessing, and curse—is a staple of the prophetic way of understanding God and the world. However, the prophets are also informed by the concerns of priests and sages. And some prophets contain apocalyptic (or protoapocalyptic) elements. Preachers need to respect the complexity of these matters.

A preacher's understanding of a specific biblical text is often enhanced by the knowledge of the larger trajectory within which it is found. A text is always more than simply an illustration of a larger trajectory, but a knowledge of the larger picture often illumines a text. Further, a specific text is often itself paradigmatic for the contemporary congregation. An encounter with a passage can awaken the congregation to an aspect of God's presence and purposes (and human response).

Just as a text is more than an illustration of a paradigm, so we iterate here that a paradigm is more than a summary of its main themes. There is no substitute for paying attention to the texts that comprise these trajectories, especially to the points at which a text does not conform cleanly to one paradigm or another.[13]

How does the preacher move from exegesis of a paradigmatic text in the First Testament to helping the congregation understand how the text illumines the life of the contemporary community? Here we suggest the hermeneutic that Sanders calls "dynamic analogy."[14] This perspective is based on two related premises. The first is that the cultural forms and worldviews of the First Testament and its people, practices, and institutions differ at many points from those of the late twentieth-century community. The second notes that while our cultural forms and worldviews differ from those of the world of the First Testament, there are underlying currents of experience that function similarly in the ancient and contemporary settings. These similar realities may go by different names in each culture. They may manifest themselves in different cultural forms. But beneath the differences, we can identify similarities at the level of experience.

A text of the First Testament makes a *surface* witness expressed in its own culture, worldview, and idiom but can be understood on a *deeper* level to contain values that transcend its particular cultural expression. The implications of this deeper level, once they are discovered and delineated, can often be transferred from one setting to another. This idea is, of course, hardly a new one. The ultimate goal of the historical-critical approach to biblical interpretation, at least when practiced by its most talented advocates, was precisely to make the ancient witness of the Israelites available and meaningful to modern believers. And like those interpreters who were deeply concerned with the Bible's contemporary witness of faith in the church, we begin with the assumption that a text intends to reveal something about God and the human response to God but does so in its own idiom and on the basis of its own cultural assumptions. The interpreter determines the possible meanings of the text within the matrix of its own worldview and then seeks the deeper witness of the text, that is those aspects of the text that transcend the particular cultural manifestation. This deeper intention of the text is thus often a clue for Christian preaching.

This perspective yields hermeneutical questions. What realities function in our world similarly to those in the world of the text? How is the situation of today's church like (or unlike) the characters, plot, or setting within the text or assumed by the text? Of course, the preacher cannot always find an appropriate analogy. But that in itself may be the subject for an excellent sermon. Preachers and congregations learn from failures.

The combination of regarding the First Testament as containing paradigms of the divine presence and of appropriating the First

Testament through the hermeneutic of dynamic analogy allows the preacher to acknowledge real differences between the worlds of the contemporary Christian listener and of the First Testament but at the same time to discover points of positive contact.

As already noted, the First Testament contains several trajectories within an overarching paradigm. The different trajectories have a common tradition in affirming the pre-eminence of the one living God. But they cast different shades of light on the divine presence and work in the world. Indeed, at times the trajectories seem to compete with one another. In such instances, preachers must have a clear theological vision that can serve as a mediating principle to help the preacher determine which text or trajectory seems most adequately to account for the divine presence in the world.[15] Christians, like our Jewish compatriots, sometimes find it necessary to say no to a biblical trajectory or text or to some aspect therein. We discuss a methodology for making such an adjudication in the next chapter.

Now we turn to a brief survey of the overarching paradigm and basic trajectories of the First Testament that are central to any act of preaching from the First Testament in the Christian pulpit. In each case we consider how each paradigm is intended to function in the listening community. What does this trajectory (or a text within it) seek to encourage in the listening community? The answers to this question are often important clues for the development of the sermon.

THE OVERARCHING PARADIGM: ONE GOD FOR ALL

In our first chapter we made the point that Israel saw itself as a nation called to reveal a God who exists for all of creation. We want now to say that this model stands at the very center of any appropriate use of the First Testament in the Christian pulpit. Though we have given a very brief and broad argument in that earlier section to substantiate this claim, the model is so important to us that it merits further discussion. This model is evaluated in different ways in the long course of the writing of the First Testament (even in the four trajectories discussed below). But it approaches the level of basic doctrine as the Christian era begins, as witnessed by its appropriation by the Jewish community then and now. Jewish prayer often begins with the opening *Baruch:* "Praised be Thou, O Lord, our God, Ruler of the *Universe.*"

The Genesis story opens the Bible to emphasize the model of the God who "created all things and called them good." The liturgical hymn of praise that comprises this first creation account is surely no attempt to argue whether or not God really did create all things in six twenty-four-hour days or in a succession of unimaginably long eons of time; or whether God "created from nothing" or worked on some already-existent matter. Such notions have exercised millions through the centuries, but the fight is of little benefit. Genesis 1 is hymn; it is doxology. One reads "lost in wonder, love, and praise," or one mis-reads. At the end of Genesis 1, the model of the God who made all and cares for all is made plain. Land and sky, water and earth, sea creatures and land creatures, sun, moon, and stars, open-seed plants and hidden-seed plants, domesticated creatures and wild creatures, human males and human females, *all* are God's creations. Not one is left out; not one is missing. God seeks for all to live together in mutual support and encouragement, being fully what God intended for it to be.

And yet we, as the ancient authors before us, know that the world in which we live is far from this balanced world of shalom designed and inaugurated by God. And they, as we, wonder why this is so. From their wondering they gave birth to the famous (infamous?) story of the garden in Eden. However the story is to be evaluated, and the possibilities appear nearly endless, the result is that human beings, through their own disobedient actions, have forfeited the world God gave them.[16] Subsequently, in a series of increasingly horrific events, from fratricide to flood-causing foolishness, from drunkenness to would-be divinity, humans prove that they are far from the design and intent of God. And as a result, the world of nature also strays from God's purposes. Yet, God shows God's faithfulness again and again by confirming the driving intent to bless the whole created order.

These great stories from Genesis 1–11 are universal in scope, the very model of the God who is our God, the God of all the world. And this remains the case, even as that God turns to another attempt to reconstitute the harmony of creation intended at the beginning by choosing Abram and Sara, not to found a nation for its own sake, but to found a nation to "bless all the families of the earth" (Gen. 12:3). The ancestral stories that follow in Genesis—the Exodus story, the continuing sagas of kings and prophets—*all* are subsumed under the search for shalom undertaken by this God who simply will not leave the chosen ones alone; they are chosen for responsibility and blessing. Their task is all too clear. When Second Isaiah announces to the scruffy little group of second and third generation Babylonian exiles that their job is now "to be a light to the nations" (49:6), he was echoing the model that remains beating in the heart of Israel. Israel's life is none other than revelatory of a God who lives for the sake of all.

Christian preachers must keep this basic model before them whenever they go to the First Testament for their preaching. This perspective yields a practical question that can be put to any sermon. Does this sermon witness to the fact that God wishes to bless the cosmos in its entirety? If the sermon denies God's desire to bless anyone or anything, the sermon does not measure up to the fullness of God's love for all. Of course, we hasten to add, this does not mean that God approves of all that happens. God sometimes requires repentance. The path to blessing is sometimes painful, for people must sometimes change. But, ultimately, as Karl Barth put it, God is *for* all.[17]

FOUR TRAJECTORIES WITHIN THE OLD TESTAMENT

Of course, it is hardly enough to hold up this central model alone as a sufficient means to appropriate the First Testament for preaching. The vast riches of the collection need also to be addressed by means of several significant trajectories by which the great variety of the First Testament may be grasped and made available for a preacher's evaluation and use. We will briefly consider four of these paradigms.[18]

The Deuteronomic Trajectory (The Choice of Love). The great corpus of literature that extends from Genesis through 2 Kings has been edited, perhaps sometime during the Babylonian exile (597–539

B.C.E.), by a group of theologians whom scholars have traditionally called the deuteronomic historians. This unknown group saw the need to provide a continuous account of the theological history of the people of Israel from the creation of the world until the loss of the nation to the invading hordes of the Babylonians. To paint this vast historical and theological canvas, they used the many resources of the tradition available to them: the ancestral stories, the Exodus traditions, the folk tales of the judges, and the rise and fall of the kings.

This magnificent picture forms the bedrock of the First Testament, and its significance can hardly be overestimated. Unfortunately, it is precisely here that Christian interpreters of the First Testament have formed their most serious misunderstandings. It is cliché to state that in this great deuteronomic story one finds the central belief that God rewards those who follow the divine commands to the letter and punishes those who do not. Thus, the First Testament is a book best characterized by "law," that is, by a kind of mechanical justice wherein God becomes a heavenly gumball machine, dispensing red balls or green ones depending on whether good deeds or bad ones are entered into the slot. We briefly discussed the implications of such a belief in chapter 1.

Multiple passages from this literature can be quoted in isolation to substantiate this claim (see, for example, Deut. 6:3; Judg. 3:7-8, and 1 Kings 8:44-51). And it is commonplace to suggest that the book of Job is a direct assault on the simplistic deuteronomic belief that God mechanically rewards the righteous and punishes the wicked. The fact that Job is in the Scripture at all is surely due in part to the fact that some ancient believers did construe the deuteronomic theology in a deterministic way. However, though some ancients understood it so, preachers hardly have reason to do the same. On the contrary, we think that the deuteronomic historians were precisely *not* believers in the works righteousness so commonly attributed to them.

The heart of the deuteronomic theology may be found in Deuteronomy 7:7-11:

> It was not because you were more numerous than all the peoples that YHWH singled you out and chose you; you were in fact the fewest of all the peoples. But because YHWH loved you and kept the oath sworn to

39

your ancestors YHWH brought you out with a powerful hand, redeemed you from the house of slavery, from the hand of Pharaoh, king of Egypt. You know that YHWH, your God, is God, the faithful God, who keeps covenant love for those who love YHWH and who keep YHWH's commandments, to a thousand generations, but who repays individually those who hate YHWH; those who reject and hate YHWH, YHWH will not delay to repay them individually. *That is why* you must keep the commandment, the statutes and the judgments, that I command you this day.

The sequence of the argument of this passage is critically important. The reason for the primary act of YHWH's choice of Israel is made plain in vv. 7 and 8. Israel had nothing itself to recommend it as the choice of God. It was weak, fewest in number of all peoples of the earth, and locked in Egyptian slavery. God chose Israel for two reasons. The first of these is simply that God loved them. This claim is overwhelmingly powerful in its utter simplicity, its unmodified clarity. The act of God is first and foremost an act of divine love. Any attempt to understand and appreciate the theology of the deuteronomic historians must begin with this claim. Following on that claim is the second and related one that God will keep the promises made to the ancestors of Israel, promises for land, progeny, and missionary service (Gen. 12:1-3). God is the promise-making and promise-keeping God, a God to be trusted "to a thousand generations," that is to say for as many generations as there may be.

From these two convictions—God loves Israel and will keep the promises made to Israel—*follows* the command to keep the commandment of God.[19] It is essential to note the order here. One is not called to follow the commandment *in order to* gain the favor of God; one follows the commandment *as the result of* God's love and promise. This order is precisely the one always affirmed to be the order of the gospel of Jesus Christ. "We love because God first loved us." It is this same order that the deuteronomic historians claim as normative for their theology, and all subsequent statements about rewards and punishments must always be read in the light of Deuteronomy 7:7-11.

A very clear warning against reading the theology in too mechanical a way is given in subsequent chapters of Deuteronomy. In 8:11-20, the people are warned not to begin to believe that the great gifts of

God to them were in fact the result of their own power, or skill, or intelligence. Then in 9:6, they are reminded that the gift of the land to them has nothing to do with their righteousness. They have amply demonstrated their stubbornness in the wilderness, their easy denials of the God who gave them freedom, and their readiness to descend to the most base form of idolatry, shown glaringly at the foot of the sacred mount of Horeb (Sinai) (9:8-21).

Again and again, throughout the unfolding history of Israel, as seen by the deuteronomic historians, the reader is warned never to forget that the origins of the whole story are to be found in the love and promise of God. Those who remember the foundational love and action of God for the community and who obey the commandments are blessed. Those who fail to follow the commandments of God have in fact rejected that love and promise and will themselves find rejection. These principles are very clear in the stories of the conquest and settlement of the promised land that are told from a deuteronomistic perspective. As the people obey, the conquest moves forward with haste. For instance, the heavily fortified city of Jericho falls in only seven days when the people remember who they are and do what God asks (Joshua 6). But Achan forgets God's pathway to blessing. Achan steals booty from Jericho. Consequently, at Ai, the people are defeated (Joshua 7). This pattern is also clear in Judges. When the people remain faithful to God, they prosper in their new land. But when they turn to other deities, their life withers (for example Judg. 2:6-10; 17:1-21:25). Nonetheless, as we have already noted, these narratives should not be read from a mechanistic perspective. Samson broke the vows he made to God. He married a non-Israelite women. But God worked through Samson in order to deliver Israel (Judg. 13:1–16:31). God is able to work through human sin in order to keep the divine promises and to effect blessing.

Many of the prophets (especially in the pre-exilic era) also assumed aspects of the deuteronomic model. These prophets assumed that God has graciously chosen Israel and has provided the guidance that was needed to lead to blessings for all in the community. But many in Israel and Judah turned away from God's guidance. Consequently, they brought destruction upon the nation. The pre-exilic prophets warn the people that the consequences of straying from the love and commandments of God will include the collapse of the nation. After the destruction of the nation, the prophets reminded the people of that warning and its fulfillment in their history. Affinities with deuteronomism are clear in the book of Hosea, for instance. God has graciously chosen Israel and acted in Israel's behalf (e.g., Hos. 11:1). But Israel was disobedient; Israel turned away from God's ways by seeking help from other deities and from pagan nations (4:1–8:14). Because Israel was disobedient, the nation would be disciplined by the loss of leadership, children, temple, and land (9:1–11:12). Repentance, however, can be the beginning of national renewal (e.g., 10:11-12; 12:1–14:9). Indeed, with God, there is plenteous mercy (e.g., 11:1-12; 14:1-3). The story of Gomer and Hosea puts this theology into narrative form (1:1–3:5).

Today's preacher can be directly helped by keeping in mind how the deuteronomic texts function. These passages are designed to cause the community to remember God's grace and love and the identity they bestow and to recognize and embrace God's faithfulness. They are also intended to help the community reflect on its response to God's love. The goal is not only for the people to be drawn to obedience (which is simply acting out their identity) but also to recognize that if they are disobedient, they can expect consequences. Often, a disastrous consequence can be averted by means of repentance and a change of heart and life. But if disobedience leads to disaster, the deuteronomic paradigm can often help a community make sense of its situation and prepare for living differently in the future.[20]

When preaching from a deuteronomic text, then, the preacher might well want the congregation to remember God's gracious faithfulness. How does God continue to cause the walls of Jericho to fall? The preacher might also want to help the community reflect on its response to the divine will. Is the congregation like those in Hosea's day who turned away from God and can, therefore, expect a curse to befall them? If yes, how can the community respond more adequately to God's purpose to move toward a life of blessings?[21]

The Priestly Trajectory (The Way of Holiness). A second paradigm of the First Testament appears at first to be a most unpromising one. Very little of the language of the priests of Israel seems to have much value for those who would preach to twenty-first-century Christians. Indeed, the opening chapters of Leviticus, the quintessential book of the priests, is a numbing enumeration of proper sacrifice down to the smallest details and appears to be of little concern to contemporary Christians. Yet, so significant a part of the First Testament can hardly be overlooked easily; we need to take account of this paradigm to assess its value as a possible paradigm for us.

Waldemar Janzen succinctly expresses the priestly viewpoint:

> According to Israel's central story, God had manifested his presence with his people to save them. Further, God continued to be present in their midst. This was experienced in the sanctuary, eventually identified with the Temple. God's presence there created a center of holy space, just as the Sabbath and the great festivals constituted holy time. To live as God's people is consequently seen, at least from the priestly perspective, as living in constant awareness and recognition of God's hallowing presence.[22]

The priests are concerned that all of life be shaped by the awareness of the presence and purposes of God. This is true in the sanctuary and worship. And it is equally true in everyday affairs. In the sanctuary the community glimpses God's holiness. In everyday life, the community practices holy living. "For I am the LORD who brought you up from the land of Egypt, to be your God; you shall be holy, for I am holy" (Lev. 11:45).

In the priestly context, the word *holy* means set apart. For the people to be holy is to be separated from those things that are inimical to God and to God's ways. To be holy is to be dedicated to God and God's purposes. It is to manifest the awareness of God in all realms of life. There was no clear distinction between the so-called sacred and secular worlds for the Israelite priests; if God created all things (a fact the priestly chapter Genesis 1 hymned with a grand certainty), then to achieve their optimum potential, all facets of human and animal life must mirror the holiness of God.

This is why Leviticus 19 and 20 so messily jumble together what we imprecisely call moral and ritual prescriptions. Demand for justice for the poor and the foreigner (19:9); laws against the immediate consumption of the fruit of trees planted after entrance into the promised land (19:23-25); and demands for compassion for all "of your kin" (19:17-18) are all given the same rationale: "I am YHWH." Indeed, for the priests, it is as grave a problem when a "man lies with a male as with a woman" (18:22) as when one eats "anything in the streams that does not have fins and scales" (11:10); the former is "detestable" and the latter is "an abomination," the two words reserved by the priests for their strongest condemnation. Both homosexuality and aquatic creatures without fins and scales mix categories: they blur the design that God had from the beginning. We might find these condemnations quite distinct; the priests would not.

But rather than argue in ways quite foreign to their thinking, we need to attempt to discover what was at stake for the priestly thinkers as they urged holiness on their people. Like the deuteronomic historians, who may have preceded them in time by several decades, the priests began with the basic model of Israel: God was the creator and sustainer of all. Furthermore, God was known in that great act of liberating Israel from Egyptian slavery. This creating and liberating God was most of all a holy God who called for the people to respond to God's liberation with lives of holiness, a purity of thought and action quite distinct from all those among whom they lived.

We must note another important similarity between the paradigms of the deuteronomist and the priest; both affirmed that the actions of God preceded any responses on the part of God's people, thus ruling out any notion that final relationship between people and God was based on right action or right sacrifice. This is made especially clear in the chapters of Leviticus referring to those things and actions judged clean and unclean. The reason why certain actions are appropriate and others are not is directly stated at 11:44-45: "For I am YHWH your God; therefore, sanctify yourselves, and be holy, for I am holy. You shall not defile yourselves with swarming creatures that move upon the earth, for I am YHWH who brought you up from the land of Egypt to be your God; you shall be holy for I am holy." We note the connecting words in these sentences: *because* I am God, therefore be holy; do not defile yourselves *for* I brought you out of Egypt.

The common move to caricature the priestly theology as one in which God's love for the people is based on the appropriate practice of sacrifice, on the timely washing of hands, or the complete avoidance of this or that animal cannot be sustained from the priestly literature itself.

We may certainly disagree with some of the specific ways in which the priests sought to tease out the implications of holiness for their people. Some of the priestly categories seem no longer to make sense. For example, we are great lovers of shrimp (John was a preacher in Louisiana, after all!), and it is difficult for us to imagine precisely why these little pink delicacies could really be in any way detestable, nor just how our eating them could serve in any way to make us unholy. But, we can only make such a claim because we do not completely share the worldview of the Israelite priests. What we need in fact to share with them is their profound desire to illustrate in all parts of their lives and in all parts of the lives of their people a holiness that matches the holiness of their God. Surely here is a worthy paradigm that the First Testament offers to Christian preachers for the twenty-first century.

The priests were asking a question any preacher should ask: how can people be holy in the midst of a world that appears so decidedly unholy? Their basic answer to this important question was: through God's gracious presence, God makes it possible for people to conform their thoughts and actions to the holiness of God. For example, people did not eat the blood of a creature because "its blood is its life" (Lev. 17:14), its very essence. To eat the blood is to usurp the prerogative of God, the giver of life. To refuse to eat the blood is to confirm your own identity and to announce to the world around you that the proper order of creation is maintained, that God is creator, and that all life is sacred and comes from God. In this example we can see that the priests' search for holiness was far more than a list of dated dietary laws and commands that need no longer concern us. Like them, we are called to discover in what ways we can be holy in a world that appears to be so completely otherwise. This call may not at all mean that we should now all refuse to eat the blood of certain creatures and claim, thereby, that we are thus holy to God. Such an appropriation of the priestly paradigm may be thoroughly beside the point for us who no longer share the specific worldview of the priests.

The priestly trajectory is designed to help the community become aware of and responsive to God's desire to hallow all of life. The priestly literature also directs the congregation to the ritual and other mechanisms by which to rid the community of defilement. It contains many prescriptions that show how to implement holiness in everyday matters. When preaching from a priestly passage, the preacher would want to help the congregation gain a fresh sense of God's omnipresence. Is the congregation responding to God's purposes through holy living as suggested by the text? That is, is the community living on the basis of God's design for the world or is the community living in unholy patterns? Can the preacher point the congregation to rituals or other practices that can help the community recover its sense of God's presence and hallowing qualities in its life?

This approach can help a preacher with a passage such as Numbers 2:1-34 that describes how the tribes are to arrange their tents while they are on the march through the wilderness to the promised land. They are to put the tent of meeting in the middle of the camp and they are to surround it symmetrically with three tribes on a side. This arrangement reminds the people in the threatening wilderness that God tabernacles in their midst; the symmetrical arrangement represents a holy world of order and balance in which each piece has its own place. The symmetry also provides defense on all sides from attackers. Within the wilderness, the community dwells secure.

The preacher might consider ways in which the congregation is in a threatening wilderness situation. What are the symbols (like the tent of meeting) that remind them of the divine presence in the midst of threat? Can the preacher point to Christian rituals and symbols that function this way? To other realities in the church and world? How can the congregation order its life so as to conform to God's will for all things to work together in mutual encouragement and support? In other words, how can the congregation organize itself for holy living? Along the way, the preacher may need to help the congregation see that holy living sets apart their values and practices from those of the prevailing culture. If so, it is all the more important for the preacher to assure the congregation of God's continued presence with them. For perspectives on other texts in the priestly paradigm, see our discussions of circumcision, the dietary laws, the temple, and blood sacrifice in chapter 5.

The Dual Trajectory of Wisdom (The Way of Order and the Way of Questioning). There have been numerous attempts to characterize the way of wisdom in the First Testament.[23] It has proved to be a slippery subject primarily because so many disparate kinds of writing have been included in its definition. Wisdom writings are normally said to include: certain Psalms (for example, 37, 49, 73, 119), Job, Koheleth (Ecclesiastes), Proverbs, Sirach, and the Wisdom of Solomon. Also, portions of many other First Testament books are said to possess various degrees of wisdom influence.[24] We choose to subsume our discussion of the paradigm of wisdom under the search for order.[25] By the search for order, we mean the search for how the cosmos is put together and how it functions and how human beings can optimally function within it. The wisdom tradition seeks after the meaning of life. What are the most important things to know and the best ways to live? On what can human beings count? Some of these writers were consumed with the search for order because the fixed order of the world assumed by the deuteronomic historians and the priests was perhaps not quite so fixed, or at least was worthy of serious exploration and debate.

But before the wisdom writers could raise their questions about the ordering of the universe by God, they had to believe that there was such an order in creation as it came from the hands of a God of order. This order was characterized by balance and wholeness, as Genesis 1 bears ample witness. Furthermore, the writers, most especially of the book of Proverbs, were convinced that this order could be discerned and appropriated by human beings as they interacted with the world. How does one discover God's design for the world and its functioning? The answer is by observing life and noting those things that are helpful and nonhelpful, community-building and community-fracturing. This belief is the reason that both very secular and clearly theological proverbs are included in the collection, because in the search for order there can be no final separation between sacred and secular. *All* is created by God, and *all* can be revelatory of that God. Their hallmark phrase, "The fear of YHWH is the beginning of wisdom" (Prov. 1:7), neatly combines sacred and secular. Right relationship to the God who makes all things leads to discernment of that God in interactions with all things. In his poem "God's Grandeur," Gerard Manley Hopkins states it clearly, "the world is charged with the grandeur of God" in such a way that we may learn to live in the world if we observe God's world rightly and interact with the world through a reflective engagement with it.

Certainly, we observe in this element of the paradigm of wisdom a kinship with the deuteronomic paradigm. Wisdom, say the sages, leads to full life, to safety in the world. In metaphors of Psalm 1, those who are wise are "like trees planted by streams of water," while those who are fools, rejecters of the order and purposes of God, are "like chaff that the wind drives away."

But this is not the only element in the way of wisdom. Order may be discernible to the wise, but a deeper and freer reflection also yielded some painful questions. How are we to explain those disordered parts of life? What are we to do when life does not follow the patterns of a reliable order? Such hard questions led certain of the writers of wisdom to question the supposedly assured order of creation.

Of course, the writers of these materials were hardly the first to raise such serious questions about the accepted certainties of the world and God. At every stage of the unfolding drama of Israelite life and thought, thinkers had dared to question the most basic convictions supposedly held by anyone who claimed to be a follower of the one God, YHWH.[26] In the very earliest stories of the ancestors, questioning stood hand in hand with faith as the patriarchs and matriarchs struggled to understand and assimilate the workings of the mysterious God who had called them to be a blessing to the nations. Abraham and Sarah both laughed in the face of the foolish promise of this God that the old couple would still have a son (Gen. 17:17 and 18:12). This same Abraham questioned the justice of God who had determined to destroy the evil city of the plain, demanding that God give an accounting, down to the last person, of any who might be righteous in the city (Gen. 18:22-33). Moses later outdid his ancestor by refusing to allow an enraged deity to destroy the chosen people by arguing that it was a shortsighted and small-minded desire on the part of God, and would do God no good at all in the eyes of the world (Exod. 32).

In response to the salutation of an angel that "the LORD is with you, you mighty warrior," Gideon, hiding in a winepress from his enemies, the Midianites, retorted that he would believe that claim more readily if he could see some proof of it. Winnowing wheat in a hole in the ground, choking in dust and chaff, this was hardly the portrait of a mighty warrior (Judg. 6:11-13)! The laments of the Psalms, the type of poem that comprises more Psalms than any other, are replete with demands for the actions of an apparently reluctant God. "How long?" is a common cry, uttered in many different ways by the anguished psalmist, and the addressee is usually God (see Pss. 4, 5, 6, 10, 13, 16, 17 among many others).

Even those great spokespersons for God, the prophets, are not free of their questions. Such uncertainties are epitomized by Jeremiah, whose forty-year ministry is riddled with pain and rejection, much of which is brought on by his deepest desire never to have been called to prophecy in the first place (see Jer. 20:7 for the sharpest statement of this reluctance). Numerous other examples could be provided, but the speakers and writers of Israel were never strangers to deep questioning.

But with the writers of the schools of wisdom we face this questioning in its most powerful form. The poet of Psalm 73 spent the first 16 verses of the poem rehearsing the absolute meaninglessness of a life wherein the wicked always seemed to get the upper hand; he only claims to move beyond this view when he is convinced in a service of worship that the wicked do finally get what they deserve in an ordered world of strict justice (73:17-20).

Koheleth (Ecclesiastes) affirms that there is indeed order in the world, but that order is so immutable that everything is fixed beyond change and as such yields only "emptiness" and "weariness." The familiar poem that states "for everything there is a season" (Eccles. 3:1-8), however much it has been romanticized in modern song, is nothing less than a hymn to an unchanging order. To see that this is the real truth of the world drives Koheleth to cry "emptiness, emptiness, all is empty" (1:2; 12:8)![27]

But the masterpiece of the school of wisdom is surely Job whose probings of the world and God bedevil and challenge readers even today. Job is the ultimate quester for order, but he neither gives in to the order of the priests, as does the poet of Psalm 73, nor does he fall into the despair of Koheleth. Job demands absolute truth and integrity from friends and God alike and never rests until he achieves it (Job 27:2-6). What exactly he *does* achieve is the subject of a vast literature, which can hardly be summarized in this brief look at Job.[28] But for our purposes it is the intensity and drama of the search itself that is important, regardless of how one assesses the results of it. Job will have the truth of things, and he will go to astonishing lengths to get it.

Commentators are fond of saying that Job "almost blasphemes" as he rails at how he has been treated. However, by the light of the paradigms of the deuteronomic historians and the priests, Job surely *does* blaspheme! What else would the deuteronomic historian think when he read Job 9:22-24?

> It is all the same! That is why I say,
>   "Blameless and wicked he obliterates.
> When disaster brings a sudden death,
>   he laughs at the sorrowing innocent.
> The earth is handed over to the wicked;
>   the faces of its judges he conceals.
> If it is not he, then who, pray tell, is it?"

In this remarkable speech Job quite directly calls into the most serious question at least one of the very basic convictions established by the first two paradigms of the First Testament. No, he does not deny that God is creator of the universe, nor that God has the power to sustain that creation. What he most seriously questions is the *purpose* of that creation. Even in the midst of a hymn to God's power, Job cannot resist raising doubts about the point of it all. Note, for example, 9:4-10, where Job describes the power of God but almost exclusively in destructive ways: destroying mountains, bringing earthquakes, stopping the sun's rising, and sealing up the light of the stars.

And the result of this belief for Job is not "the heavens are telling the glory of God" (Ps.19:1), but "Look, he passes by me, and I do not see him" (Job 9:11). God's creation is not revelatory of God's presence and power for Job; it rather obscures God and whatever purposes God may have for the creation. In a rising crescendo of fury, Job assaults the basic belief that God is in fact on the side of the divine creation, and by doing so Job represents a terrible but certainly possible conclusion when the basic belief in the goodness and the power of God confronts an apparently exemplary human life gone seriously wrong. In this search for order, either Job has done something quite terrible to deserve his ash heap and broken piece of pottery, a claim strictly denied both by God and the teller of the story (1:1, 8; and 2:3), or God is at best mistaken about Job or is at worst monstrous.

The poet may offer the reader a way off the horns of this terrible dilemma in the speeches of God by reframing the entire discussion. Both Job and the friends agree that God is primarily in the business of rewarding the righteous and punishing the wicked, but the words of God suggest that this too simple way of understanding God's governance of the world needs a deeper reflection.[29]

So, wisdom offers two general possibilities for preaching. The first possibility is to work from texts that affirm the order of the universe.[30] Preaching on such wisdom texts might lead the congregation to live with confidence as the text leads them to see reliabilities in life. Psalm 127, for instance, reminds the congregation that a safe home and a large family come from God. A safe home and a large family are symbols of personal security. How does today's home become a place of safety? In today's world, with overpopulation an increasing danger, the preacher might want to employ the hermeneutic of analogy to locate a means other than a large family whereby God provides for personal security. Nonetheless, the preacher can still ask, what is built into the fabric of life around us that helps us to live without fear and to be open to the fullness of life? When a place functions in that way, it is a gift of God. The brutal fact, of course, is that some in the congregation do not enjoy such homes. Indeed, for some the home is the place of deepest fear. Some people in the congregation, or some-how related to it, may be homeless. Can the preacher legitimately indicate how God provides a "safe place" for those whose homes are fearful and for those who have no homes? Does God provide a community outside the conventional family structure or the conventional social pattern that serves as a "home"? Or is the preacher more honest in turning to a lament or other expression of anguish?

Some passages in Wisdom literature call congregations to learn of God and the good life by looking closely at their own experience. Indeed, in the language of systematic theology, experience becomes a source of revelation for some wisdom writers. A text could become a lens through which to reflect on how the congregation's experience mediates the divine presence and purposes. Proverbs 2:1-22 is a tightly constructed poem that promises this very thing. The fruit of the search for wisdom is "the knowledge of God" (2:6). In this case, a major work of the preacher is to help the congregation analyze its experience and name those aspects that are revelatory.

Wisdom, of course, is a feminine word. Wisdom itself is frequently personified in the Wisdom literature in feminine form (for example, Prov. 1:20-33; 3:13-18; 8:1-36). Wisdom in its feminine dimensions is becoming increasingly important in contemporary theological discussion. As a correlate, the presence of wisdom in sacred scripture is contributing to the fresh energy to many Christian communities to respect women, to treat women justly, and to regard feminine experience as a norm and source for theological reflection. Some Christians are using Wisdom as a name for God. But many laypeople (and some clergy) are unacquainted with these aspects of wisdom in the Bible and in books that are outside the Protestant canon in which wisdom is prominent (especially the Wisdom of Solomon and Sirach). Many congregations would be enlarged in faith and practice by sermons that expose the congregation to this dimension of the biblical tradition.

The other model for appropriating the Old Testament in the mode of questioning is offered by Job. In fact, we would call this homiletical approach *the way of questioning*. For the deuteronomic historians and the priests, certain convictions have reached the level of ontology; one should not question the creative, sustaining, loving nature of the one God of the universe. However, this element of the paradigm of wisdom announces that such questions are not only possible but also even necessary if faith in this God is to be sustained and enriched. After all, it was not to the friends of Job, those loud defenders of at least a type of deuteronomic orthodoxy, however caricatured, to whom God appeared. It was Job himself, that brash questioner of central theological convictions, to whom God came and who was finally called "right" by the same God (42:7). These facts should warn us that a proper wrestling with the First Testament may at times be a bruising match, one from which we may emerge with a decided theological limp.

When preaching on Job and other questioning texts, the preacher may want to show how attentiveness to Job's situation helps us recognize similar situations and questions in our own setting. How can Job's honesty and probing help us articulate our own questions and pain? The minister faces a special challenge when preaching in a Joban vein. The preacher surely wants to bring a word of healing and hope (much as Job received at the end of the book that bears his name). But this word cannot come too glibly or too quickly, lest it preempt questions that still need to be asked or pain that still needs to be processed. Too much good news too soon can be like suturing a wound with infection still inside. For a time, the surface of the wound looks clean; the wound appears to be healing. But soon enough, the infection restarts its inflaming work.

The Trajectory of Apocalypticism (The Way of Radical Hope). Among the thirty-nine books of the Protestant First Testament, not one is wholly representative of the kind of literature called *apocalyptic.* Indeed, discussions of apocalypticism and *protoapocalypticism* in the First Testament are usually confined to Daniel 7–12, some portions of Isaiah 24–27;, 34–35; 56–66, and selected parts of Zechariah 9–14. Isaiah 40–55 and Ezekiel 40–48 are sometimes added to protoapocalyptic literature.[31] But out of this relatively limited body of writing it may appear peculiar to attempt to delineate a fourth paradigm. However, apocalyptic writing and thought is present in the First Testament. Furthermore, it became increasingly prominent in Jewish life in the years between the testaments and in the period of the Second Testament itself.[32] Apocalyptic theology played a significant role in the formation of Christian theology.[33] Hence, it is certainly worthy of a brief discussion.

As in the scholarly discussion of wisdom, there are several different ways in which apocalyptic thought might be characterized. We choose to discuss it under the title of radical hope. Apocalyptic literature is born in the fire of repression. From the standpoints of apocalyptic theology and apocalypse as a literary genre, the fullest example in the Old Testament is Daniel 7–12. The book was collected as a response to the radical Hellenizing demands of the Seleucid monarch, Antiochus Epiphanes IV (middle of the second century B.C.E.). In the typical style of such writing, the author employs a series of fantastic images and metaphors—beasts, clouds, heavenly figures—in order to say one quite simple thing: the victory of God is assured in the face of terrible evil. No force in the world—however powerful, however appalling, however seemingly invincible—can defeat the power of God. And those who have faith in that certain fact will themselves be ultimately victorious, though they may suffer a martyr's death in this life. It is hardly accidental that the first possible reference to a human resurrection after death in the First Testament is to be found in Daniel 12:2.[34]

Here is a radical hope indeed, an ultimate hope against an earthly hopelessness. These portraits of hope were instrumental in the formation of post-biblical Judaism and emerging Christianity. Both traditions needed all the hope they could muster in the face of a Roman empire headed by a long series of oppressive rulers. The most monstrous of these were concentrated in the first century C.E., namely Caligula, Nero, and Domitian, each of whom proscribed Judaism or Christianity or both during their three brief reigns. From apocalypticism then came the way of radical hope.

It is a tragedy for preaching that the powerful apocalyptic imagery of the Bible has been usurped by certain Christian groups who would reduce the material to a game of predicting the world's future. Though apocalyptic material is certainly future-oriented, the basic concern of the trajectory is the specific ways in which the future of God impinges upon our present. Hope for the future had an immediate pastoral effect. The apocalyptists believed that the world was broken and needed fixing. In their eyes, the situation was so serious that only God could fix it through a cataclysmic invasion of history (an apocalypse). God, the power above all powers, would exercise divine power, eliminate evil and establish a realm of righteousness. When God's rule was established in its fullness, even death would lose its power. This hope allowed communities to endure and to be faithful.

At one level, preaching on an apocalyptic text is quite straight-forward. Apocalyptic theology is designed to encourage hope, especially among those for whom hope has grown dim. Almost everyone needs such encouragement from time to time. The preacher needs to explain the imagery of the text; our experience is that congregations find this fascinating. Preachers can locate analogies between the situation of the hurting ancient community and the situations of their own communities. The preacher can affirm that God's will for life transcends the immediate circumstances. Can the preacher point to signs of hope? For instance, perhaps the minister can describe a contemporary situation of despair that parallels that of the congregation but through which God has proven faithful. Of course, clergy need to decide whether they believe that God will actually intervene in history in a cataclysmic way (as envisioned by the apocalyptists) or whether this symbol is a surface expression of a deeper Christian hope. Some Christians find it hard to anticipate such a historical cataclysm but can still affirm that God will continue to work with the world and its situations until all things are conformed to the divine will of love and justice for all. No matter how grim a situation may be, God never gives up.

The imagery of apocalypticism gives the preacher an invitation to be imaginative. In fully developed apocalypses, the writers communicate their messages through images. Perhaps the preacher might think about the imagery used by these writers: clouds, beasts, and dragons, to name a few. These pictures are attempts to make the realities of which they speak present to the imaginations of the writers' generations. Though the contemporary generation does not often use such imagery, we can use them analogically. What are images that conjure up similar realities for us? For instance, what are images that bespeak evil for us as graphically as the beast and the dragon of the apocalyptic texts? It is not enough, however, to create images of evil. In order to internalize the hope of apocalypticism, the preacher must locate images of hope and encouragement that are as deeply touching, and as believable, as those of evil and destruction.

Apocalypticism is especially valuable for social criticism. Apocalyptic texts hold out a vision of the world as the way God wants it to be. The preacher can use the apocalyptic vision of the last days as a measure of the world as it is—with its distortions, oppression, lies, idolatry, and brutality. Apocalyptic hope reminds the community not to confuse its present world with the world God wants. Far from offering "pie in the sky by and by" apocalypticism pronounces judgment on many contemporary social realities.

Daniel 8, for example, is a vision of animals who controlled Palestine. A ram (the Medo-Persian empire) is conquered by a male goat (Alexander the Great) whose descendants are in turn pushed out by a little horn (Antiochus Epiphanes). These animals all have great power that they exercise for human abuse. But God breaks the power of Antiochus. Can the preacher find analogous images to the ram, the he-goat, and the little horn? What are experiences similar to being under Antiochus's repression that are familiar to today's congregation? And how shall we image God's rule over these harsh realities?

Clergy sometimes face a special problem when preaching from apocalyptic texts. Apocalypticism came to expression among communities that felt themselves marginalized and oppressed. Apocalypticism comforts those who are treated cruelly. In today's culture, the comfort of apocalypticism should not be used to allow cruel people to continue in their cruelty. When faced with people who are cruel or who are implicated in cruelty through their jobs or investments, the pastor might turn to apocalypticism as a forceful reminder of God's will for justice in all relationships.

Monarch, Priest, and Prophet. A cross-trajectory concern deserves mention. Some scholars speak of a royal consciousness in contrast to a prophetic one.[35] These figures appear in all four of the trajectories we have discussed. Hence, monarch and prophet are not so much paradigms in themselves as they are functionaries within the other trajectories.

All of the trajectories assume the existence of a monarchy in Israel. Prophets and priests play particularly important roles in three of the paradigms (deuteronomic, priestly, apocalyptic). What is the relationship of the monarch, the priests, and the prophets? The relationship is similar in the case of each trajectory although some of specific nuances are different.[36] The monarch is charged with enacting justice in the community. The priests are charged not only with helping the community be aware of the presence of God and with presiding over the liturgical life of the community but also with helping the community remember its sacred stories, laws, and traditions.[37] The prophets function rather like ombudspeople who monitor the degree to which the monarch and the priests (and the rest of the community) are adequately performing their responsibilities.

All of these roles could be corrupted. The monarchy could lose sight of its responsibility and become self-serving. This particularly happened when Israel's monarchs turned away from Israel's own understanding of the monarch as a servant among servants and took on the values and practices of other ancient Near Eastern sovereigns. The monarch could even lead the community into exploitation that basely violated the heart of Israel's understanding of community. The priests, likewise, could perform their duties without a vivid awareness of transcendent reality and so as to fatten their own pockets at the expense of the poor. Prophets could be co-opted by monarch and priest so that they did nothing but pass the hand of blessing over illicit values and activities. In such circumstances, conflict often developed between the classical prophets of the Bible and the monarch, priests, and royal prophets.

The Four Trajectories in Summary. We claim that the four central paradigms of the First Testament are the *deuteronomic,* the *priestly,* the *way of wisdom,* and *apocalypticism.* In brief, Christian preachers may learn from these four. From the deuteronomic paradigm, we learn that God's choice is made primarily out of love, pure and simple. From the priestly paradigm, we learn that all of life is called to be holy and pure in the light of the holiness of the one who creates and sustains all of life. From the way of wisdom, we learn both that there is a recognizable order and purpose in the world of God and that the serious questioning of that order is crucial to the life of faith. From apocalypticism, we learn of a radical hope that can sustain us in the face of our hopelessness and that criticizes many of our institutions and practices. These are the central paradigms of the First Testament, gifts to the Christian preacher to enrich and ennoble the proclamation of the gospel of the God of Israel and Jesus Christ.

Now that we have outlined our understanding of the central theological content of the First Testament, we will explore points of continuity and difference between the people and literature of the First and Second Testaments and the church of today. This exploration is necessary in order that Christian preachers may begin to see ways that the above paradigms can inform their modern sermons.

THE TWO TESTAMENTS AND
THE CONTEMPORARY CHURCH

Vast differences persist between the world of the Bible and our own world, particularly in terms of culture and worldview. Indeed, the critical study of the Bible over the last one hundred and fifty years has made us amply aware of this vast gulf. There is little need to delineate these features here. Whenever one attempts to interpret the biblical record, the interpreter's policy should be to avoid ripping the material out of its unique cultural matrices. To seize the text out of context prompts reading ideas and prejudices from one's own time and place into the material, thereby transmuting the biblical witness into something it clearly was never intended to be.

As we begin this journey—from First Testament to Second Testament to present day—we focus on religious similarities and differences. First, in both testaments one finds a monotheizing process—movement toward the confidence that one God creates and sustains the universe. This model stands as an ontological conviction for both testaments.

Second, the biblical record provides us with a religion of grace wherein the singular and awesome God is revealed as a God of love, choosing the people solely on the basis of that love, a love that urges devotion to God and one another but does not coerce it.[38]

Third, one finds in both testaments an overwhelming concern for justice and equity in the world of God. This great concern is found in all parts of the First Testament (see, e.g., Gen. 18; Lev. 25; Amos; Job) as well as the Second Testament (see, e.g., Jesus' treatment of the "least of these"; Paul's movement toward equality in Galatians 3; and the sharp demands of Revelation 18 for economic justice). These calls for justice should be echoed in our own preaching now.

Fourth, a radical hope in the face of hopelessness characterizes people at various moments of both testaments. Abraham's hope for the future of the promise becomes so great that he is willing to give up the visible reality of it, in the person of his own son, believing that God would still bring the promise to fruition, even though he, Abraham, had no way of knowing how it was possible at all. The author of the Letter to the Hebrews in the Second Testament captured this same radical hope by finding in the example of Abraham a perfect reflection of that very hope. And in Revelation, in the face of Roman tyranny, John records that hope, which can even transform a martyr's death. The Second Testament fairly vibrates with such hope. For example, Romans 8 strains the boundaries of language with its desire for God's future.

Fifth, we saw in the school of Israelite wisdom the way of the divine order of the world and the way of radical questioning. These important strains are often underemphasized or simply avoided in discussions of the two testaments, but they are too significant to suffer such neglect. The latter is obviously prominent in the First Testament, as we saw above, and it is far from unknown in the Second. For example, sharp questions about the future return of Jesus in glory were arguable in some New Testament communities. For instance, Mark 13:14-27 enumerates supposed signs of the future, and is juxtaposed with the warning that "no one knows the day or the hour, neither angels, nor the son" (Mark 13:32). With the latter quite astonishing statement, one could imagine that the nascent Christian community was being warned about future speculations about the return of the Lord. This section, in addition to other similar ones in the Second Testament, suggest that the way of questioning did not cease with the time of the First.

As for the former, wisdom's perspective on God's ordering of the world formed the matrix in which the influential Christology of John's Gospel is to be understood. The personification of the figure of "Woman Wisdom" in Proverbs 8 originated a discussion of this ordering principle of the world. This notion of a personified Wisdom, becoming now a creative force with God, moved through the Wisdom of Solomon (chapters 10–11 particularly) and into the Fourth Gospel where Jesus is identified as the *logos,* the "Word" of God, "without him not one thing came into being."

With these five similarities, however true we think them to be, there is a danger. We could easily take the above convictions and facilely conclude that the two testaments are completely synonymous and that Judaism and Christianity are the same religion. John Holbert participated over a year's time in a Jewish-Christian dialogue group, made up primarily of very well-educated lay people, deeply committed to their respective faiths. One of the Christian members of the group said during one of the meetings, "I have always felt that I have been as much Jew as Christian; our beliefs are so similar, our ways of life so much the same." This romantic notion can easily be carried too far. We believe that the essences of Judaism and Christianity are similar. Yet, Christians are not Jewish. Our initiation rites are vastly different; our practices of piety are quite different; and our canons are different. Indeed, some aspects of biblical Israel and some forms of contemporary Judaism are thoroughly foreign to Christians, for example: circumcision, dietary laws, and many of the practices of the temple that have been preserved in the synagogue. Each of these examples would generate a spirited discussion among representatives of the various kinds of contemporary Judaism, of course. But even so, Christian involvement in such a discussion would need to incorporate sacred texts and perspectives not shared by many in the Jewish community.

For example, a discussion of dietary laws from a Christian perspective would need to take seriously the dream of Peter in Acts 10:9-16 where he is urged to "arise and eat" food formerly forbidden to him. Also, Paul's demand that Gentiles not be forced to follow kosher practices before becoming Christian would need to be taken into account. Furthermore, the Christian understanding of circumcision would be vastly different from the Jewish one, given the ways in which the two traditions reflected on this practice in the post-biblical world leading up to our own time. In short, very few contemporary Christians would find any of the above practices *necessary* for their faith and practice.

In the face of these clear and important differences we recognize that we Christians are not Jewish, and, just as important, we recognize that our Jewish brothers and sisters are not anti-Christians or "half-Christians" or "wanna-be" Christians, or "hidden Christians." They are Jewish; they are members of a distinct world religion. And we recognize that the Jewish community reads the First Testament in ways different than we Christians read it. Nevertheless, Christian preachers can effectively and appropriately utilize the paradigms of the First Testament for our Christian preaching without in any way denigrating or caricaturing that part of the Bible, knowing full well that when we do so we are using it in ways that our Jewish friends may or may not applaud.

JESUS CHRIST AND THE OLD TESTAMENT

The relationship between Jesus Christ and the First Testament is a significant theological question. By Jesus Christ we mean less the historical Jesus (and the factual questions about his birth, life, teaching, death, resurrection, and exaltation that surround the historical Jesus) and more the Jesus Christ of faith as he appears in the literature of the Second Testament and in the preaching and teaching of the church.[39] Indeed, in this sense Jesus Christ is a paradigm of divine presence and purpose.[40]

In the stories and traditions about him, and in the sayings from him, the church experiences the divine presence. For the church, speaking about Jesus Christ evokes the knowledge and awareness of the God of Israel, the universal God.[41] The church quickly became and has remained a Gentile community. Thus, we say that the preaching of Jesus Christ pre-eminently reveals the divine presence, purpose, and power to the Gentile world. As Schubert Ogden puts it: Jesus Christ re-presents God to the church.[42]

Through Jesus Christ, the church learns that God is gracious to it even as God is gracious to biblical Israel and to Judaism. The church learns further that God calls the church in ways that are similar to the divine call to Israel. God's activity in Israel is paralleled through God's activity in Jesus Christ. The First Testament furnishes the basic vocabulary and the conceptual framework within which to understand the nature and purpose of God's presence in Christ and the church. Further, the First Testament is larger than the Second Testament. It was written over a much greater span of time and deals with a broader range of life's situations and concerns. Therefore the First Testament often helps enlarge the church's understanding of the divine presence and its effects in the world.

In this respect, we would say that the "new convenant" is new not in the sense of superseding the old, but is new in the sense of the mode of presence it describes. Jesus Christ is now a mode of divine presence with the Gentile community. This mode does not at all abrogate the old but extends and exists alongside it. It is new not in quality but in focus and in manner of implementation.[43]

We admit that this way of relating the event of Jesus Christ to the First Testament is dependent on a much more complete theological discussion than we can provide here. We admit that the Jewish community may find our appropriation of their sacred literature in this way peculiar. Because we so deeply respect that community we owe it to them to clarify our real differences as well as our real similarities. Still, this way of identifying paradigms and their deeper intentions seems to us a useful way of dealing with continuity and difference while at the same time respecting the integrity of the First Testament.

With these theoretical underpinnings now in place, we turn to a practical analysis of the ways in which we suggest sermons from the First Testament may be effectively and appropriately shaped and given.

CHAPTER
THREE   Allen

TWELVE STEPS TO THE SERMON
ON THE OLD TESTAMENT

When a family buys a VCR, they follow the owner's manual for step-by-step directions in order to operate it. But, after using it for several weeks, they operate the VCR by second nature.

This chapter is much like an owner's manual. It presents twelve steps to developing basic sermon ideas on a text from the First Testament.[1] This approach emerges from the concerns of the previous chapters and looks forward to the exegetical moves, remarks, and conclusions of later chapters.[2] Preachers who use this pattern will likely adapt it to their own theological frames of reference, styles of working, and personalities.

We illustrate in two ways. First, we follow Psalm 110 as a case study through the twelve steps of the method.[3] Psalm 110 is an interesting study in its own right, and it also plays an important role in early Christian literature. Second, we briefly consider other texts.

1. DETERMINE THE LIMITS OF THE TEXT

One of the most basic rules of exegesis is to determine the limits of the text; a natural starting point and a natural ending point. The delimited text should be a meaningful unit of understanding. Still, the congregation may need to know some of the storyline, ideas, or information from the larger context in order to grasp the import of a specific passage. The preacher can supply this kind of background with supplementary remarks at the time of the reading of the text or in the sermon itself.

Psalm 110 is a complete literary unit. To take another example, 1 Kings 19:1-18 is also such a unit. This second example is the story of the revelation of the presence of God in sheer silence to Elijah on Mount Horeb. However, in the Common Lectionary the text was chopped into three pieces and spread across three Sundays, thus inhibiting its natural movement. In the Revised Common Lectionary in Year C, the text has been located on a single Sunday, but the reading contains only vv. 1-4 and 8-15. In order to honor the fullness of the text, the preacher must supply the missing details.

2. RECALL PRIOR ASSOCIATIONS WITH THE TEXT

Preachers typically have some preassociations with a text. These may be conscious or unconscious. They may come from direct association with the text or by transfer of association from a similar text. Preunderstandings may emanate from official church pronouncements, from recognized Bible expositors, from the memory of a childhood Sunday School class, or from barbershop lore. A preacher needs to become cognizant of these associations and to reflect on them so that they will not predetermine the preacher's conversation with the text and the direction of the sermon. Investigations of the text may confirm preassociations or may enlarge or correct them.

For instance, a preacher might naively think that the reference to the creation of the woman from the rib of the man in Genesis 2:18-25 shows the subordination of the woman to the man. However, a careful reading of the text, especially in light of Genesis 1:27-28 and 3:16, reveals that the man and the woman are created to live in mutuality and interdependence.

Christian preachers sometimes preassociate Christ and the church with texts from the Hebrew Scriptures without reflecting on the meanings of those texts in their own historical and literary contexts. Psalm 110 is often cited in the earliest Christian literature in order to speak of Christ (e.g., Matt. 22:44; Acts 2:34; 1 Cor. 15:25; Eph. 1:20; Heb. 1:3). Consequently, it is natural to think of Christ when encountering Psalm 110 in the psalter. However, to do so is to import associations into the text that were not present in pre-Christian Israel. Reading Christ into the Psalm may short-circuit ways in which the Psalm, as a song of Israel, might be instructive to the church.

Recalling prior associations with the text may also be useful in the sermon itself. The preacher might want to share with the congregation her or his changes of perception as a way of helping the congregation recognize the possibility of changing their own perceptions. "When I began the preparation of this sermon, I thought . . . but now, after study, I think . . . ."

3. IDENTIFY THE MAJOR TRAJECTORY(IES) OF THE OLD TESTAMENT OF WHICH THE TEXT IS A SPECIFIC CASE

A passage is usually a specific instance of one of the larger trajectories (or some combination thereof) mentioned in the previous chapter: the world of Deuteronomy, the priestly tradition, wisdom, or apocalypticism. The text may not directly signal its paradigm to the reader. But the text may presuppose the paradigm. Often, the preacher's awareness of the paradigm will help clarify points of interpretation and will help the preacher describe and evaluate how the reader would view God and the world and would behave in the world if the reader were to adopt the viewpoint of the text. The preacher can ask, "What is the vision of God and the world in this trajectory and how does the text manifest that trajectory and lead the reader to participate in its vision?"

The preacher must be careful not to reduce the text to a mere illustration of the larger trajectory. A text has its own perspectives and qualities that can be discovered only by digging into the text in its particularity.

Psalm 110 is commonly called a royal psalm. Scholars debate the time of its origin. In its present form and use, however, it partakes of the priestly paradigm. The interpreter, therefore, looks for how the text leads the community to become aware of God's presence and to respond to God's desire to hallow the whole of life, i.e., by helping all relationships and experiences correspond to God's design. What role does the monarch play in hallowing life?

How would the preacher know that the psalm is a part of the priestly paradigm? The text itself provides the clue when it notes that the monarch of the nation plays a priestly role in the community (v. 4). [Table 1 correlates books of the Old Testament and the four major trajectories.]

This step can particularly help preachers get a sense of the big picture within which to view a text. Many of the proverbs, for example, seem to be little more than common sense observations about life with few genuinely theological roots. But awareness of the larger worldview of wisdom, as summarized in the previous chapter, enables the preacher to appreciate the theological depth beneath the surface of the text. An underlying conviction of the sages is that God has ordered the universe with wisdom that reveals the divine will. That wisdom can be discovered by reflecting on life. Proverbs 3:30 advises, "Do not quarrel with anyone without cause, when no harm has been done to you." This text presumes that this is the divine will. One of the purposes of wisdom is to create a community of encouragement and support. Quarreling, especially without cause, frustrates this environment.

Table One

BOOKS OF THE OLD TESTAMENT CORRELATED WITH THE FOUR TRAJECTORIES

This table correlates books of the First Testament with the four trajectories discussed in chapter 2. While most of these correlations are clear, a few are imprecise. Some of the prophets participate in both the deuteronomic and priestly trajectories (with occasional touches of wisdom and protoapocalyptic included). We mark books that are especially hybrid with an asterisk (*). Of course, few books are "pure" examples of a single trajectory. Individual Psalms belong to the different trajectories and must be identified individually.

Deuteronomic	*Priestly*	*Wisdom*	*Apocalyptic*
Deuteronomy	Genesis	Job	Isaiah 24–26[b]
Joshua	Exodus	Proverbs	Isaiah 34–35
Judges	Leviticus	Ecclesiastes	Isaiah 56–66
1 Samuel	Numbers		Zechariah 9–14

Recalling prior associations with the text may also be useful in the sermon itself. The preacher might want to share with the congregation her or his changes of perception as a way of helping the congregation recognize the possibility of changing their own perceptions. "When I began the preparation of this sermon, I thought . . . but now, after study, I think . . . ."

3. IDENTIFY THE MAJOR TRAJECTORY(IES) OF THE OLD TESTAMENT OF WHICH THE TEXT IS A SPECIFIC CASE

A passage is usually a specific instance of one of the larger trajectories (or some combination thereof) mentioned in the previous chapter: the world of Deuteronomy, the priestly tradition, wisdom, or apocalypticism. The text may not directly signal its paradigm to the reader. But the text may presuppose the paradigm. Often, the preacher's awareness of the paradigm will help clarify points of interpretation and will help the preacher describe and evaluate how the reader would view God and the world and would behave in the world if the reader were to adopt the viewpoint of the text. The preacher can ask, "What is the vision of God and the world in this trajectory and how does the text manifest that trajectory and lead the reader to participate in its vision?"

The preacher must be careful not to reduce the text to a mere illustration of the larger trajectory. A text has its own perspectives and qualities that can be discovered only by digging into the text in its particularity.

Psalm 110 is commonly called a royal psalm. Scholars debate the time of its origin. In its present form and use, however, it partakes of the priestly paradigm. The interpreter, therefore, looks for how the text leads the community to become aware of God's presence and to respond to God's desire to hallow the whole of life, i.e., by helping all relationships and experiences correspond to God's design. What role does the monarch play in hallowing life?

How would the preacher know that the psalm is a part of the priestly paradigm? The text itself provides the clue when it notes that

4. DIG INTO THE TEXT ITSELF

One of the most important steps in exegesis is digging into the text itself. The interpreter seeks to discover and experience the specific vision of the passage through study of its content and assumptions. What should this text evoke in the minds and hearts of the listeners when they hear it in terms of ancient setting, literary style, and presuppositions? So as not to belabor this process (probably already familiar to the reader), we subdivide it into three phases.

(a) *Describe the setting of the text in its immediate literary context and its historical context* (insofar as the latter can be determined). How do these contexts provide perspectives that help the preacher enter into the world of the text?

The immediate literary context is of little use in making sense of Psalm 110. Although the historical context is debated, most scholars think that Psalm 110 was used at the time of the coronation of the sovereign. This coronation may have taken place as a part of the annual renewal of the covenant between God and the community. After the end of the monarchy, this Psalm was sometimes used in Jewish literature to describe an ideal future ruler.

Both literary and historical contexts come into play when interpreting the famous vision of the resurrection in the valley of dry bones in Ezekiel 37. By the time he writes Chapters 33–48, Ezekiel is in the Babylonian exile. Ezekiel's worldview has elements of the priestly trajectory and those of the deuteronomic trajectory and yet charts a course that moves beyond them.[4] In chapters 1–24, the prophet clarifies the circumstances that led to the exile: Israel has been disobedient. In chapters 25–32, the prophet lays bare the disobedience and doom of nations near Israel. But in chapters 33–48, Ezekiel looks forward to the restoration of Israel. Chapter 37 depicts God's promise to end the Exile and to breathe new life into the community.

(b) *Examine the language of the text.* How would an ancient listener hear the words, images, themes, and idioms of the passage? What are the particular shades of meaning in the body of literature of which the text is a part, as well as the overarching paradigm within which the text is found? Do the words of the text call forth associations with texts, stories, images, or ideas found elsewhere in the First Testament or in the ancient Near East? At this point, there is no substitute for going over the text word by word with the help of a concordance, Bible dictionaries, and commentaries. Often a single word or phrase will reverberate with associations that deepen the preacher's understanding.

A caution: an energetic morning with the concordance, the Bible dictionary, and the commentaries will usually generate far more exciting material than can be worked into a single sermon. The preacher must exercise focus and limitation to take into the pulpit only material that serves the particular sermon. Extra material can be filed for future sermons.

Psalm 110 is loaded with such associations. For the purpose of illustration, we discuss only two. In v. 1, God says to the monarch, "Sit at my right hand." We turn to the article on "right hand" in the Bible dictionary. The right hand is a place of authority. Some scholars also think it refers to taking a seat beside the Ark of the Covenant at the time of enthronement. So, we turn to the entry on "ark." The Bible dictionary reveals that the Ark is a primary symbol of God's presence, faithfulness, and power. The sovereign's rule is thereby guaranteed by the divine. In v. 4, the monarch is declared "a priest forever, according to the order of Melchizedek." The concordance leads us to the source of this citation (Gen. 14:18) where Melchizedek is described as the Canaanite ruler-priest of Salem who blessed Abram in the name of the God of Israel. By calling forth this association, Psalm 110:4 expects that the rule of a monarch will also be a blessing to the community. A biblical commentary reminds us that the essential work of the priest is to help the people become aware of the divine presence in their midst. Sovereign rule is to have this priestly dimension.

To take another example, the prophets are filled with talk about justice. Like other prophets, Jeremiah laments that the community has failed to practice justice in behalf of the orphan and the needy (5:28). God, however, is altogether just (9:24) and acts justly both toward the nations and toward Judah (23:5; 33:15). Jeremiah calls the community to practice justice (21:12; 22:3). People today often hear the word justice in terms of Western legal practice: a person or community gets what it deserves. As our commentary on justice in the next chapter shows, however, this perspective distorts the Hebrew notion of justice. In the latter, justice is a relational term that summarizes how God wants a community to live. The just community is one of mutuality, encouragement, and support. It is a community in which all relate to God and to one another in the way that God intended from the very beginning. Indeed, the fullest picture of the just community in the Bible is Genesis 1, where all created entities function together in mutual support.

(c) *Experience the text from the standpoint of its genre.* One of the most important discoveries in recent biblical interpretation and homiletics is that the genre and content of a text cannot be separated. The genre (e.g., narrative, prophetic oracle, wisdom saying, and apocalyptic vision) is not simply the container of the meaning of the text but is an integral part of the meaning.[5] In fact, the experience of receiving the text in its own genre is a part of the meaning of the text for the listener. Different genres affect the hearer in different ways. The preacher can ask, "How does this text touch the listener, given the ways in which its genre functions? How does the text attempt to move the heart, mind, and will of the community?"

Psalm 110 is a hymn. The reading of this Psalm evokes the memory of singing it. In corporate singing, the whole self is stirred. The congregation associates the content of the hymn with the feelings stirred during its singing. Of course, today's scholars cannot reconstruct the tune of Psalm 110. (We surmise that the tune was much more like the folk tunes of Palestine today than like the Bach chorales of our worship.) However, today's congregation can imagine what it might be like to sing this Psalm as the monarch is enthroned and thereby can experience the multimedia affirmation of the divine promises in this Psalm to the priestly-ruler and, thereby, to the community.[6]

Daniel narrates the story of the three youths in the fiery furnace (Dan. 3:1-30). The reader identifies with the youths, thereby experiencing their confrontation with Nebuchadnezzar, as well as their resolve to faithfulness, the intensity of the fire, and the divine providence in its midst. At the time of the Antiochene persecution (168–

165 B.C.E.), this story offered the community a vision of how to understand its own life. The challenge of Antiochus and Hellenization confronted the community. If they choose to remain faithful to God, they will experience the fire of persecution. But they can count on God's sustaining presence to lead them through the fire.

In addition to helping the preacher become more sensitive to the interpretation of the text, this step may provide clues to the development of the sermon (see step 12 below).

5. SUMMARIZE THE VISION OF THE TEXT

Using the data gathered in the previous step, the preacher summarizes (a) the surface vision of the text, and (b) the deeper vision of the text. As noted in the previous chapter, the surface vision is the straightforward meaning of the text in its own worldview, whereas the deeper vision includes those aspects of the text that are expressed in the language and idiom of its worldview but which transcend that worldview. The latter is particularly important if the text is intellectually or morally problematic. The deeper vision may allow the text to speak a positive word to the contemporary congregation when its surface vision appears unpromising.

At the surface level, Psalm 110 inspires confidence in the monarch of Israel as divinely appointed. The text encourages the congregation to recognize that God will rule the community, in part through the rule of the sovereign. Hence, the Psalm has the further effect of encouraging the community to be loyal to the sovereign and to experience divine blessing through the royal administration.

At the deeper level, the text bespeaks the divine promise to be faithful to the community and to bless it. In this case, divine faithfulness is expressed in the mode of the human institution of the monarchy. In Israel, the ruler of the community represents the divine will for justice in all relationships (Psalm 72). Yet, while the text speaks specifically of the enthronement of the sovereign of an ancient nation, it speaks more deeply of God's intention to use human institutions to bless communities with justice. It promises the divine presence to institutions that promote justice.

6. ANALYZE THE TEXT THEOLOGICALLY

As we have noted, the various biblical trajectories and texts make specific witnesses that do not always cohere. Of this, Paul Hanson asks, "Does not pluralism consign communities of faith to a sea of relativism within which they must lay hold of whatever ideological flotsom the currents of time send their way?"[7] Hanson responds that a Christian community can overcome the threat of infinite relativity if it has a transcendent theological vision within which to understand specific biblical paradigms and texts.[8] This vision articulates the nature of God and of God's purposes in the world in a comprehensive way. It is informed by the witnesses of the Bible and church history but it transcends them.

For the writers of *Holy Root, Holy Branches,* this vision is informed by three main sources. The deep witness of the overarching paradigm (discussed in chapter 2) is that God wills for the cosmos and all its inhabitants and parts to live together in relationships of mutuality, encouragement, and support. From the Reformed tradition (among other places), we are reminded that God's love is universal and unconditional. This is consistent with Holbert's Wesleyan tradition, whose theme hymn affirms to Jesus, "pure, unbounded love thou art"[9] and with Allen's heritage in the Campbell-Stone movement that reads the Bible " . . . with the eyes of the understanding fixed solely on God himself, his approbation and complacent affection for us."[10] While neither of us is a doctrinaire process theologian, the following criteria show that we have been touched with its influence.

The preacher analyzes the text theologically to determine the adequacy of the witness of the text.[11] To facilitate this conversation, we pose three criteria.[12] The use of these criteria is illustrated here and repeatedly throughout the rest of the book.

(a) *Appropriateness to the gospel.* The gospel is the news of God's unconditional love for each and all (including nature) and God's call for justice for each and all. The relationship between the text, the gospel, and the contemporary community has many possibilities that can be named only by sensitive listening to the various parties involved. A text may invite the contemporary community to see that its understanding of God's love and justice are too limited. Such a text may press the community to see that God loves others and wills justice for them in ways that the church has not recognized. Or the witness of the text may be more limited than the gospel. The text may deny God's love or justice for some. If so, the text is not fully appropriate to the gospel. Many texts combine these two possibilities as they assert God's love and justice for some but deny them for others. In this case, the preacher has the delicate responsibility of helping the congregation affirm the appropriate aspects of the passage even while correcting its limitations.[13]

Psalm 110 falls into the last category. It confirms God's love and will for justice for Israel. However, vv. 5-6 deny unconditional love to Israel's enemies. The psalm declares that God will fill the nations of Israel's enemies with corpses. The deep intention of the text is to affirm God's faithfulness. This is appropriate to the gospel. But one of the surface means whereby this faithfulness is enacted is destruction. This is hardly an expression of unconditional love for Israel's enemies. The preacher can thus both affirm aspects of the text and correct other aspects. This approach raises another question for the preacher: if God is not faithful through killing our enemies, then how can the community understand divine faithfulness?

(b) *Intelligibility*. Intelligibility has a double focus.[14] It refers to the coherence of Christian statements with one another. Christian statements cannot contradict one another and remain intelligible or coherent. The preacher is obliged to ask, "Is the vision of the text (and the sermon) consistent with other Christian beliefs?"

Intelligibility also refers to the degree to which the text makes sense in the light of the way in which the contemporary community understands the world to operate?[15] Contemporary Christians ought to be able to believe the ideas of the sermon without suspending disbelief in what they otherwise accept as true.[16] The contemporary community's perceptions of the world are modified from time to time as the human family discovers more about the universe and its operation. However, the preacher and the congregation are called to interpret the text in the light of their best perspectives on the world at the time, remembering with humility that their perspectives are not absolute. The preacher is still obliged, then, to ask, "Does this vision of the text make sense in the light of how I think the world operates today?"

We qualify these notions of intelligibility in two ways. For one, a biblical trajectory or text may cause the community to reevaluate its framework of coherence and its notions about how the world works. A passage may critique how we think about the world.[17] Texts may cause the community to see that its perceptions are too limited—or too large. For another, a text may be nonintelligible (or intelligible) on the surface, but it may not be intelligible (or nonintelligible) at its deeper level.

For the most part, Psalm 110 is intelligible. From the standpoint of compatibility with the contemporary understanding of the world, it is reasonable to believe that God can be faithful through human institutions. Except for its claim that God will fill the nations of Israel's enemies with corpses, Psalm 110 coheres with the gospel.

In 1 Samuel 5:1-12, the Philistines capture the Ark of the Covenant and place it in their temple beside the statue of their deity, Dagon. In the night, the Ark beats up Dagon, eventually cutting off Dagon's hands. At the surface level, this text is not intelligible. A nonmotorized object cannot beat up another nonmotorized object. However, the text makes a deeper and more intelligible point: the God of Israel is more powerful than other gods.

(c) *Moral plausibility.* Moral plausibility calls for the moral treatment of all involved in the vision of the text and its implications. In particular, the preacher asks, "Does the text call for all who are affected by the vision of the text to be treated as if God loves them unconditionally and as if God unreservedly wills justice for them?"

Psalm 110 is morally plausible with respect to Israel but not so in its attitudes towards Israel's enemies. In fact, a number of texts in both testaments founder on moral plausibility in their attitudes towards the treatment of others in the human family.

Psalm 58 is an example of a morally implausible text. The psalm is a prayer for God to curse the worshiper's enemies by breaking the teeth in their mouths. The psalmist pleads for them to vanish like water that runs away, to become like grass that is trodden underfoot, and to dissolve like the snail into slime. This prayer denies God's love for the enemy and wishes horrible things to happen to the enemy. The text is probably a countercurse that is designed to counteract a curse pronounced upon the worshiper by the enemy. Nonetheless, the content of the prayer is simply inconsistent with the gospel of unreserved and unmerited love.[18]

7. LISTEN FOR ECHOES OF THE TEXT IN THE NEW TESTAMENT AND IN CHRISTIAN LIFE BEYOND THE BIBLE

The preacher listens for echoes of the text in the Second Testament and in the subsequent life of the church. These may be quite direct, as when the Second Testament explicitly cites the text. Or the echoes may be somewhat indirect, as when the Second Testament alludes to a text. Further, the church sometimes uses a text, image, or theme from the First Testament in Christian theology or liturgy.[19]

By using a concordance, the preacher can often locate instances when the Second Testament refers to the First. The preacher identifies key words in the First Testament passage, looks them up in the Second Testament, and investigates the passages in which they occur to determine whether the Second Testament actually makes use of the text from the First.[20] For instance, in Acts 18:18-23, Paul cuts his hair to keep a vow. By looking up hair and vow in the concordance, the preacher quickly discovers that Paul was enacting a Nazirite vow described in Numbers 6:1-21. In the midst of a discussion of church discipline, Paul admonishes the Corinthians to clean out the old yeast because Christ, the Paschal Lamb, has been sacrificed. By looking up these terms, the preacher discovers that they are drawn from Exodus 12, especially vv. 15, 3-8, and 21. The foundation of Paul's ethical exhortation, then, is to understand Christ as the Paschal Lamb of the church. The preacher will often get help from secondary sources, such as the commentaries or the Bible dictionaries. We encourage preachers to pursue their instincts in this matter, as well. A preacher will often "feel" a connection between a text in the First Testament and a text or theme in the Second. Of course, the results of a potential intuitive discovery must be critically examined to determine their accuracy.

The preacher must soon make a key decision. If the text from the First Testament has echoes in the Second, should the Second Testament be brought into the sermon? Usually the preacher can cite good reasons for responding to the question both affirmatively and negatively. But the preacher can responsibly answer that question only after understanding how the text is used in the Second Testament.

If the text from the First Testament does appear in the Second, the preacher will want to notice how it is used in the Second Testament. At this point, we anticipate chapter 6 by positing three possible relationships between texts when the Second Testament echoes the First.

(a) The First Testament may help interpret the Second. The language of the First Testament may help the church name its experience and see how the traditions of the First Testament are confirmed, interpreted, extended, and adapted for the church.

(b) The Second Testament may interpret the text from the First as a prophecy that is now fulfilled. The passage from the First Testament expresses a promise that, according to the early church, was not made good until the coming of Christ. At other times, the prophecy offers interpretive categories that help the church explain Jesus Christ and its experience without diminishing the First Testament or the life of the people who wrote it.

(c) The use of the text in the Second Testament occasionally implies a relationship of contrast, even supersession, in the two testaments. In this case, the Second Testament allegedly exposes the inferiority of the First Testament and (or) of Jewish people, beliefs, practices, and institutions.

These categories sometimes overlap. The Gospel of John, for example, interprets Jesus and the Christian life in categories that are drawn almost exclusively from Judaism. Yet John is polemical towards many Jewish people and some of their convictions.

The connection of texts in a lectionary is a subcategory of this discussion. If the text from the First Testament appears as one of the lectionary readings for the day, the preacher must reflect on the relationship of the lection to the other lections for the day. Are the texts genuinely related to one another, either directly or indirectly? Or are they essentially unrelated? If the former, the preacher must decide whether to comment on this relationship either in connection with the scripture readings or in the sermon itself. If the latter, the preacher needs to be careful not to miseducate the congregation nor to violate the integrity of the lections by leaving the impression that the texts are related when they are not.

Psalm 110 is cited more frequently in the Second Testament than any other passage from the First Testament. Each use of the psalm has its distinctive aspects.[21] Most instances fall into the first category above (a. The Old Testament helps interpret the New). The psalm explains the relationship of God, Christ, and the church. Christ manifests God's rule in the church much like the monarch manifests the divine sovereignty in Israel. One can see this, for instance, in Ephesians 1:20.

Mark 12:35-37 is an example of the second use above (b. The Second Testament regards the First as prophecy fulfilled). Mark depicts David as the author of Psalm 110. David, under the influence of the Holy Spirit, prophesied that the Christ would be superior to the son of David (i.e., Israel's sovereign). The reader recognizes that Jesus fulfills the hope of the psalm.

Hebrews 7 is an example of the use of the psalm to show that Jesus and Christianity have superseded Judaism as in the third category above (c. A relationship of contrast between the testaments). Hebrews 7:15 uses Psalm 110:4 to show that the priesthood of Jesus is superior to the levitical priesthood.

Some texts from the First Testament echo in the life of the church outside of the Second Testament. The crossing of the Red Sea, for instance, is associated typologically with baptism in some theological traditions. The preacher might need to discuss such an association to help the congregation discern critically how the association is or is not germane to the sermon.

8. ESTABLISH THE GENERAL DIRECTION OF THE SERMON

The preacher now establishes the general direction of the sermon. This step has two important dimensions. One is determining the general theological content of the message. The other is determining whether to bring the Second Testament (or some other component of Christian origin) into the homily.

If the text is appropriate, intelligible, and morally plausible the preacher asks, "How does this passage help the community perceive and respond to God's presence and purposes?" If the text is inappropriate, unintelligible, or immoral, the preacher may envision an encounter with the text that will be of benefit to the congregation. For example, the sermon may critique an intractable text so as to help the congregation discern misperceptions of the text.

When a text from the First Testament echoes in the Second, there are no simple rules for determining whether to bring the echoes into the sermon. A preacher ordinarily ought to take into account the occasion of the sermon, the needs of the congregation, the prominence of the passage from the First Testament in the Second, and in Christian consciousness, as well as the time needed to explain the relationship of the two passages. On a major Christian holy day, it may be important to carry forward the text into the Second Testament. If the congregation suffers from a misconception about the passage, the preacher may feel the need to discuss this misconception in the light of the Christian reflection. The minister may want to bring material of Christian origin into the sermon when the passage from the First Testament has become so closely associated with a passage in the Second Testament or with themes or practices of the Christian life that the congregation uncritically thinks of the passage in Christian terms.

We recommend that preachers first explore the possibility of letting a passage from the Hebrew Bible speak on its own. When the preacher brings the Second Testament or Christ or Christian doctrine or practice into the sermon, let it be for specific and significant reasons.

A preacher could easily think that Psalm 110 is irrelevant to the church in the United States today. We do not have a monarchy. Even when remembering that the categories "church" and "state" as separate entities are contemporary and not ancient, the preacher may be uneasy with the close alliance between religious and political leadership implied in the psalm. Further, liberation theologians and others have heightened our sensitivity to the abuses of power by hierarchical authorities such as kings and queens.

However, the deeper vision of the text, as outlined in step 5, suggests that a sermon on Psalm 110 might examine ways in which God seeks to express the holy will for justice in the community through human institutions and movements.[22] God promises to be faithful to such initiatives. A sermon could encourage the congregation to identify such movements and to have enough confidence in the divine will to pursue them unrelentingly. If the preacher decides that it is important to bring the Second Testament into the passage, the sermon might help the congregation discover how the church experiences such divine initiative and faithfulness through Christ.

Zechariah 14 is a protoapocalyptic passage that predicts a cataclysmic event that will end the present evil era of world history and inaugurate another age in which all things are in accord with the divine rule. In the new world, even horses and cooking pots will be holy. Many late twentieth-century Christians find it unintelligible to think of God intervening in history in such a cataclysmic way. However, the deeper vision of the text serves as a principle of social criticism by which to evaluate our present social order and, thereby, to remember that things are not as God wants them to be. The text also reminds us of God's unremitting will to help the world conform more closely to the divine intention. The text lures the community to respond positively to God's efforts. Even if today's congregation may not hold Zechariah's vision of a cataclysmic intervention, they must not lose sight of the deeper point that God wills for the world to manifest fully a loving, just, supportive quality of life and that God is ever working toward that goal.

In addition, Zechariah 14 echoes in the Second Testament. For instance, several images from Zechariah 14 appear in the so-called little apocalypse of the Synoptic Gospels (Matt. 24:1-51 and parallels). The sermon might make the point that, because of its knowledge of

God through Christ, the church joins Zechariah in recognizing the brokenness of the present age and in hope for the new.

9. THINK ANALOGICALLY

As we noted in the previous chapter, the hermeneutic of analogy rests on two foundation stones. First, it recognizes differences in paradigm, culture, and expression between the worlds of antiquity and today. But second, it also recognizes that at the deepest levels of human awareness, ancient and contemporary people are often very similar. Beneath differing paradigms, cultures, and styles of expression there is often common orientation to life. The similar feelings and awarenesses may go by different names, but their feeling and effect are closely related. Therefore, the hermeneutic of analogy seeks to bridge the gap between ancient and contemporary communities by locating language and events in contemporary culture that function similarly to those in the text.

The congregation will probably feel the most direct affinity to the wisdom trajectory discussed in chapter 2. Indeed, several wisdom texts do not require much in the way of analogy. The Song of Songs, for instance, can provide a direct entry to a discussion of sensuality and sexuality. Many in the congregation will likely be quite distant from the apocalyptic trajectory. As we said in chapter 2, it is important for the preacher to be especially sensitive to analogies with apocalyptic and protoapocalyptic passages. The deuteronomic and priestly paradigms both call for creative analogical thinking for these trajectories to provide help for today.

When preparing a sermon on Psalm 110, a preacher might ask how the congregation experiences threats to the just life. What institutions or movements are seeking justice in today's world? How can the congregation join them? How is God faithful to their initiatives? What does God promise to such a congregation? If the preacher concludes it is important to deal with Ephesians 1:20 in conjunction with Psalm 110:1, a leading question might be, "How do we experience the sovereignty of God (as expressed through Christ) over the principalities and powers of the world?"

To take another example, consider Hosea (whose book has affinities with the deuteronomic model). Is the relationship of the church and its identity similar to that between Hosea and Gomer (and between God and Israel)? If so, what are the points of similarity? How has the church abandoned aspects of its faithful devotion to God and its witness? Perhaps the church has made unholy alliances with forces in the cultures, joined in the worship of Baal, or forgotten God. What word of promise can the preacher offer the community? What can the congregation do to join God in the work of restoration? Here, the deuteronomic emphasis on repentance is key.

10. TRACE THE EFFECT OF THE PREACHER'S CONVERSATION WITH THE TEXT

Preachers might look again at their responses to step 2. How has the preacher's conversation with the text affected her or his understanding of it? At the least, the exegesis and subsequent reflection ought to have deepened the preacher's perception. At the other end of the spectrum, the process of engaging the text may have brought the preacher to an understanding of the text that is 180 degrees from the preacher's starting point. Will the congregation be enriched if the preacher brings these changes of perspective into the sermon?

11. STATE THE CORE OF WHAT THE PREACHER WANTS TO SAY IN A SINGLE INDICATIVE SENTENCE

One of the most revered axioms of homiletics is that the preacher should state the core idea of the sermon in a single sentence. This sentence goes by many names (e.g., proposition, big idea, focus statement, thesis, sermon in a sentence). Out of the exegesis, theological analysis, and hermeneutical reflection, the preacher distills a single idea that will be the centering point of the sermon. This sermon in a sentence summarizes the good news that will come from God through the sermon.

The summary sentence normally has the following characteristics. (a) In grammatical terms, it is indicative in mood. The indicative describes what is. It is the mood of present reality. For example: God loves you. The indicative contrasts with the imperative, the mood of command. For example: you should love God. The priority of the indicative in the construction of the sermon mirrors theological reality. God first acts in our behalf. God's action is indicative. We then respond to the divine initiative. Of course, the preacher might come upon situations that call for a sermon whose dominant note is the imperative, but even then the preacher should make clear the content of the indicative on which the imperative is based. (b) The sentence should be as simple and uncomplicated as possible. The sermon tends to become more complicated, and even convoluted, as this sentence becomes more complex. (c) God is ordinarily the subject of the sermon in a sentence since the sermon is primarily news from and about God. (d) The verb is normally an activity of God in behalf of the community. (e) The predicate is often a result of the actions of God. The predicate sometimes includes an indication of the congregation's response to God.

A possible sermon in a sentence for a message on Psalm 110 is:

God is acting to bring justice to our community by means of [specific circumstances or people that the preacher can name].

The sermon could relate the monarchy to the quest for justice in the community. The sermon might help the congregation recognize impulses towards justice in its own world that function similarly to the monarchy in antiquity. How might the congregation experience these impulses as demonstrations of divine faithfulness?

12. SELECT A FORM AND MOVEMENT FOR THE SERMON

The preacher will frequently find it useful to reflect consciously on possible structures and movements for the sermon. Such reflection allows the preacher to shape the sermon so that it has the best chance to be received positively by the listeners. For example, if the congregation is likely resistant to the direction of the homily, the preacher may want to avoid antagonizing them at the very beginning of the sermon with a bald statement of the main idea of the sermon. The preacher may want to shape the sermon so that the congregation eases into the subject and, thereby, has a greater chance of being receptive to it.

Because sermon form is one of the most widely discussed aspects of preaching today, we do not dwell on it here. However, we call attention to an approach to preaching that is especially promising for sermons on the Hebrew Scriptures. Recent homiletics emphasizes the possibility of letting the literary genre and function of the text suggest the design of the sermon.[23] The preacher notices how the text communicates its genre. The preacher designs the sermon to function similarly. Sometimes the text can actually provide a structure for the sermon. For instance, this is often true of narratives. The story of Jacob's encounter with God at the Jabbok (Gen. 32:1-32) unfolds in a series of scenes that could easily become a series of subunits in the sermon. Scene by scene, the preacher might make analogies with the contemporary setting. The experience of hearing the sermon then becomes sequentially similar to that of hearing the text.

At other times, the function of the text may suggest an approach to the sermon. Psalm 110 seeks to awaken the awareness of the congregation to the divine will for justice and to God's trustworthiness in the search for justice. The experience of singing the psalm (or of hearing it) kindles such awareness and feeling. How can the preacher use ideas and images in the sermon to kindle similar ideas and feelings?

A step-by-step approach to the preparation of the sermon cannot guarantee that preachers will engage a text at a significant level. Indeed, a preacher's most stunning insights sometimes seem to come out of the blue. And the repetition of a single pattern of engaging the text, week after week, can have a narcotic effect on preacher and congregation. Even the most disciplined exegesis cannot expose all the riches of a single text in the Hebrew Bible in a given week. But an exegetical pattern can often help carry the preacher's imagination across the occasional homiletical wasteland. It can help intensify those infrequent moments on the exegetical mountaintop when the preacher can see the promised land.

CHAPTER FOUR

TEXTS AND THEMES FROM THE OLD TESTAMENT

In chapters 2 and 3, we offered a number of abbreviated comments on texts in order to suggest the potential for preaching proposed in this book. In this chapter, we explore several texts exegetically to give fuller illustration. These texts are drawn from the range of trajectories in the Old Testament. They do not lead to the knotty hermeneutical and theological problems that are associated with the texts that we discuss in chapter 5. In terms of the twelve-step process enumerated in the previous chapter, these investigations end at about step 8 (establishing a general direction for the sermon) with some general remarks at the level of step 9 (thinking analogically).

In keeping with the paradigmatic approach articulated in chapter 2, we comment on how knowledge of the trajectory illumines our understanding of the specific text. We also indicate possibilities for how the particular passage can function for the listeners as a paradigm of God's presence and purposes.

In addition, we bring a new element into the discussion. We look at how texts within trajectories and from different trajectories interpret similar subjects. Toward this end, we have selected four themes that are fundamental to the Old Testament and that cut across the various paradigms: creation, *hesed* (steadfast love), the deliverance of Israel, and justice.[1] This additional exercise is important in two ways. First, it shows how a motif can be developed within a trajectory. Like a prism, different texts within a trajectory refract the theme with different colors. Second, it demonstrates how texts from the various trajectories share much in common but also develop their own shades of interpretation; sometimes the individuality of trajectory or text is subtle but quite forceful. We conclude the discussion of each theme with possibilities for preaching that theme. A congregation's theological reservoir will often be deepened by hearing sermons that compare and contrast how different texts and trajectories treat the same theme.[2]

Preaching on Creation

Our discussion of creation focuses largely on the priestly tradition to illustrate how a theme develops within a single trajectory. In connection with the last text, we comment on the importance of the motif of creation to apocalypticism.

Genesis 1. In a previous chapter we claimed that the central model to be discerned in the First Testament is that of one God for all.[3] The church has from its earliest days borne witness to this centrality in its creeds that nearly all begin with an announcement of God the creator: "I believe in God, the Father Almighty, maker of heaven and earth"; "We believe in the one God, maker and ruler of all things."

From the fact that God creates flows other beliefs about God: God sustains the creation; God judges the creation; God redeems the creation. When we proclaim that God is creator we at the same time claim that no one else, least of all ourselves, is ultimately creator. This claim puts God at the center of all striving and effort and effectively relativizes our human attempts at ultimacy. Further, Genesis 1 reveals the character of the cosmic community God intended: all things in mutual relationship and support.

For the preacher, Genesis 1 is an ideal starting point from which to work with big pieces of the current world jigsaw puzzle: ecology, the environment, the nature of community. In regard to the latter, what message is more needed in a day when both individuals and nations claim well-nigh heavenly authority for their own policies, their own economic ideas, their own national aspirations, their own racial superiority, and their own individual autonomy? At the time this passage was given its present form by the priestly theologians, Israel was in chaos. This passage assures all communities in chaos that an abiding and trustworthy reliability lies beneath the chaos. In any era, Genesis 1 can open the door to a conversation about the relationship between religion and science. This topic is timely to the late twentieth century in the light of the resurgence of the discussion regarding evolution and creationism.

Because we have already spent some time with Genesis 1, let us turn to several other texts in which the motif of creation is crucial in order to see how these can enlarge a congregation's understanding of this vital notion.

Exodus 14. It may appear odd to address this famous deliverance text under the category of creation, but a closer look gives the reason. On the second day of creation, according to the account of Genesis 1, God "*separate[s]* the waters from the waters" (v. 6). On the succeeding day, the separated waters, now existing below the dome of the sky, are "gathered together into one place, in order that the *dry ground* might appear" (v. 9). As the days of creation unfold, it becomes clear that the dry ground (the habitable earth) is the special place of the creative work of God.

This creation scenario forms the backdrop for Israel's deliverance at the Sea of Reeds (that, like Genesis 1, is shaped by the priestly hand).[4] The separation of waters and the appearance of dry ground lie at the heart of the descriptions. Both vv. 22 and 29 say that the Israelites go into the sea "on *dry ground,*" the same Hebrew word found in Genesis 1. In Exodus, we further witness the *dividing* of waters as the saving action of God. However, in this case, two different Hebrew words are used to describe the action of dividing and separating. Nevertheless, the creator God of Genesis is now portrayed as the saving God of Exodus, and the divine actions of creation and salvation are related. This tradition connects the creation of God directly with the salvation of God.

We witness a similar scene in Joshua 3:17. The Israelites enter the land of promise through a division of waters, this time of the Jordan river, and once again on "dry ground" in the middle of the Jordan. With this further repetition of the creation themes of the division of waters and the creation of dry ground as the place of salvation, the tradition here adds the notion of the promise of future rest for the people of God. God is creator, redeemer, and sustainer of the people into the future.

The preacher could use this motif to show that God's universal intention (expressed in Genesis 1) is not vague and amorphous but comes to expression in particularity (the people of Israel crossing the Sea of Reeds). Further, God is no clockmaker who set the world in motion and then retired. Can a preacher help the congregation identify how God continues to create in our world after the priestly pattern? These texts also open a window on the relationship between creation and redemption; redemption allows relationships to be the way God intended at the beginning. A Christian preacher may also see in this theme a significant part of the theological backdrop to the initiation rite of Christian baptism. From the waters of chaos, divided by the power of God, emerges onto dry ground the redeemed initiate.

Psalm 8. In Psalm 8, a meditation on Genesis 1 and characteristic of the priestly trajectory, the poet first hymns the majesty of the name of God, the ineffable YHWH. It would have been predictable for the poet merely to list the creative actions of God as proof of God's majesty. But the thought moves in a different direction.

The meaning of this remarkable passage appears to be as follows: God has placed the glory of the divine name "above the heavens," that is, in a spot unattainable by any human being. Yet, this divine glory is best protected against its foes by—of all things—the cooing of suckling babies! Indeed, these soft baby sounds will "silence the enemy and the avenger!" What are we to make of this anomaly? We would argue that this seeming incongruity between the world's might (foes, enemies, and avengers) and the epitome of weakness (a suckling child) reveals the scope and character of divine power. The suckling child of God is more powerful than the enemies' armies.

The more famous incongruity that follows in vv. 3-8, namely the distinction between the vastness of God's creation and the tiny insignificance of a human being in it, shows us again that in the creation of God things are seldom what they seem. The insignificant human is in fact "little less than God" and God has "given them (rule) dominion" over the remainder of the creation.

When the poet concludes the poem with the identical hymn to the majesty of God's name, our understanding of what that means has been sharply altered in a way that is attractive to the contemporary preacher. God's majesty is demonstrated in the way God exercises power and in God's relationship with the human community. The preacher, then, might help the congregation reexamine its perception and use of power. This theme has obvious echoes in the New Testament. For instance 2 Corinthians 4:7 reads "We have this treasure in clay jars [cracked pots?]" so that it may be clear that this extraordinary power belongs to God and does not come from us.

Isaiah 45. The great unknown poet of the Exile of Israel, the so-called Second Isaiah (who is influenced by the priestly theology), offers to us further explorations of the theme of creation. In chapter 45:12-13 the poet uses the fact of God's creation of the world as an argument against those who would deny God's astonishing choice of the pagan monarch, Cyrus of Persia, to be God's Anointed One, the Messiah. The argument goes: if you agree that I, God, "stretched out the heavens" without counsel or help from anyone (45:5-6), then I can call whomever I choose to do my work of salvation, even one who has never heard of God, indeed, does not know God's name (45:4). The implications of such an argument are staggering for those of us who would in any way limit the power or provenance of God. The preacher can ask, "Whom is God using in our own day? Is God using a Cyrus?"

Isaiah 51. Isaiah 51 turns to creation to ground future hope for the exiles. At creation, God cut Rahab (a chaos-monster) in pieces. Later God dried the sea so that the redeemed could cross over. "In the same way, the ransomed of YHWH shall return and come to Zion with singing and everlasting joy shall be on their heads." Sorrow will vanish (Isa. 51:9-11).

One of Holbert's first instructors in Old Testament, Professor Kermit Schoonover, was fond of saying that much of the hymnic language of Isaiah could be summarized by "Do it again, YHWH!" The prophet implores God to "cut into pieces" whatever Rahabs are alive today and to dry up the sea again so that God's people may return home to everlasting peace.

Isaiah 51 is influenced by the priestly tradition, but we see in it a root notion of apocalypticism. The act of creation is the paradigm of the act of eschatological redemption. As God acted in the past, so God will act decisively in the future. Indeed, the end time (the eschaton) will be like the beginning time (the world as it was at creation). This notion provides the preacher with a wonderful way to image the eschatological hope (and to answer the question that comes up in every pastorate, "What will heaven be like?"). Further Isaiah sees the continuing reliability of the created order as ground for hope in deliverance. People can be hopeful because God has sustained creation, and, indeed, continues to create within it.

Sermon Series on Creation. The theme of creation might be explored in sermons over several Sundays. An important series could relate the priestly vision of the created world to contemporary ecological and environmental concerns.[5] A series could also relate creation and redemption. Several of the texts could be used to reveal the character of God and the inter-relatedness of God's activity in the world: creator (Genesis 1), redeemer (Exodus 14), sustainer (Isaiah 51), and bringer of a hopeful future (Isaiah 51). Another series might focus on the extent and nature of divine power (Genesis 1; Psalm 1; and Isaiah 45).

Preaching on Hesed *(Steadfast Love)*

We now explore a motif that describes God's relationship with the people of Israel: *hesed.* Its most common English translation is steadfast love (the RSV and the NRSV). This notion encompasses the grand thought that YHWH loves the people with a love that cannot be broken or withdrawn. It lies at the heart of Israel's understanding of the nature of God, the God of Jesus Christ.

Exodus 34:6-7. After the people of Israel have disobeyed the first commandment (Exod. 20:4-6) by molding and worshiping a molten calf (Exod. 32:4), Moses returns to the holy mountain, and in an astonishing scene convinces the furious YHWH not to obliterate the erring people (32:11-14). Then this same Moses, having saved his wretched people, insists that God forgive them for their evil and goes on to offer his own life for theirs if God refuses to forgive (32:32). Moses urges God to go with the people as they move toward the land of promise. God first promises that "the Presence" will go with them, but Moses demands proof of the presence (33:12-17). God agrees, but still the cheeky Moses is not satisfied. "Show me your glory" (33:18)!

This insistence appears to be little less than the desire to be shown the very essence of the creator of the world!

Remarkably, God does not directly deny Moses' arrogant request. In fact in Exodus 33:19 Moses is told that the basic thing about YHWH is grace and compassion, given by a God who is utterly free. But Moses, and we, would know more. And in 34:6-7 more is given.

> YHWH is both filled with *hesed* and acts with *hesed*. YHWH is a compassionate, merciful, and gracious God, slow to anger, filled with *hesed* and faithfulness, keeping *hesed* for the thousandth generation by forgiving iniquity, transgression, and sin; but by no means clearing the guilty, visiting the iniquity of the parents upon the children and the children's children to the third and the fourth generation.

God's compassion and grace evidence themselves in *hesed*, which is best demonstrated by God's comprehensive forgiveness of "iniquity, transgression, and sin," the three terms most often used to announce Israelite rejection of God and God's demands. And this forgiving *hesed,* as well as its accompanying "faithfulness," is kept by YHWH "for the thousandth generation," a future time unimaginable in its vast length, while God's just judgments against those clearly guilty last only to an easily foreseeable "third and fourth generation."

This passage, and the priestly understanding of *hesed* that it defines, is of immense value to today's preacher. For the preacher stands before a congregation of sinners. God's will is to forgive our evils even beyond our imaginings. It is God's very nature to forgive, and because that forgiveness moves far into our futures, we can be certain that God wills to be in convenant with us, will abide with us, and will show love to us over and over again, despite our constant iniquities, transgressions, and sins. The preacher's task is to help the congregation recognize and admit its sin, and, more important, to help the members of the congregation accept the promise of this text. One of the preacher's challenges is to image *hesed* so that the congregation feels it in the depths of their beings.

The abiding care of priestly *hesed* is in stark contrast to the sentiment, still intoned in some Christian circles, that the God of the First Testament is "only a God of judgment and wrath." Indeed, the "amazing grace" of *hesed* provides the preacher with an opportunity to show a continuity between the testaments.

Micah 6. The relatively short prophecy of Micah is unmatched in its denunciations of the evils of Israel and Judah and their capital cities, Samaria and Jerusalem. Oracle upon oracle denounces the evil of societal injustices, including theft of property (2:2); the stifling of the prophetic word of God (2:6-7); oppression of the powerless by the powerful (3:1-3); corruption of the priests and the prophets (3:11); and corrupt business practices (6:10-12). Yet, this catalogue of wickedness is interrupted in chapter 6 by a justly famous scene where the God of all the earth summons the evil people to dispute with them and to remind them of what is required if they are to remain the people of God.

In vv. 3-5, God describes the state of reprobation into which Israel has fallen. How is it possible that these children of the God of *hesed* are acting as they are in the face of all of God's multitudinous saving deeds on their behalf? God has provided leadership for them, saved them time and again from powerful kings, potent prophets, and (the story mentioned is found in Numbers 22–24) a dangerous wilderness. How are they to live as the people of this God?

Traditional and extraordinary sacrifices will no longer serve to satisfy the demands of the aggrieved God, so, the mountains and the foundations of the earth announce what God demands in 6:8.

> God has told you, mortal one, what is good.
> What does YHWH want from you?
> Is it not to do justice, to love *hesed,*
> to walk in submission to your God?

In this imaginative dispute the meaning of *hesed* is extended for us. The nature of God to maintain a faithful relationship with God's people, should call forth from those people actions of justice. These actions are in sharp contrast to the horrors of the society that Micah has described. Proper recognition of the basic nature of God must lead to a search for justice; such a search would be a direct sign of genuine submission to this God. In short, genuinely to love God is precisely to do justice (see Jer. 22:15-16 for another statement of this truth).

Micah's call to justice reminds us of the deuteronomic paradigm. The community is called by divine *hesed*. However, that love calls for obedience. Israel is disobedient. Its collapsing life is a sign of its curse. In this context Micah emphasizes that while *hesed* is a quality of God, it is also to be manifest in the relationships of the people with one another.

When turning to Micah 6, the preacher might stress the priority of God's steadfast love for understanding the community and its actions. The sermon might bring out parallels between the actions of the people in Micah's day and the actions of people in our own day. Does the contemporary culture stifle the word of God? Oppress the powerless? Allow corruption among priests and prophets? Engage in corrupt business? Are these practices resulting in a curse (i.e., in the decay of the community's life)? The preacher can point to practical ways that obedience can institute *hesed* in our affairs today.

At one point, however, the preacher may take a different tack for our day than Micah did in his. The corruption in Micah's day had reached the point that doom was inexorable. It is not clear that the preacher should reach the same conclusion concerning today's church and society. It appears that our world has time to repent. The knowledge of God's *hesed* for us gives us the confidence to do so.

Jonah. The tiny story of Jonah has generated a large volume of commentary over the years with even the central meaning of the book much in dispute.[6] This is as it should be with a great work of imaginative literature; no single theme can begin to exhaust the riches of any such work. Our contention is that the primary concern of the author is to make fun of the self-serving hypocritical prophet, Jonah, by skewering him on his own supposed system of beliefs.

Jonah is called to preach to Nineveh. But the prophet's ship encounters a storm. The pagan sailors are saved. Jonah himself is saved. Jonah gets to Nineveh and preaches and the Ninevites (and their cows!) are saved. Jonah is enraged! Enraged about what? It might be that he feels God has made a fool of him by not destroying the city as

Jonah had announced. But there is a fuller reason. In his rage he prays to God in 4:2.

The prayer suggests that Jonah is not simply angry because he has been made the fool. He is angry because he recognizes that in a world of a God of *hesed,* even Ninevites might find their way into the favor of God. In short, Jonah would rather die than worship in the same pew with a Ninevite. God's insufferable desire to save, to maintain covenant love, with any and all, is just too much for Jonah.

Though God tries still to teach the rascal the truth with the fast-growing and fast-dying magic plant (4:6-11), we cannot know Jonah's response to the rhetorical question that ends the story: "Should not I pity Nineveh?" In a brilliant strategy, the writer leaves the listening community to answer the question. The writer hopes, of course, that the listeners will answer "Yes."

The preacher can ask, "Who are the Ninevites to us?" How does it affect our attitude toward them (and our relationship with them) to realize that divine *hesed* is as much for them as for us? Jonah's unwillingness to welcome God's steadfast love for sinful Nineveh also corrupted his own life; Jonah wanted to die. How does the embrace of God's *hesed* for those whom the congregation finds distasteful help the congregation itself? Indeed, as the story of Jonah concludes, the listeners are warned not to be like Jonah! Join the sailors and the Ninevites, both people and cows, and worship the God whose *hesed* is to the thousandth generation.

Ezra 7. As the book of Ezra opens, Ezra is in exile. But in Ezra 7, the Persian ruler Artaxerxes gives permission for Ezra to return to Jerusalem. Ezra, priest and interpreter of the law (and exemplification of the priestly paradigm) can lead the people in returning to the way of God. What makes this return possible? According to 7:28, God has placed *hesed* in the heart of the Persian monarch. Ezra is enabled to perform the work that God has given him to perform only because God made it possible by the gift of steadfast love, albeit in its surprising expression in the heart of Artaxerxes.

How, the preacher might ponder, does God's steadfast love enable the congregation to do what it is called to do? Can the preacher point to instances that are as concrete in our setting as the movement of God through Artaxerxes?

Series on Hesed. A series of sermons on this theme might demonstrate that the God of the First Testament is a God of never-failing love for all. Such a claim gives the lie to any neo-Marcionite ideas that the First Testament God is alien from the God of Jesus Christ. The first sermon might remind the congregation that the nature of God is precisely _hesed,_ a love that forgives sin and will not let the congregation go (Exodus 34). The next sermon might help the congregation understand what it means to love _hesed_ in our communal relationships (Micah). The third sermon could encourage the congregation to understand the universal scope of divine _hesed_ (Jonah). A final sermon could lead the listeners to understand how God's _hesed_ works specifically for them (Ezra). A fifth sermon might connect the _hesed_ of the First Testament with the steadfast love of God experienced by the church through Jesus Christ.

The Deliverance of Israel

The theme of the deliverance of Israel from the horror of Egyptian bondage is central to much of the First Testament. It comes up in all four trajectories.

Exodus 1–2. It is remarkable just how the First Testament so often begins its greatest stories. We are not confronted by the tramp of mighty armies or the roar of huge crowds of people. This dramatic flair is a portrait often given by the productions of Hollywood biblical epics, but such pictures are quite alien to the Bible. The story of the beginnings of the nation of Israel introduce a lying husband, his powerful wife, and a succession of scheming, self-serving characters. The entry into the land of promise begins with the secret visit of two spies to a house of ill repute, well-known in the city of Jericho, and their subsequent protection by the madam of the house, Rahab. Of course, Christians ought not to be surprised by these tiny beginnings to great stories. We believe that our story includes a birth in humble circumstances, in a backwater village.

As Exodus 1 begins, we read of a tiny group of Israelites enslaved by pharaoh, but finally saved by God through the unlikely actions of a desperate mother, a vigilant sister, two wiley midwives, and the pharaoh's own daughter. The infant Moses is not only nursed by the mother who thought she had lost him forever, but she is paid out of pharaoh's pocket to do so.

Several important points should be noted about this amazing and surprising tale. First, five women save the baby Moses, a remarkable turn of events in a patriarchal world. Second, deliverance comes in wholly unexpected ways and by wholly unexpected means. Not only are the women surprisingly involved, but pharaoh's own foolishness and uncontrollable rage lead directly and ironically to his undoing. Third, humor is prominent, and humor of a very broad, slapstick variety, from clownish kings to brash women. A sermon based on this text can make good use of this humor as a significant part of the story's presentation. (For homiletical use of these points, see the sermon, "The Surprise of Deliverance," in chapter 7.)

As a preacher moves toward a sermon on Exodus 1–2, she or he will want to keep clearly in mind the possible dynamic analogies thrown up by this story. With whom should the congregation identify in the narrative? Are we pharaoh, grasping desperately for a power that is never ours? Are we pharaoh's daughter, playing a role in a larger history of which we are not fully aware? Are we Moses' sister, rushing up to the place of power, urging it to go in ways that it would not go on its own? Are we the Israelites whom God is even now delivering? The priestly theologians envision a God whose scope can easily encompass any of these points of identification.

Amos 9:7-10. The theme of deliverance speaks of God's unalterable will to save the people. The story of the Exodus from Egypt forms the backbone of YHWH's commitment to the convenant people for the deuteronomic thinkers. But is this commitment unshakable? We saw in our previous discussion of *hesed* that God's commitment to the people *was* unshakable, but that persistent human unwillingness to heed the call of God for justice and wholeness for all could result in God's anger and disciplinary measures. The prophet Amos describes such results in memorable and terrifying words.

In his fifth chapter Amos pleaded with the people of Israel to "seek the LORD and live" and to stop attempting to find God in the discredited temples of Samaria. The people have claimed that their God is with them, no matter what they do. Their gross injustice, so vividly catalogued by the book of Amos, goes unrecognized and unacknowledged. They believe that as long as they go to the temples regularly, bring the requisite sacrifices and offerings, YHWH will be satisfied. Amos would convince them otherwise.

They have apparently based their certainty of God's presence and favor on the story of the Exodus from Egypt. God acted on behalf of our ancestors then; God will act in the same way toward us, the heirs of those long-ago slaves. Amos sharply disagrees. God brought the Philistines from Caphtor and the Arameans from Kir (9:7-8). In effect, Amos has with one withering stroke undercut the people's appropriation of a central claim of their faith. The belief that God acted *uniquely* for Israel in its exodus from Egypt is expressly denied by the prophet; YHWH acts like that on a regular basis with all sorts of people. Why, God even performed an exodus for the Philistines (Israel's long-hated enemy!) and for the Arameans (Israel's current enemy!).

And another thing, Amos goes on to say. Your continuous claim that God has chosen you as special people is correct, but the content of that specialness is not what you think it is (3:2). God's choice of Israel is not for some sort of comfortable, undemanding relationship. God has chosen Israel to model God's way in the world, the way of justice and righteousness, the way of *hesed*. Israel of Amos's day has turned away from its responsibility. Obedience is needed to make room for blessing. As we saw in chapter 2, this calling forth of worthy lives by the love of God is the very essence of the deuteronomic paradigm.

Preaching from this text might identify ways in which the congregation and its larger culture claim divine sanction even while practicing injustice and idolatry. Is the community living on the basis of cheap grace? Or does the community function without any reference to transcendent values? A sermon on Amos 9 might further urge the congregation to reflect on how they regard the scope and activity of God's gracious work as privately and exclusively theirs. The preacher might further ask, "Are we living up to our calling to model God's way in the world?"

It is all too easy for sermons from Amos, or from any of the great prophets of Israel, to turn into expositions of works righteousness. "If we do justice, *then* God will bless us once again." The preacher needs to help the people remember that the doing of justice is not possible apart from God's prior gift of *hesed*, a fact made clear in both the paradigms of Deuteronomy and of the priests.

Isaiah 43. The priestly Isaiah uses the motif of deliverance from Egypt as a type of the deliverance from the Exile. In Isaiah 43:1-7 the prophet reassures the community that as God acted in the past, so God will act again. Isaiah here emphasizes the uniqueness of Israel, how YHWH chose them and defeated other nations in order that Israel might become a "light to the nations" (49:6). In 43:14-24, the prophet again recounts God's victory over the Egyptian warriors at the Sea of Reeds as the basis for Israel's hope in the future. But a homiletical surprise comes in v. 18: "Do not remember the former things. . . . I am about to do a new thing!" The new Exodus will be greater than the old.

This use of the memory of deliverance for a people still clearly in need of deliverance should give an important clue for the use of the theme in our own day. Discouraged communities today still need to be reminded that the Exodus is a type of what God is doing among us. But God does more than repeat the past. God fashions in continuity with the past but God's new thing has its own freshness and delight. The roots of the apocalyptic paradigm obviously draw from such springs.

The contrast between the uses of the memory of the Exodus by Amos and Isaiah is instructive. Whereas Isaiah needed to bolster the faith of a sagging Israel in the sixth century B.C.E., Amos needed to puncture the pride of a sinful Israel in the eighth century B.C.E. Amos's congregation did not need the comfort of Isaiah's word; it needed the shocking discomfort of Amos's word. The preacher must ask, "Which is the more needed emphasis in my congregation at the present time?" In the relative wealth of many of our congregations, preaching deliverance might be an announcement of cheap grace. But in many disheartened mainline congregations, who feel themselves going into exile in the larger culture, such a message might be just right. In the language of James A. Sanders, the preacher determines the degree to which a community needs support or challenge.[7]

The preacher who takes Isaiah's message supportively might probe for points at which the congregation feels that its possibilities are shut off. Can the preacher point to ways in which God is working to create a new future?

Sermon Series on Deliverance. One series might take its inspiration from these texts we have discussed. The first sermon (Exodus 1 and 2) could focus on the character of God as a delivering God. The second sermon (Amos 9) might focus on misuses of the stories of the Exodus. The third sermon (Isaiah 43) could help the congregation enlarge its understanding of what to expect from God's delivering work today.

Another series might take its cue from the ancient model of *lectio continua* (reading of sections of the Bible in sequence and commenting homiletically upon each section as it unfolds in the reading). The series would move sequentially through the scenes of the Exodus story itself. For example, the series might begin with Exodus 1–2 (the surprising means of deliverance). The next sermon might focus on the revelation of the divine name as the clue to God's delivering activity (Exodus 3). Another sermon might highlight God's use of the unlikely Moses and God's provision of Moses for the task (Exodus 3–4). From there, the preacher could go to the confrontation with pharoah (Exodus 5–11). The series could conclude with messages on the Passover (Exodus 12) and the departure from Egypt and the crossing of the Sea of Reeds (Exodus 13–15). Along the way, the preacher would want to comment on Jesus Christ as continuing the work of deliverance in the church.

John Holbert has found that narrative sermons are especially congenial to preaching on deliverance.[8] The preacher tells the biblical story and interweaves the contemporary story with it. A sermon on the crossing of the sea, for instance, might tell the biblical story while pausing along the way to weave in ways in which the preacher sees God making a way through the sea for people today. By using the narrative form, the preacher stays close to the form of the biblical material itself. As the annual retelling of the Passover saga shows, well-told stories have the power to build and sustain communities and to be adapted to new situations while maintaining continuity with the old.

Preaching on Justice

The motif of justice is prominent in the Old Testament and in the consciousness of the contemporary world. The word most often translated "justice," *mishpat,* is found often in writings that cover the whole range of trajectories in the Hebrew Scriptures. The call for justice in all human relationships is at the heart of the preaching of the prophets. Our discussions of Micah 6 and Amos 9 demonstrate this motif.

Genesis 18:16-33. This priestly text sharply raises the question of the definition of the term under consideration. With the laughter of Abraham and Sarah ringing in the divine ears, God sends two angels to investigate reports of evil in Sodom (18:17-19). Meanwhile, God has a tiny inner dialogue concerning whether to tell Abraham what God is about to do (18:17-19). God decides to tell Abraham because Abraham needs to know in order to fulfill his role to be a blessing to all the nations (Gen. 12:3). Genesis 18:19 suggests a way that Abraham will be such a blessing; Abraham is to command his children and his household to do righteousness *(tsdaqah)* and justice *(mishpat).*
A sloppy reader might believe that works righteousness is advocated here. However, we need to be reminded that God has always made the first move in the stories dealing with Abraham and Sarah, from the initial call in Genesis 12 to the promise of the gifts of land, progeny, and blessing.

Exactly what these two terms mean is explored in the remarkable story that follows. As the two angels move toward Sodom, "God still stood before Abraham." Abraham and God engage in a marketplace haggling session over the future of the city. Abraham boldly raises the question of justice with God. As he begins, he issues a sharp demand. "Must not the judge of all the earth do *mishpat?*" What Micah says that God requires of us (Mic. 6:8), Abraham now says is required of God. The implication is that if the judge is not just, then attempts at justice at the human level mean very little.

Abraham's questions reveal his definition of justice. Quite simply, at the surface level, the righteous cannot fare as wicked in a world of justice. When innocent ones are treated as wicked ones, the world has descended to moral meaninglessness, and any attempts at moral behavior are finally pointless. But at the deeper level, it is crucial to Abraham that God is just, that is, is One who does what is right. For God to be just is to act in integrity with God's own purposes. For the priestly writer, these are revealed dramatically in Genesis 1. (Indeed, the world created by the end of Genesis 1 is the most precise picture of the just world in the priestly corpus: a just world is one in which all relationships are ordered the way in which God wants them be in community and mutual support.) As the debate over Sodom proceeds, it becomes clear that God will not in fact destroy a place as long as even one righteous person can be discovered. God will not act against God's own purposes.

Of course, Genesis 18 is only one side of the many-sided box of justice. Contemporary people know, even if they have not read Job's ruminations on this question, that righteous ones *are* often destroyed with wicked ones in our terrible world. But note carefully what Abraham is trying to say. His question is profoundly theological. He wants to know that *God* will not purposely act in an unjust manner. If he can know and believe this fact, then it makes sense for humans to strive to do the same. Job will accuse God precisely of acting as Abraham insists God cannot act (Job 9:22-24), thus raising the terrible possibility once again that God may in fact not be just. The questioning paradigm of the wisdom school rises to question Abraham's demand for the certainty of justice.

Preaching on Genesis 18 offers the preacher a marvelous opportunity to reflect on the character, integrity, and trustworthiness of God. Justice in the human community (and in the natural world as well according to the priestly writers of Genesis 1) is rooted in the justice of God. This text, then, exposes the ground of all Jewish and Christian talk about justice. The preacher can ask, "How does our community experience this aspect of divine justice?"

Of course, if one is preaching only a single sermon on this passage (or some other text that centers on justice as a property and activity

101

of God), the preacher should raise Job's question. If the preacher does not do so, she or he will be the only person in the sanctuary who does not have Joban questions close in mind.

1 Kings 3. According to the deuteronomic historian(s), who have evidently edited this material, Solomon began his reign at a time of great religious confusion. Because no temple had yet been built where the God of Israel could be appropriately worshiped, the people were "sacrificing at the high places" (3:2). Solomon, too, offered copious sacrifices at the high place of Gibeon, and, after one such huge offering, God appeared to the king in a dream, urging the king to "ask what I should give you." The pious Solomon announces to God that God has been good to David, Solomon's father, with the result that David "walked before you (God) in faithfulness, in righteousness, and in uprightness of heart."

Solomon asks for only one thing. "Give to your servant a listening heart [this expression is sometimes translated 'discerning mind'] in order to judge your people, by discerning between good and bad; for who is able to judge this your great people?" (3:9). God is greatly pleased that Solomon asked for the ability to discern rather than asking for riches or power. As a result, God gives Solomon his desire for right judgment and throws in riches and power as a bonus! After Solomon wakes from the dream, he hurries off to Jerusalem, where he will later have the temple built, and offers sacrifices at the place that soon would be the only appropriate place to do so.

In this story, *mishpat* is the ability to discern good and bad. But note that Solomon does not ask for this skill only for his own purposes. He wishes to place this ability in the service of the people of God. Indeed, Solomon teaches us that right judgment is best used for others and that judgment, *mishpat,* is best observed in actions of faithfulness, righteousness, and uprightness of heart.

This text is an ideal occasion for the preacher to lead the congregation to a model for critical theological reflection. In today's confusing theological and moral climate, congregations ask Solomon's question. How can we discriminate between the ways of God and the ways that run contrary to God? The congregation seeks to know how to act in *mishpat.* The text cannot provide a framework to answer every question, but the background of *mishpat* does suggest a norm with which to begin: those things are of God that are faithful to God's intention. For the deuteronomists, this purpose is primarily to create a community in which all live in covenant with God and with one another for mutual blessing. Indeed, the deuteronomic corpus repeatedly stresses that the just community is one that cares for *all* of its members. Any who are unblessed testify to the lack of justice in the community. Of course, on a specific issue, the precise application of this norm (or other norms) may be debated. But the preacher can profitably stress this communal norm as a starting point.

The preacher could easily hold up Solomon's prayer as a model for today's Christians. Solomon asks from God the ability to discern good and bad. Few Jewish or Christian people receive lightning bolt answers to this request. But by opening the window of consciousness to God in prayer, they offer their hearts, minds, and wills to the living presence that is the source of justice.

The Book of Job. No discussion of the theme of justice in the First Testament would be complete without at least a brief glance at the book of Job. For our purposes, it is neither possible nor necessary to attempt a full analysis of the poet's exploration of the concept. We limit our discussion to the most basic level, and thereby demonstrate how the paradigm of wisdom that we called the way of questioning is important for anyone who wishes to tackle justice homiletically.

We focus our reading of Job on two texts only. In chapter 9, a pivotal one for the overall argument of the book, Job quite directly accuses God of gross injustice. In 9:22-24, Job answers Abraham's question of Genesis 18:25 in the negative: the God of all the earth does not do justice. Quite the contrary, says Job. The God of all the earth thwarts justice, "covering the faces of its judges" (using the noun form of the verb from which our key term comes) and, even worse, laughing uproariously at the dying, whether innocent or righteous. Job has looked at his own life of exemplary goodness, and instead of receiving the expected reward of God's favor, he has received an ash heap and a broken bit of pottery. He concludes that God is not just.

Turning now to the first speech of God in chapters 38–39, we are perhaps shocked to hear that God apparently cares nothing for Job's concern about justice and injustice in human life. This is all the more surprising since at least two of Job's so-called friends, Bildad in his first speech at 8:3 and the latecomer Elihu at numerous places in his long speech (see 34:4, 12, 17 for example), proclaim flatly that "God does not pervert *mishpat*." If what they say is true, then Job is being punished and there can be only one explanation: it is Job who has perverted justice, not God, who by definition cannot.

With the argument so clearly drawn, we might have expected God to weigh in on the side of the friends, thus defending the divine honor. But whatever else God does in the first speech, the issue of justice is not addressed, either directly or indirectly. God, in effect, points at the mysteries and wonders of the divine creation and asks Job whether he can do anything like it or whether he in fact knows anything at all about it. God's "answer" to the debate about justice is: "Look at the ostrich!" However much this response has proven satisfactory to many commentators, who say that God has rightly put the little pip-squeak in his place, telling him to shut up, Job was not impressed. His answer to the divine bombast is 40:4-5.

But the divine speech has had one desired effect; Job has been vanquished. In the presence of the awesome power of the creator God, Job admits he is small and unable to answer or talk anymore. But this admission in fact admits nothing more than Job has said throughout the dialogue. He has always known that he could never talk to God as an equal. He has always feared that if God would ever deign to address him directly, God would ask questions that no one could answer and would not really listen to what Job has been saying (see 9:13-19 for a clear expression of Job's fears). One of the greatest ironies of the story is that God's first speech has proved Job right about God! God *does* ask questions Job cannot answer, and God apparently *does not* listen to what Job has been saying. Is Job in some sort of horrible and ultimate sense right about God? If Job ended at this point, any talk of divine justice would be moot.

The second speech of God moves in a different direction. Here it turns out that God has been listening to Job after all (40:8). Job's immediate answer to both of these rhetorical questions is yes. But we suggest that Job should look again at the questions. First, exactly what is God's *mishpat*? Is it what Job and the friends all think that it is? Is it rewards for the righteous and waste places for the wicked? Is that all? We suggest that one of the functions of God's second speech to Job is to begin a redefinition of the key term. When God asks Job to "look at Behemoth" and to "consider Leviathan," God opens to Job the divine throne room, and what is to be found in there is not a great gumball machine that doles out rewards and punishments in some mechanical way, but a God who struggles with the created order—a God not far above it all, but a God directly engaged with it all. Job, and we, need to think again about the basic definition of God's justice.

As for the second question of God, the options between condemnation either for God or for Job apparently do not exhaust the possibilities. In a world not ruled by a mechanical God of reward and punishment, the category of condemnation may be fully inappropriate. In short, we would argue that 40:8 and the subsequent second speech of God puts the entire discussion of justice on a different track. Though it does not provide any simple and straightforward answers to the issues, it does urge that the old attempts at answers are not fully satisfying and new avenues must be explored if those dead ends are to be avoided. The "comfort" of the book is the assurance that the divine presence continues.

What then does our analysis of Job add to the discussion of justice for preaching? It presents a larger context in which the discussion of justice needs to take place. It exposes weaknesses in simpler formulations of the issues. When Abraham demanded that the God of all the earth be just, he was referring to the basic insistence that the righteous and wicked not be swept away indiscriminately by a God of indifference. The poet of Job has run this claim out to its logical conclusion: what should we think when precisely that, an innocent punished, has happened? His "answer," we suggest, is: the question needs to be reframed. What is God's *mishpat*?

Does the answer that Job received satisfy today's hearer? If so, how can the preacher's listeners experience it? Perhaps the preacher could construct an image that does for people today what the speeches of God were intended to do in the days of Job. How can the preacher shape the sermon so that the sermon itself mediates the sense of God's living presence to the congregation?

Sermon Series on Justice. A preacher might address the theme of justice in five sermons. The first, perhaps starting with Genesis 18:16-33, could deal with the just character of God. A second sermon could follow Solomon (1 Kings 3) in trying to understand the meaning of justice in community. A third sermon could come from one of the prophets (for example, Amos 5) to show how the concern for justice is immediately pertinent to our social order. A fourth sermon could raise Job's questions. A final sermon could bring this theme into the New Testament where the dawning of the rule of God and the incorporation of the Gentiles into the people of God and the hope of return of Jesus in glory all demonstrate God's will for cosmic justice. Indeed, the apocalyptic paradigm, which underlies much of the New Testament, has concern for justice at its core. The apocalypse is the full and complete revelation that God is truly just in the way that transcends the concerns of Abraham and Job.

The various themes we are examining overlap one another and interpret one another. In our brief examination of justice we found references to our earlier look at *hesed,* which in turn referred us to our discussion of deliverance. The First Testament's material may often be seen as a vast interlocking web; if you touch one part of this web, many other parts, even those seemingly some distance away, will vibrate with possible interpretive interest. And in the process, you will get to be better friends with the Bible.

CHAPTER
FIVE *Allen*

TEXTS THAT APPARENTLY OFFER LITTLE OR NOTHING TO THE CHRISTIAN PULPIT

Some of the literature of the First Testament appears to be antiquarian or of interest only to the Jewish community, such as texts that deal with circumcision, the dietary laws, or the design and practices of the temple. Other texts raise difficult theological and moral questions. For instance, should Christians join several psalmists who pray for God to wreak vengeance on their enemies? In this chapter, we discuss approaches for dealing positively with such material.

While we were preparing this chapter, a thoughtful pastor asked, "Why preach on these passages in today's congregation?" The pastor pointed out that many congregations have lost their sense of Christian identity. This pastor's congregation receives a large number of visitors who are curious about what the Christian faith might offer. "How would a sermon on not boiling a kid in its mother's milk help these people?"

We reply that such texts are not likely to be a weekly staple of parish preaching. But good reasons abound for turning to them from time to time. Encounters with these passages often offer perspectives on God and the world that are valuable to the Christian community. Congregants encounter some of these passages in the lectionary or in their own daily Bible reading. This biblical material often causes listeners or readers to be curious or troubled; the sermon can respond to congregational questions. Further, the Second Testament frequently presupposes passages, images, and themes from this material. The more Christians know about the First Testament, the better they can appreciate the Second. Finally, many Christians think of Judaism in caricature as a religion of rigid legalism and works righteousness. Christian interpretation of difficult texts sometimes contributes to this problem. Preaching on such texts can help dispel this notion and can help the church recognize that its own origins are in a religion that is gracious, just, and loving and whose practice is dynamic.

Material That Appears to Be Antiquarian or of Interest Primarily to the Jewish Community

These texts can be approached with the exegetical method and hermeneutic articulated in chapters 2 and 3. The preacher first gets a clear picture of the text. The preacher then identifies the vision of the passage in both its surface and deeper dimensions. The identification of the deeper dimensions usually establishes a bridge between the passage and the contemporary Christian congregation through analogy. (If a text does not yield a satisfactory analogy, the preacher might then ask, "What do we learn from the example of this passage that is helpful to our understanding of God or Christian faith or practice?") It is sometimes important for the preacher to follow the interpretation of a text, image, or theme into the Second Testament. This is particularly true when the congregation is familiar with the reference in the Second Testament or when the reference in the Second Testament is theologically important.

Some Christians value texts from the First Testament that deal with ethical matters but devalue texts that deal with ceremonial practices. This is not a helpful contrast. In Jewish thought, ceremony and ethics are often related.Ceremonial rites portray the paradigm that generates ethical guidelines. Ethical behavior is often a way of responding to the vision that is portrayed in liturgy.

We look now at examples. These are patterns of interpretation that can be applied to other texts.

Circumcision. The priestly trajectory gives us the present form of Genesis 17:1-8. God initiates an everlasting covenant with Abraham and Sarah. In 17:9-27, God assigns circumcision for all males in the community. (In ordinary Jewish custom, this sign applied only to males. In other religious traditions, however, women have been

108

marked physically through excision and infibulation.)[1] Circumcision is a sign with a double meaning: (a) those who bear it can rely everlastingly on God's promises; and (b) they agree to abide by the covenantal stipulations. Circumcision creates a physical condition that serves as an identification and reminder for the circumcised. Abraham is obediently circumcised. By reading the rest of the story, the reader knows that God proves faithful to the covenant represented by the sign. Hence, the reader is encouraged to appreciate circumcision and its symbolism.

Most interpreters of Genesis believe that this part of the text was given its present form by the priestly community even though the practice of circumcision is much older. (Scholars debate the original purposes of circumcision.)[2] Other passages in the First Testament that mention circumcision generally assume the priestly meaning (for example, Exod. 12:48-49; Lev. 12:2-5; Josh. 5:2-7).

The deuteronomic Moses uses circumcision figuratively. "Moreover, the LORD your God will circumcise your heart and the heart of your descendants, so that you will love the LORD your God with all your heart and with all your soul, in order that you may live" (30:6). To circumcise the heart is to repent of stubbornness, to trust in God, and to obey God's directives (10:12-22; see also Jer. 4:1-4; 9:25-26). The deuteronomist does not downplay the physicality of circumcision but makes it clear that the full meaning of circumcision is manifest in divine promise and in human trust and obedience.

At the surface level, circumcision hardly seems applicable to Christians. But at a deeper level, circumcision is a sign that God provides for the Jewish community for its benefit. The circumcised can always remember who they are (beloved of God through the covenant) and what they are to do (be faithful to God).

When preaching on Genesis 17:9-27, then, the preacher might emphasize God's covenant with the community. God provides signs to remind the community of God's faithfulness and our response. What signs function similarly in the church? Commentators often see similarities between circumcision and baptism (note Col. 2:11-12). Baptism is a gift of God for our benefit. Baptism assures us of God's unconditional love. When we are baptized, we signify our willingness to accept this love and to live according to its designs.

Many of today's listeners will remember that the Second Testament discusses circumcision. Hence, the preacher may want to turn to the Second Testament. Few early Christian writers belittle circumcision as such. Those who are critical of circumcision usually critique not the condition itself but its misunderstanding or misuse by Gentile Christians.

Paul, for instance, inveighs against the circumcision of Gentiles but he does not deny the validity of circumcision for Jewish people. In Galatians 2:1-20, Paul favorably recalls the agreement with the leaders of the church at Jerusalem that they direct a ministry to Jewish people while he spearheads a Gentile mission. When Paul says that "real circumcision is a matter of the heart" (Rom. 2:29), he stands in the tradition of Deuteronomy and Jeremiah.[3] For Paul, the central reality in the First Testament is God's promise of blessing to Abraham and Sarah, a promise for Jews and Gentiles alike. Circumcision is irrelevant for Christians because it came after this promise. Circumcision was given for the Jewish community. It can still function as a sign in Judaism, but it is not a necessity for Gentiles who are received into the promise through Christ (Rom. 4:1-25).

Likewise, Luke regards circumcision as normative for Jewish people (including Jewish Christians). But circumcision is not necessary for Gentile Christians (Acts 15:19-29; 21:15-26).

The Christian preacher, then, should not debunk circumcision. Instead, the preacher can rejoice with the Jewish people that God has given them this sign. And the preacher can help the congregation appreciate the comparable signs that God gives us.

Dietary Laws. The dietary laws of Judaism are discussed at length in the Bible only in Leviticus 11:1-47 and Deuteronomy 14:3-21 (although they seem to be assumed elsewhere, for example Isa. 66:17; Ezek. 4:9-15; Dan. 1:1-21). Jewish food practices are sometimes described as "keeping kosher." While not applied directly to food customs in the Hebrew text, the related Hebrew words well describe the purpose of these customs, for they mean "fit" or "appropriate."

Later Jewish discussions on the appropriateness of Jewish dietary observance spring from Leviticus and Deuteronomy.[4]

Both central passages in the Hebrew Bible divide the animals of the world into clean and unclean. The clean animals are fit for consumption and for use in religious rites (for example, sacrifice in the temple) while the unclean are not. The preacher's first task is to describe the clean and the unclean. Leviticus presents a classification based on categories. Land beasts are clean if they have cloven hooves and chew the cud (11:2-8). Aquatic creatures are clean if they have fins and scales (11:9-12). Some flying animals are permitted while others are not (11:13-23). Swarming things are generally forbidden (11:29-38). The list in Deuteronomy is simpler but in much the same spirit. Further, the Jewish community elaborated patterns for slaughtering and preparing meat and for keeping milk and meat separate. These latter traditions are based on the prohibition against partaking of blood (Lev. 7:26-27; 17:10-14).

Scholars posit several different theories to account for the origins of the dietary laws.[5] Some contend that the laws are arbitrary. Others think that they were designed to encourage healthy eating. Some believe that they were intended to teach human beings a kind of reverence for life. In this view, the laws had an ethical origin that limited the Jewish right to kill; the law prescribed methods of swift and relatively painless slaughter. This would help tame the human instinct for violence and killing. Whatever their origin, the present contexts of the dietary laws indicate that the dietary observances are part of the calling of the community to be holy (Lev. 11:44-45; Deut. 14:2, 21).

For illustration, we focus on the laws in Deuteronomy. These laws take their place in the deuteronomic paradigm (discussed in chapter 2). Israel's holiness is the gift of God (14:12). Holiness results from God's gracious initiative. To be holy is to be set apart for God's purposes. For Deuteronomy, holiness is more than a cultic concern. It is God's gift for the whole of the community's life and can be expressed in every arena of existence—worship as well as personal and social behavior.[6] There is a concrete illustration of these themes in chapter 2.

How does the notion of corporate holiness illumine the dietary laws? The deuteronomist is consumed with the passion to eradicate idolatry from the community (12:1–13:18). The essence of idolatry is to confuse categories, to mistake one thing for another. The idolater mistakes the penultimate (the idol) for the ultimate (the true God). For Deuteronomy, holiness sets the pattern for the whole of life; everything has its proper relationship with other things. These relationships are revealed in the order of creation. When people, things, and events are in their proper relationship, then the community manifests God's purpose and is blessed. But when these relationships are confused, the people fall under a curse.

The dietary regulations in Deuteronomy 14 reveal how to hold categories of animals in proper relationship, and hence, how to keep idolatry and curse at bay. The clean animals are clean because they "conform fully to their class" whereas the unclean animals mix or confuse the classes.[7] At the surface, the classification scheme of Deuteronomy (and Leviticus) may seem arbitrary. Why should cloven hooves and cud-chewing determine cleanliness? But at a deeper level, these "regulations introduce into the life of holiness and purity a concern for the order and structure of things, the recognition of difference and sameness, and a desire to maintain things as God has created them."[8]

The idea that the deuteronomic dietary laws are intended to discourage idolatry is strengthened by two additional observations. First, the immediate context prohibits the Israelites from adopting pagan customs of mourning (14:2). Second, some of the unclean foods were used in the religious life of Israel's neighbors. The pig and the snake, for instance, were symbols among some idolatrous peoples. Boiling a kid in its mother's milk was likely a fertility rite of the Canaanites.

The dietary laws thus had several positive effects. To follow the rules of cleanliness and the dietary laws is to commit oneself to God's design for order and blessing, while to partake of the unclean is to invite curse. These instructions "would have been like signs which at every turn inspired meditation on the oneness, purity and completeness of God."[9] Each meal reminds the community of God's promises and of the community's need to respond in kind by maintaining all the dimensions of the covenantal life. Each encounter with the animal world reminds the community of the need to maintain proper relationships in all arenas of life.

The early church did not make the dietary practices normative for Christians. Luke, for instance, invokes a heavenly vision to indicate that these laws are not for the church (Acts 10:1–11:18). Mark critiques aspects of Jewish dietary practice very pointedly (Mark 7:1-20).

However, preachers need to be careful not to misrepresent the intention of the dietary regulations. The Jewish community has never envisioned obedience to its food customs as a means to earn God's favor. Instead, the food practices are a gift from God to help the community. Thus, preachers need to be careful not to denigrate the dietary laws of Judaism as examples of works righteousness. Christians do not follow the dietary laws. But neither should we make fun of them or misrepresent them.

On the positive side, the church desires for life to unfold in proper relationships. Today's preacher might search for realities in today's world that are comparable to the classification of creatures into the clean and the unclean. Where do we run the risk of confusing categories and of inviting chaos into our community?

Dietary practice serves as a daily reminder for the Jewish community of the divine presence and the need for the community to respond to that presence in every sphere of life from the dinner table to major moral decisions. The food laws were especially valuable in a setting in which the temptation to idolatry was ever present. Today's culture is at least as charged with possibilities for idolatry. The preacher might help the congregation identify moments and practices that can daily help the church nurture its consciousness of the divine presence and its daily need for witness.

Obedience to the dietary laws has helped the Jewish people through the centuries to remember that some choices are not available to them if they are to live out their identity. This is dramatized and reinforced in their daily adherence to the limited choices of foods. Further, the constant recognition of restriction is a way of making peace with finitude; Jewish people cannot have and do all things. The preacher could explore points at which Christian identity functions similarly. What are points at which our choices for values and behavior are limited by virtue of our Christian connection? How do such limitations contribute to order and blessing for the Christian community and for others? And in a world in which people are constantly tempted to think of themselves as infinite, restriction comes as genuinely good news.

The Temple at Jerusalem. The temple at Jerusalem is one of the fundamental places of Hebrew tradition. One of the most frequent Hebrew designations for the temple is "house of God." This reveals the temple's primary function: to be a dwelling place for God. Scholars forcefully point out that in ancient Jewish thought, God is present everywhere and is not restricted to the temple. But the temple is a visible representation of the divine presence and its promises. The temple is a place where the community can count on encountering that presence.[10] But why should Christians be concerned about a sacred place that was destroyed in 70 C.E.?

Many scholars think that the temple building, and its location on Mount Zion, functioned as a "cosmic mountain." Ancient civilizations lived much closer to the edge of survival than today's First World residents. People of antiquity feared being overwhelmed by chaos. The cosmic mountain was a point where the heavenly world touched the earthly world and guaranteed the survival of the latter. As long as Mount Zion (and the temple) was intact, the community believed that its world was secure.[11]

The temple is a microcosm of the universe. "The ascent of the Temple mount was considered to be something more than simply a change of locale. It was, in fact, a way of entering a different kind of existence, marked by closeness to God, a life at the very center of the cosmos, the point on which the world is balanced, a true paradise."[12] The temple is a microcosm of a universe that is predictable because of God's trustworthiness.

In addition, the temple was an important political and economic reality. The first temple was built at the time that political power in Israel was consolidated in Jerusalem in a single household. Its bank was a major player in economic Palestine. The temple not only symbolized stability in the social order but implicitly authorized the rule of the sovereign. But the temple was not a license for *carte blanche* royal exercise of power. The essential work of the monarchy was to effect divine rule (justice) in the community. The temple was thus the symbol not only of royal authority but of the service to which that power was to be put. Several of the prophets complained that misuse of royal power contributed to the downfall of the nation. The presence of the temple by itself could not guarantee national security.[13]

This complex of symbolism illumines Haggai. The community has returned from exile. They have rebuilt their homes but they have not reconstructed the temple. Consequently, the prophet claims, God has sent drought upon them (1:7-11). When the community rebuilds the temple, God will end the drought and restore the life of the community. Fertility will return (2:1-19). The king will be firmly established and the community can look forward to social stability (2:20-23). (Note similarly 1 Kings 8:22-53).[14]

At the surface level, texts from the First Testament that focus on the temple at Jerusalem appear to have negligible value for Christian preaching. Not only was the temple a peculiarly Jewish institution, but it was destroyed in 70 C.E. Further, the temple gets mixed reviews in the Second Testament.[15] Paul seems unconcerned with the temple of Jerusalem (although he speaks of the church as a temple in 1 Cor. 3:16-17 and 2 Cor. 6:16-18). On the one hand, the Gospels assume that the temple played an important role in Judaism. On the other hand, the Gospels often portray the temple in a negative light. Some of Jesus' opponents come from the temple. Jesus castigates the money-changers and the temple leadership for improper practice of temple life. The priests are implicated in the death of Jesus. Jesus predicts the destruction of the temple. When the veil of the temple is torn, the temple loses its religious force. Matthew summarizes the synoptic view, "Something greater than the temple is here" (12:6). For John, the real temple is Jesus himself (2:13-22). Hebrews claims that the heavenly sanctuary of Jesus has replaced its earthly, shadowlike counterpart (8:1–10:18). And John the Revelator's vision of the eschatological world has no need of a temple (21:22-27).

These views of the temple are understandable as a part of the early church's interpretation of how it separated from its parent religion whose primary architectural symbol (the temple itself) was destroyed. Yet, such images have contributed to many Christians devaluing the temple at Jerusalem.

Today's Christian community in North America does not have an architectural symbol that is as compelling as the temple in Judaism of antiquity. Nonetheless, the symbolism of the temple at Jerusalem can still speak to Christians at deeper levels. The temple is a *place* where the community becomes aware of the divine presence and purposes. God is not limited to the temple. But particular places can alert the church to God's presence and purposes. The preacher might identify such places. The church building sometimes serves in this way, but the preacher might want to help the congregation name other places that have a temple-like quality.

As cosmic mountain and microcosm, the temple represented God's faithfulness in preserving the cosmic order. The experience of being in the temple helped one live confidently from day to day in the midst of a world threatened by chaos. This experience is quite similar to the feeling of the contemporary population as it lives in the face of rapid social upheaval, economic uncertainty, mind-boggling technological change, and illnesses that can turn the most outwardly secure life into chaos. The preacher might describe the symbolism of the cosmic mountain and the elements of the temple and then posit symbols from our world that give us similar confidence in the face of our uncertainties. In the midst of divorce, for instance, people speak of sitting in the sanctuary prior to the beginning of worship and feeling reassurance. The place itself communicates constancy.

The temple also exemplifies political stability and authority while reminding the community of the divine purpose of justice for all. Yet, the fact of the temple does not automatically guarantee that political rulers carry out the divine will. On the one hand, the preacher might ask, "What people and movements in our culture call attention to the concern for justice that is embodied in the temple?" In fact, true political stability comes only through universal justice. On the other hand, the legacy of noncritical union between church and state in the

United States ought to make the preacher careful not to say grace automatically over particular politicians or governmental structures. The preacher would want to call attention to the importance of human faithfulness to the divine purpose. The temple can be a norm by which to measure all uses of political power.

This point is similiar to the one the deuteronomic Solomon makes in his prayer at the dedication of the temple in 1 Kings 8. He assures the community of God's faithfulness to Israel and to the temple (8:22-26). But he also reminds the congregation that God is not limited to the temple (8:27) and that the practices of the temple life are connected directly to the well-being of the community (8:28-40; 44-52). Indeed, Solomon reminds the Israelites that God hears the prayers of the foreigner. Implicitly, then, the prayer warns the readers against thinking that they have an automatic, exclusive claim on divine blessing. The practice of the temple is a norm by which to gauge their daily life at home, school, work, and play.

Blood Sacrifice. Passages from the First Testament that deal with blood sacrifice suffer from handicaps in Christian consciousness. Christians have little understanding of the theory and practice of sacrifice; Christians frequently misconceive it as magic or as a form of works righteousness. Since sacrifice belongs to a dead institution (the temple) and since the sacrifice of Christ has "superseded" Jewish sacrifice, few Christians are interested in these arcane passages. Some believers regard the practice of blood sacrifice as theologically repugnant. What kind of God would require the offering of blood to change the divine disposition toward humankind? Further, many contemporary people are blood-phobic. Texts that describe or assume the practice of blood sacrifice cause some people to experience a negative visceral reaction. They avoid such feelings by avoiding such passages.

Yet, the religion of the First Testament generally assumes that blood sacrifice is important.[16] For instance, blood itself plays a prominent role in the Exodus (Exod. 12:1-27) and in the ratification of the covenant at Sinai (Exod. 24:1-18). Blood sacrifice is a key element in the worship of the temple.

Scholars propose many different and sometimes conflicting theories on the origins of blood sacrifice in Israel.[17] However, the priestly writers (perhaps building on older traditions), who gave the fullest and most recent exposition of the sacrificial system in the First Testament, put forth a perspective on blood and sacrifice that is easily understandable and that helps us make positive sense of the rite. The key is Leviticus 17:11, "For the life of the flesh is in the blood; and I have given it to you for making atonement for your lives on the altar; for, as life, it is the blood that makes atonement."

The principle that life is in the blood, and that life belongs to God, means that Israel's access to blood is restricted. According to the priestly viewpoint in Genesis 1:29-30, God originally intended for the human family to be vegetarian. Leviticus 17:1-16 regulates slaughter. Animals are killed in (relatively) humane ways. Even when animals are slaughtered for food, the slaughter itself takes place with the community aware of the presence of God.[18] The blood of animals taken for food is to be poured on the ground as a sign that it belongs to God. The human being cannot practice gratuitous killing of other forms of blood-life. Murder is particularly despicable. However, the law of restriction applies even here. The community may put the murderer to death but it may *only* put the murderer to death (and may not kill the murderer's family or clanspeople).

Leviticus 17:11 is clear that the purpose of blood sacrifice is to make atonement. Human beings violate the purposes of God. When God's purposes are violated, the stability of one's own life and the life of the community are threatened. According to the priestly rationale, blood sacrifice is a means that God has ordained in order to assure the community of forgiveness and the continuation of divine faithfulness.[19]

Scholars debate whether the sacrifice actually changes God's disposition toward the community from one of wrath to one of favor or whether the sacrifice is intended to reveal God's continuing (and unchanging) faithfulness to the worshiper.[20] Donald Gowan shows that the primary effect of blood sacrifice *on the worshiper* is to be a sign of atonement. The sacrifice signals the people that God accepts the community despite their sin.[21] The life force itself can be trusted to continue to support the community even in the wake of transgression.

Victor Turner points out that symbols that are charged with meaning can release intense emotional energy in worshipers.[22] Emotionality becomes coupled with intellectuality; emotion increases the vitality of thought; thought harnesses the surge of emotional dynamism. The result is passion that touches the depths of the human soul. Although it may seem strange to late twentieth-century North Americans, blood was such a symbol in the priestly world. The worshiper brings the sacrificial animal and sees the blood (representing life) in contact with the symbols of the Holy God (the altar). This releases the deepest human associations. Israelites, seeing blood in the intellectual framework of atonement, experience assurance at the depths of their beings.

Christians often point out that some Israelites criticized the practice of sacrifice. Samuel speaks for this viewpoint, "Surely, to obey is better than sacrifice" (1 Sam. 15:22). However, such critics seldom rejected sacrifice as such. They objected to persons practicing sacrifice without a corresponding attempt to embody the fullness of covenantal life.[23] Sacrifice is grossly misused when a member of the covenantal community makes sacrifice but then oppresses the poor.

The earliest Christian literature uses the symbolism of sacrifice to help interpret the death of Christ. For example, among Paul's metaphors for the death of Christ we find the paschal lamb (1 Cor. 5:7) and "a sacrifice of atonement by his blood" (Rom. 3:25). Some churches associated the Lord's Supper with blood sacrifice (1 Cor. 11:25; Matt. 26:28). Hebrews envisions the death of Christ as a sacrifice made once and for all; henceforth, the human race has no need of sacrifice (Heb. 9:6–10:31). Of course, scholars debate the precise relationship of the Jewish theologies of sacrifice to the death of Jesus in the different strands of the Second Testament.[24] At the least, interpreters agree that the sacrifice of Jesus is a sign of God's love that functions for the church much like the practice of sacrifice in Israel of antiquity.

When preaching on a text from the First Testament that refers to blood sacrifice, the preacher might do four things. First, the preacher probably needs to help members of the congregation to name their visceral repulsion at the mention of blood. If they name it, they can probably deal with it and be able to hear the rest of the sermon. If they do not, the feelings of revulsion may prevent them from being able to tune into the message itself.

Second, the preacher might want to help the congregation realize the restrictive dimension of Jewish sacrificial theology. Far from commending wanton killing, Jewish thinking was intended to preserve and honor life.

Third, the preacher might describe the symbolism of blood in the Jewish tradition. With sufficient descriptive power, the preacher may be able to help the congregation recover a vivid sense of blood as life force. What analogies can the preacher identify from the world of the listeners that will help them understand and feel the power of blood?

Fourth, the essential work of the sermon is to help the congregation discover that the purpose of blood sacrifice was to help the community grasp God's unyielding love, grace, and trustworthiness. In this respect, the preacher may want to lead the congregation to remember the depth of their own sin. For the listeners' appreciations of blood sacrifice may be proportionate to the depth of their own self-knowledge of sin. In the language and imagery of another worldview, the ancient text still speaks a contemporary word: God is with you and wills good for you.

Christian preachers are sometimes tempted to criticize Jewish sacrifice, especially since Jewish sacrifices were repeated. "After all, Christ died once and for all." While the latter is true, Christians have repeated rites, too. For instance, most congregations contain a weekly confession of sin and an assurance of pardon. This weekly repetition is similar to the Jewish practice of regular sacrifice. If the pastor is compelled to bring the sacrifice of Jesus into the sermon, the pastor could take care to show the continuities between the death of Jesus and Jewish sacrificial practice.

A sermon on a text that depicts blood sacrifice places the listener several steps removed from the physical symbol of blood. Nonetheless, a sermon that draws on blood symbolism in a descriptive and evocative way can release powerful emotions (as Victor Turner describes). When coupled with a compelling interpretation, it can touch the depths of the self with the depths of divine love.

TEXTS THAT OFFER LITTLE TO THE CHRISTIAN PULPIT

Material That Is Theologically Inappropriate, Unintelligible, or Immoral

Some material from the First Testament is problematic because of its theological, intellectual, or moral content. These passages, themes, images, and ideas seem to be inappropriate to a gospel of unconditional love and universal justice or seem to be unintelligible or seem to authorize immoral treatment of some created entities. When faced with such texts, the preacher has a fourfold responsibility.

The first is to help the congregation understand the claims of the text.

The second is to help the community see why the text came to expression. Even if today's Christians cannot agree with a text, they may develop a sympathetic understanding of why the people of antiquity came to the conclusion voiced in the text. Often this is a point of contact between text and congregation. Today's people may have thoughts or feelings similar to those expressed in the text. "Have you ever felt like the psalmist . . . ?"

The third is to help the listeners identify the inadequacies of the passage. What is wrong with this text from the standpoints of appropriateness to the gospel, intelligibility, or moral plausibility? The preacher may get some help at this juncture from the First Testament itself. The preacher can sometimes bring the difficult passage into dialogue with other passages that offer different perspectives. For instance, the preacher who is troubled by the exclusivism of Ezra-Nehemiah might bring those books into dialogue with Ruth. Further, the Hebrew Bible contains overarching perspectives that help critique the claims of single texts. As we noticed in chapter 4, God's *hesed* calls into question any text that denies God's faithfulness to any creature.

These latter approaches may be very helpful in the sermon. Instead of a frontal assault on the text (which may raise the ire of listeners), the preacher might bring the text into dialogue with texts and perspectives from the First Testament itself and thereby encourage the congregation to raise its own questions about the adequacy of the passage. This helps the congregation realize that the preacher is not arrogantly standing in isolated authority over the text; the congregation is not the first to wrestle with a passage. Such solidarity with the communities that gave birth to the Scriptures may give the hearers a greater sense of freedom to question the text. Of course, for the sake of integrity, the preacher eventually must call a spade a spade. But the preacher may not need to begin by playing a trump card the congregation will resist.

The fourth is to move from negative criticism of the text to positive preaching of the good news of God's unconditional love for all and God's unfailing will for justice for all. While the text itself may not articulate an encouraging word, the sermon needs ultimately to offer the community good news from God. We are not suggesting that a sermon should take its cues from Pollyanna and avoid bad news at all costs, far from it. In order for the good news to be heard in its fullest depth and clarity, we sometimes must hear the bad news in its awful depth and clarity. But the preacher is ultimately called to speak the gospel.

In all phases, the preacher needs to avoid being cavalier. A text is a genuine other. In addition, many Christians have a view of the Scripture that discourages disagreement with the text. Others are simply unaccustomed to hearing a preacher take issue with a text. Such listeners may dismiss a preacher whom they perceive to be playing fast and loose with the Bible. Let the preacher deal with difficult material tenderly and with compassion for people ancient and contemporary.

The preacher may be tempted to criticize or dismiss difficult passages because they do not appear to measure up to Jesus Christ or the Second Testament. This tactic is often problematic. It probably misrepresents the relationship between Christ, the Second Testament, and the First Testament. It presumes that the picture of God and religion in the Hebrew Bible is inferior to that of the church and that the First Testament is discontinuous with Christ and the church.

The appeal to the superiority of Christ often blithely overlooks images and ideas in the Second Testament that are every bit as problematic as those of the First. For example, Christians sometimes criticize the killing of members of the human family in the divine name in the First Testament (see below). Yet, for all their horror, such acts of violence do not last long. People are killed. They suffer as they die, but they die quickly. But some in the early church speak of people in torture for prolonged periods (for example, Matt. 13:36-42; 24:45-51; 25:14-30; Rev. 20:7-15).

Preaching on an intractably difficult text also models theological method for dealing with other problematic passages. We turn now to examples.

Texts that Depict the Brutal Treatment of Human Beings (or others) Without Censure

Some texts depict human beings treating others very brutally. The abusers are not always censured. Often the lack of censure is the result of assumptions of the ancient world. While understandable against the background of the cultural mores of antiquity, such texts are neither appropriate to the gospel nor morally plausible.

For example, in Numbers 25, Israel is on its way to Canaan but a plague has settled on them because of idolatry and unfaithfulness. God charges Moses to execute the idolators. An Israelite (identified as Zimri in Num. 25:14) took a Midianite woman into his family. Phinehas saw this violation of the community's code. Taking a spear, Phinehas entered the tent and killed both the Israelite and the Midianite by piercing them through the belly. This turned back God's wrath. Phinehas was rewarded for being jealous for God and for making atonement.

When faced with such a test, the preacher would first clarify its claims. The passage claims that idolatry and intermarriage are unfaithful but it approves of Phinehas's act.

Second, the preacher might help the congregation understand that two important issues are in the background. The priestly understanding of purity is the framework within which to understand Phinehas's action. Phinehas is not simply a capricious thug. He is acting in a priestly way for God. Indeed, Waldemar Janzen notes that the emphasis of the story does not lie in Phinehas's act of killing. The stress falls on Phinehas's zeal for God and for his atoning work. Phinehas has prevented the life of the people from further disruption by halting the sexual relationship between the Israelite and the Midianite.[25]

However, third, the preacher must critique this text. No amount of explanation can take away the brutality of Phinehas's act. Phinehas denied God's love for Zimri and the Midianite. The fact that God apparently sanctioned the action only intensifies its horror.

Fourth, the preacher needs to set forth the good news of the gospel in contrast to the bad news of the text. God loves Israelites. God loves the Zimris and the Midianite women. And God loves the Phinehases of the world. God wishes for all to live in encouragement and support. God wishes to bless them and does not ask for violent actions such as Phinehas's. A God of universal, unconditional love works in constructive ways.

Vicious portrayals of divine activity. The Hebrew Bible sometimes portrays God acting in ways that trouble contemporary people. In passages that especially puzzle contemporary Christians, God hardens pharaoh's heart (e.g., Exod. 4:21; 7:3; 8:15, 32; 9:12, 34; 10:20, 27; 11:10; 14:4, 8) so that the slavery in Egypt is prolonged. God actively authorizes suffering and death. For instance, at the Sea of Reeds, the text says plainly, "As the Egyptians fled before it [the waters engulfing them], the LORD tossed the Egyptians into the sea." Not one Egyptian remained alive (Exod. 14:21-29). When taking the promised land, Joshua confronts a large army. God speaks, "Do not be afraid of them, for tomorrow at this time I will hand over all of them, slain, to Israel; you shall hamstring their horses, and burn their chariots with fire" (Josh. 11:6).

Passages such as these contradict the notion that God's love is unconditional and universal and that God wills justice for all. The preacher will want to help the listeners understand this contradiction.

However, the preacher may want to assist the congregation in understanding the function of such texts in their ancient settings.[26] Typically, these passages communicate three things to the reader. For one, they demonstrate God's faithfulness for Israel. For another, they show that God is more powerful than any other deity. For still another, the passages stress that God is the gracious source of Israel's strength. For instance, the hardening of pharaoh's heart serves several purposes. It reminds the reader that God was ultimately in control of the events that led to the Exodus. It answers the question of why pharaoh was reluctant to release the Hebrew slaves when confronted by the plagues. By delaying the Exodus, God works even more potent deeds. This increases the hearer's sense of awe and trust in the power of God to do what God promises. In the case of the Exodus itself, God fights for the Israelites by drowning pharaoh's army. And when Israel is conquering the promised land, God fights the holy war. Victories result not from Israel's cunning and muscle but from divine agency.

These passages thus show that God's purposes cannot be thwarted. The material encourages the community to have confidence in God. This may hint at a hermeneutical connection. Even if the preacher does not believe that God operates through the hardening of a pharaoh's heart or through holy war, the preacher can still ask, "How does God act in our world? How can I help the contemporary community understand God's use of power today? How can I offer the listeners a sense of genuine confidence that God will achieve the divine purposes?"

It is crucial for the preacher to point out that such passages do not authorize the contemporary community to practice violence against evil. Our world and our continent are beset with violence and fear. On the basis of such passages, it would be natural for Christians to think that God blesses the use of violence against the violent. But violence is always inappropriate to a God of gracious love. Contemporaries may encounter evil of such monstrous proportions that they conclude it can only be checked by the use of force. If so, the violence should be accompanied by a deep sense of sorrow and repentance; violence should never be glorified.

God's judgment upon Israel (and upon the nations) is a subcategory of this discussion. The Old Testament frequently reports that Israel and the nations fall under the judgment of God. This judgment often has painful, destructive consequences. How shall the preacher handle such texts? It is helpful to recall that for the deuteronomists and the priests, judgment is remedial. God has shown gracious love to Israel and cut a covenant with Israel. When the people are obedient to the covenant, they are blessed. When they are disobedient, they fall under judgment and are cursed.[27] The curse is not usually for its own sake but is for the sake of awakening the community to the fact that it has strayed from the path of blessing. Most of the prophets and other theologians of Israel point to repentance as the means whereby the community renounces disobedience and becomes obedient and on the pathway to blessing (for example, Deut. 4:25-31; Amos 5:14-15).[28] This is the conceptuality within which to understand prophetic oracles of judgment (and other texts that speak of God's judgment on Israel).

This model suggests that a goal of preaching on such texts is to help the congregation discern points at which it is obedient and disobedient. At points of obedience, the preacher can help the congregation rejoice and call the community to redouble its efforts. At points of disobedience the preacher can explain the meaning of repentance and help the congregation identify concrete actions of repentance. The preacher needs also to warn the congregation that its disobedience can lead to unfortunate consequences. The preacher thus seeks not simply to excoriate the people but to awaken them to the seriousness of their situation and the bitterness of its consequences so that they can repent and turn to God and the pathway to communal and personal renewal.

Other prophets speak in situations in which destruction has already occurred. The community is bewildered as to why they have collapsed. The prophet then uses this conceptuality to offer a pastoral interpretation of *why* the nation has fallen on hard times. Essentially the prophet says, "You are in this mess because you were disobedient." The prophet points to God's faithfulness as the source of hope for a future that is filled with the possibility of blessing. Isaiah 40–55 is such a text.

Judgment often results in painful, destructive consequences. It is crucial to recognize that judgment is never capricious. It always follows disobedience. As the nation is collapsing, Jeremiah interprets the human role in invoking the collapse. "Your ways and your doings have brought this upon you" (Jer. 4:18).

What is God's role in acts of judgment that result in negative consequences? Commenting on Jeremiah 4:18, Bernhard Anderson offers a helpful perspective on the divine part in some oracles of judgment. "In one sense, the 'wrath of God' is not so much God's intervention to punish as it is *withdrawal* from a rebellious people, leaving them to suffer the destructive consequences of their own actions and attitudes. It is, one might say, a kind of self-destruction."[29] While this is a creative hermeneutical move, there are passages in which God actively and directly inflicts pain and even death upon Israel. For example, in the parable of the vineyard, God says, "And now I will tell you what I will do to my vineyard, I will remove its hedge, and it shall be devoured" (Isa. 5:5). Habakkuk notices that God is rousing the Chaldeans (Hab. 1:6).

It follows from our theological remarks earlier in this chapter that God cannot be the direct agent of such destructive activity. It would violate God's integrity and God's purpose of universal love for God to do harm. Nor, as Anderson suggests, can God completely withdraw from a situation; God is omnipresent and ever working for the good of all in the situation.[30]

However, these passages are still instructive for today's congregation. They remind the reader that when people and communities violate the divine call for love and justice, those persons and groups suffer consequences. The preacher can help the congregation understand that God does not willfully foment bad consequences on them. But their violation of divine purpose limits God's ability to work positively in their midst. They take up values and patterns of behavior that create injustice and chaos. The entire community suffers. Psalm 81:11-12 moves in the direction of this line of thinking. "But my people did not listen to my voice; Israel would not submit to me. So I gave them over to their stubborn hearts, to follow their own counsels."

The preacher might thus lead the listeners to reflect on aspects of their lives and culture that are disobedient and that would lead to the curse. God does not wreak havoc on them; pain results from the collapse of their own values and practices. God does everything God can do to awaken the community to its plight and to turn away from its destructive path. But God cannot prevent a body of people from choosing their own unfortunate destiny.

The preacher might want to help the congregation recognize that in such situations God grieves and does all that God can to help all who fall under the curse. But sometimes, they (we) must take their own medicine and trust in God's presence to help us move beyond the disasters of our own making. The preacher's ultimate word, then, is hopeful. For despite the desperate circumstances that a community creates for itself, God is ever present to begin restoration.

Once in a great while, a preacher encounters a situation that has fallen into so deep a pit that it cannot be changed. The preacher might then assure the community that God feels each of their pains and that God is faithfully with them. No one dies abandoned and alone.

Imprecations. An imprecation is an invocation of a curse upon one's enemies. The most familiar imprecations are in the Psalms. For instance, "O God, break the teeth in their mouths; . . . Let them be like the snail that dissolves into slime; like the untimely birth that never sees the sun" (Ps. 58:6-8). "Pour out your indignation upon them, and let your burning anger overtake them" (69:24). Psalm 83 asks God to do to the psalmist's enemies "as you did to Midian, as to Sisera and Jabin at the Wadi Kishon, who were destroyed at En-dor, who became dung for the ground" (83:9-10). Psalm 109 is one of the most thorough and savage of the imprecations. "May their days be few; may another seize their position. May their children be orphans and their wives widows. . . . May their posterity be cut off; may their name be blotted out in the second generation" (109:8-9, 13). Perhaps the most famous imprecation is Psalm 137:8-9: "O daughter of Babylon, you devastator! Happy shall be they who repay you with what you have done to us. Happy they be who take your little ones and smash them against a rock."

These sentiments contradict many passages from the hands of the early Christians. Paul, for example, counsels, "Bless those who persecute you; bless and do not curse them" (Rom. 12:14). Likewise, Luke's Jesus says, "Love your enemies, do good to those who hate you, bless those who curse you, pray for those who abuse you" (6:27-28). But much more than contradicting singular passages from the Second Testament, the imprecations are inappropriate to the gospel itself. For they explicitly ask God not only to deny divine love to one's enemies but actively to do harm against them. The preacher needs to help the congregation understand this contradiction.

At the surface level, these passages seem to have no positive value for the Christian pulpit. But the congregation's encounter with these passages can be significant and positive.

George Mendenhall points out that some people in antiquity assumed that retribution of the kind sought in the imprecations was essential for a moral universe.[31] A fundamental conviction of the ancient community is that God rules. The psalmists, however, experience malevolent power that appears to have come from a source other than God. God must demonstrate God's superiority to the malevolent power. In particular the psalmist has suffered injustice. Retaliation vindicates both the psalmist and God for it demonstrates both the justice of the complaint of the psalmist and the justice (and power) of God. These passages, then, are not the whimpers of spoiled, vindictive children; they are pleas for the moral order of the universe to be manifest. Contemporary people share this longing. Can the preacher help the congregation voice its yearning for a moral universe in terms that do not call for damage to the offending parties? Indeed, if damage and destruction are to befall all who offend God and order, then all persons should prepare to be cursed.

The preacher can also point out that the Hebrew Bible itself contains thoughts that run against the grain of the imprecations. This is not a simple case of Second Testament against First but of the First Testament containing ideas that critique the unfortunate qualities of the imprecations. James A. Sanders notes that while there is no "categorical commandment" in the First Testament "to love one's enemies, there is certainly none to hate one's enemies." Indeed,

> . . . a spirit of international good will under the universal sovereignty of God is the very basis of such thinking as is found in Ruth; Isa. 19:19-25; 40–55; Jonah (cf. 1 Kings 20:31; 2 Kings 5:20-23). The theme of the biblical doctrine of election from the early chapters of Genesis is that through Israel the rest of the world may be blessed (Gen. 12:1-3; cf. Jer. 4:1-2). Jeremiah, in his letter to the exiles in Babylonia bids them pray for the peace and welfare of their enemies and captors. (Jer. 29:7)[32]

Further, the Second Testament contains savage statements that are as bitter as the imprecations of the First Testament. For instance, in the book of Revelation, the souls who have been slaughtered on account of the Word of God cry out, "Sovereign Lord, holy and true, how long will it be before you judge and avenge our blood on the inhabitants of the earth?" (6:10). And 2 Thessalonians affirms, "For it is indeed just of God to repay with affliction those who afflict you" (1:6).

The preacher can also encourage the congregation to recognize that the imprecations never authorize the one praying to carry out the curse against the enemies. Human acts of vengeance are never legitimized by these texts. Those who prayed the imprecations evidently agreed with the deuteronomist (among others) who had God say, "Vengeance is mine . . . " (32:35). We believe that God never acts against people in the ways requested in the imprecations. Whether or not that is true, these passages do not authorize vigilante actions. God is the only authorized agent.

The imprecations are not precise models for Christian prayer. It is simply inappropriate for a Christian to pray for difficulty to befall another person. Nevertheless, the content of these prayers reminds the community of an important aspect of prayer: human beings can be completely honest with God. The psalmists, evidently, are hurt and enraged; they pour out these feelings in unhindered clarity to God. The honesty of these prayers maintains the integrity of the relationship between the worshiper and God and enables God to relate to the root of the worshiper's concern.

However, rather than actually praying for God to curse the enemies, it would be better for Christians to acknowledge their pain and anger with the same candor as the psalmists but to frame their desire for God to do harm to their enemies so that it is clearly a statement of the feelings of the worshiper and is not a request to God. For example, "O God, in my heart I wish that I could ask you to cause my opponents to drop dead." (This might be a good way to begin a sermon on this concern.) This would express the essential feeling but would not leave the congregant in the awkward position of praying for violence to occur to another person. The sermon might help the congregation think about ways to express feelings of hostility in prayer.

Some writers point out that these passages have a therapeutic function.[33] The texts allow the community to "vent" intense hostility in a "safe" context. Indeed, rage against the enemy in prayer not only releases tensions in one's own heart but lessens the likelihood that the worshiper will try to do physical damage to the enemy. Violent feelings expressed in ritual often diminish the impulse to act violently outside the ritual context. The sermon can help the worshipers recognize and deal with hostile feelings toward others. The preacher may want to encourage worshipers to locate means of processing their negative energies outside the worship setting.

Some of these texts are evidently countercurses (for example, 109:17-18). An enemy has cursed the psalmist. In order to protect the community from the enemy's curse, the psalmist calls forth a countercurse on the enemy. One's own curse should neutralize the curse of the enemy. This introduces an intriguing homiletical possibility. Today's church is sometimes beset with "curses" from those outside who do not appreciate its witness. Sometimes one group of members within the church wish hardship on other members. How does the preacher suggest that the church "protect" itself in such situations? Does it bash those who disagree, perhaps polarizing and exacerbating the situation? Or does the church seek to "protect" itself from the curses of others (and from curses within its own house) by working toward a larger community that is free of the conditions that call forth curselike attitudes and behaviors? Justice and reconciliation may be the most effective countercurse.

The discussion of the texts, themes, and images in this chapter has a provisional character. For the history of biblical interpretation teaches that today's certainties may be called into question by tomorrow's discoveries, questions, and situations. And, today's questions may be resolved by tomorrow's perspectives and discoveries. The text that seems antiquarian in June may be the clue that unlocks December's theological dilemma. The passage that was a familiar, trusted theological thoroughfare on Saturday night may collapse into a sinkhole with Sunday's headline. Nonetheless, preachers are called to make the best sense of the text that they can in the light of the fullest knowledge of God that they have. Fortunately, the Bible (at its best) reveals a God whose love and justice always find a way to come to expression, even when frustrated by the church's misinterpretations.

CHAPTER
SIX

Allen

WHEN THE TESTAMENTS COME TOGETHER

The Second Testament often calls forth associations with the First. One scholar has identified over sixteen hundred citations of the First Testament by the Second.[1] In addition, there are many more allusions. Moreover, passages from the Second Testament sometimes cite or allude to the literature of Second Temple Judaism (material mainly written after 400 B.C.E. and not included in the Protestant canon, e.g., Apocrypha, Pseudepigrapha). These texts helped shape the consciousness of the early church much like the First Testament. Further, the testaments sometimes come together in a lectionary that assigns readings from the two parts of the Bible on the same day.

We first consider recent shifts in this discussion. We then turn to how the preacher might understand the relationship between texts from the two testaments when the Second cites or alludes to the First (or to the literature of Second Temple Judaism) and when the two meet in a lectionary.

Recent Shifts in Understanding the Relationships of the Testaments

In order to reflect on the relationship between texts from different testaments, the preacher must recognize occasions when the Second Testament draws on the First. A preacher can ask three questions of any text in the Second Testament in order to help recognize and interpret citations and allusions to the First Testament (and to the literature of Second Temple Judaism).

1. Does the text from the Second Testament contain citations or echoes from the First Testament (or from the writings of Second Temple Judaism)?[2]

2. If so, what are these allusions and where are they found in the literature of Judaism? (These may be specific texts, images, themes, or associations common to the ethos of the Hebrew Bible and the literature of the Jewish people.)

3. How does the passage in the Second Testament make use of these associations? How is our understanding of the text enhanced by the awareness of the relationship of the earlier and later material?

A major shift is underway in scholarship regarding the reasons for the early church's use of the First Testament.[3] C. H. Dodd claimed that the early church used passages from the Hebrew Bible in order to defend the gospel in the face of its critics.[4] Recently, however, scholars have seen that the authors of the Second Testament more often use the scriptures inherited from Judaism in order to interpret the meaning of Christ, the church, and the Christian life.[5]

In the first century C.E., Jewish writers employed a variety of methodologies in order to interpret the significance of their sacred texts and traditions. These included typology, allegory, commentary, midrash, and targum. Early Christians employ some of these methods in the Second Testament.

The wording of a citation of the First Testament in an early Christian writing is sometimes different from its original in Hebrew, Aramaic, or the Septuagint. Did these Christians use versions of the older texts that are now lost to us? Did the early Christian scribes cite these materials inaccurately from memory? These cases may sometimes be true. But a recent scholar has noted that in many such instances, the form of the quotation of a text in the Christian corpus is the result of a Christian writer making use of a literary convention that was common in antiquity: consciously rewording quotations or references in order to show how the citations fit the purpose of the first century writers. Christopher Stanley calls these "interpretive readings."[6]

However, the scribes of the early church *allude* to the sacred texts of Judaism more than they directly cite such texts. A word or a phrase evokes a memory from the Jewish ethos. The early Christian writers use this allusion to interpret some aspect of Christ or the Christian view of the world.

Some contemporary pastors and scholars point to the misuse of the First Testament by the Second (at least according to the canons of today's historical-critical and literary-critical exegesis). Some of today's folk point to occasions when the Second Testament seems genuinely to understand the context and original points of the earlier sacred texts. The preacher will want to examine specific texts in the Second Testament from the perspective of these concerns. Nonetheless, there are instances in the later testament when the use of material from the earlier testament is clearly arbitrary from the standpoint of today's historical and literary criticism. Yet, such instances are normally examples of the writer of the Second Testament making use of an interpretive methodology that was commonly accepted in the ancient world. It is anachronistic for contemporary people to expect ancients to exhibit the best of contemporary biblical scholarship. We need to understand the ancients on their own terms.

Some scholars think that when the writers of the church cite or allude to a verse or passage from the inherited Scripture, they mean to call to mind the larger context in which the material is found.[7] This seems to be the case frequently but not universally. When coming upon a reference to the older testament in the newer, the preacher ought always to ask if the reference calls to consciousness the larger context in which the reference is found. If so, how does the larger context enhance our understanding of the text?

Broadly speaking, the church is in the interpretive tradition of Israel. For in the period when the Hebrew Bible itself was being written, an author often reinterpreted older traditions in order to show their contemporary significance.[8] For example, the Chronicler revised the history of the books of Samuel and Kings. As we noted in chapters 2 and 4, Jewish writers often regarded God's actions in the past as paradigmatic of God's actions in the future. Isaiah 40–55, for example, depicts the release of the captives from exile as a new Exodus. This is precisely what the church intended in its use of the First Testament: to show how God has acted afresh in Jesus Christ.

When the Second Testament Cites or Alludes to the First

When the text for the sermon from the Second Testament makes direct or indirect reference to the First, the preacher can frequently think of the relationship between the two testaments as falling into one of three general categories. (1) The Second Testament cites or alludes to the First to interpret positively God, Christ, or the church. (2) The Second Testament regards a passage from the First as a prophecy that is fulfilled in Christ or the life of the church. (3) The Second Testament corrects or rejects a part of the first.[9] These categories can combine.

A caveat. It is axiomatic in scholarly circles today to note that specific authors of the Second Testament often draw upon the First Testament in their own special ways. Paul and Matthew, for instance, each make use of the Septuagint. Paul and Matthew have much in common, but they also read the Old Testament with their own nuances of interpretation. One cannot always simply speak of "the" New Testament's use of the Old. It is better to speak of how particular writers of the New Testament use the Old. The following three categories may be helpful, but they should be brought into dialogue with an individual author's perspective on the Old Testament.

1. *The Second Testament cites or alludes to the First in order to interpret positively God, Christ, or the church.* As noted earlier, most of the uses of the First Testament by the Second presume that the purposes of God through Christ and the church continue the work of God begun in creation and attested in Israel. The writers of the Second Testament often call forth stories, images, themes, and other associations to name the significance of God, Jesus Christ, Christian faith, and life.

Richard B. Hays describes how this operates for Paul.

> The vocabulary and cadences of the Scripture—particularly of the LXX [Septuagint]—are imprinted deeply on Paul's mind, and the great stories of Israel continued to serve for him as a fund of symbols and metaphors that condition his perception of the world, of God's promised deliverance of his people, and of his own identity and calling.[10]

The same phenomena are true of most other writers of the earliest Christian literature.

The Second Testament may contain either a direct citation from the tradition or a reference that, while not a direct quote, is still immediately apparent. For example, in Romans 4, Paul pursues an exegesis of the story of Abraham in order to show that the promises that God made to Abraham are good for the church. Paul brings this to unmistakable clarity. "Therefore his [Abraham's] faith was reckoned to him as righteousness. Now the words, 'it was reckoned to him' were written not for his sake alone, but for ours also" (Rom. 4:22-23).

Matthew 21:1-11 (Jesus' entry into Jerusalem), for example, cites Psalm 118:26, "Blessed is the one who comes in the name of the LORD!" The psalm offers thanksgiving to God for deliverance from battle and is part of a liturgy used when entering the temple. Verse 26 is a choral blessing on the person entering the temple. By using this text, Matthew urges the reader to recognize Jesus as one through whom God's deliverance is coming.

We can also see direct evidence of the influence of Jewish tradition when the Second Testament makes use of Jewish interpretive practices. For instance in Luke 18:1-8, the parable of the widow and the unjust judge, Luke makes use of the typical Jewish practice of arguing from the lesser to the greater. If an unjust judge will give justice to a widow (the lesser), think how much more God will give justice to the faithful (the greater).

In addition to direct references from the First Testament that should be obvious to the contemporary reader, early Christian sources contain many more allusions that would likely have registered in the consciousness of the ancient receiver but that may not be obvious to today's Christian. These include the use of a word, a phrase, an image, or a pattern of thought. Richard Hays refers to them as echoes: expressions that cause the consciousness of the hearer or reader to associate an aspect of the text in the Second Testament with aspects of the Jewish tradition.[11]

Revelation 4:1-6 illustrates these echoes. This text is a vision of the throne room in heaven. It consists of a series of brief images. Each image threads a particular strand of memory into the mind and heart of the hearer from the First Testament or from apocalyptic writings. The whole passage gains its meaning by weaving the many images into a single cloth of impressions and associations. To change the metaphor, we get the meaning of the passage by identifying each of the echoes on their separate tracks and then listening to the whole tape to get their full sound. We now consider representative elements of this vision.

In Jewish writings, heaven is the place where God dwells. In apocalypticism, heaven is the realm in which events on the earth are controlled. Events on the earth are either actively initiated by God in heaven or they are permitted by God. At the very beginning of the text the listeners realize that they are in the place where their destiny is controlled. A throne is in the center of the place. The throne reinforces the sense of power and authority. The throne is surrounded by a rainbow. This element reminds the reader of God's promises to Noah and to the whole human community. After the flood, God pledged to Noah to continue the life support structures of seed time and harvest. God has been faithful to this promise.

The big throne is surrounded by twenty-four small thrones on which sit elders dressed in white robes; they represent the twelve tribes of Israel and the twelve apostles. The heavenly vision is true for all of God's people. White is a color characteristic of those who are in heaven's embrace. The elders sit on thrones and wear crowns indicating that they, too, have power. They are to exercise power in their limited spheres after the manner of God who exercises power in the cosmic sphere.

The throne issues flashes of lightning and peals of thunder. These cause the listener to remember the presence and revelation of God at Sinai and in other theophanies. As the law revealed God's will for Israel, so the vision in this book reveals God's will for the cosmos. Lightning and thunder bring forth a feeling of awe in the reader.

Seven flaming torches burn in front of the throne. The number seven in biblical parlance often represents completeness. The torches provoke the reader to remember Revelation 1:16, 20. There, John recalled Zechariah's use of the lampstand for the community of Israel and applied that image to the church. In chapter 4, the torches represent the spirits of these churches. What are these spirits? Many apocalyptic theologians believed that God had appointed a guardian angel for each human community. The angels mediated providence (and judgment) to the communities. Hence, the reader sees that the guardian angels for the churches are in the immediate care of God and, hence, can be trusted to watch over the church in its earthly pilgrimage.

A sea of glass, like crystal, is in front of the throne. In some ancient Near Eastern mythology, the sea is associated with chaos. In heaven, however, the power of chaos has been calmed. The chaos is quiet as glass. The church need not fear the manifestations of chaos that sweep into it on the earth because the heavenly counterpart of chaos has lost its destructive power.

The total effect of these images is to communicate to the reader a wonderful sense of divine power, promise, and providence. God is in control of the events of the world and promises to bring the church safely through them. John's church was in a situation of chaos. John himself was in prison and his church was either being persecuted or it feared the threat of persecution. Caesar—rapacious, idolatrous, and violent—occupied the throne on the earth. But this vision exposes his pretentiousness. This vision encourages the church to make its way through its earthly suffering and toward the apocalyptic fulfillment of God's purposes.

Ephesians 4:1-6 exhorts the church to maintain its unity. The theme of oneness permeates this passage: one body, one Spirit, one hope, one Lord, one faith, one baptism, one God. The hearer of this text will immediately recollect Deuteronomy 6:4-9 that states one of the central convictions of the Jewish tradition: God in Godself is one. The oneness of the church is rooted in the oneness and integrity of God. At this point, Judaism and Christianity share a common core.

The preacher can scarcely make sense of John 1:1-14 without referring to Proverbs 8:22-30; Sirach 24:1-22; Wisdom of Solomon 7:22–8:1. These texts help the reader see that the Johannine Christ functions for the church much like wisdom in Israel.

When preaching from such texts in the Second Testament, the preacher will want to help the congregation discover the background of the text in the Hebrew tradition and how that background is illuminating. Because of the lack of familiarity with the Bible in the church today, the preacher may need to provide background information for the congregation.

Of course, the preacher must examine critically the Christian uses of Jewish texts in the Second Testament. Even when the Christian use of a text intends to be continuous with the Jewish use, the early Christian writers occasionally distort the ancestral text. For instance, 1 Timothy 2:13-14 makes reference to the Fall. "For Adam was formed first, then Eve; and Adam was not deceived, but the woman was deceived and became a transgressor." First Timothy understands itself to be in continuity with the story of Genesis 3:1-6 and expresses a view held by other writers of the period (e.g., Sirach 25:24). But when read on its own terms, Genesis 3:1-6 arguably indicates that the man and the woman are equally transgressors.[12] In this case, the preacher needs to help the congregation understand the distortion of the First Testament in the Second.

2. *Texts from the First Testament regarded as prophecy fulfilled in the Second.* Many Jewish writers from 300 B.C.E. to 200 C.E., particularly those influenced by apocalypticism, believed that the Jewish Scriptures contained prophecies that predict the future. Many of the first Christian authors subscribed to this belief. However, as Dodd remarked, early Christian writers do not generally regard the texts that they treat as prophecies "as a kind of pious fortune telling."[13] More often, the hermeneutic of prophecy and fulfillment is intended to help the church see that God's action in Jesus and the church is an extension of God's actions in Israel. As we shall see, this hermeneutic is often strongly typological.[14]

The older testament itself contains texts of predictive prophecy.[15] Jeremiah, for instance, predicted the destruction of Jerusalem (7:14; 26:1). And, indeed, the temple fell. Some of these predictions have yet to come to pass. For example, Isaiah looks forward to the wolf dwelling with the lamb (11:6-9). When early Christian writers use predictive prophecy, they reflect their Jewish heritage.

While early Christian writers occasionally seem to view predictive texts from the First Testament woodenly and without regard for context, we notice a more frequent situation. The writers of the Second Testament frequently select predictive texts in which the situation in the passage from the First Testament is similar to the situation of the church. Frequently, the specific verse or verses cited in the Christian book seem to call to mind the larger context from the Hebrew Bible.[16]

Matthew 1:23 uses Isaiah 7:14 in this way. In Isaiah's day, "the heart of Ahaz [the leader of Judah] and the heart of his people shook as the trees of the forest shake before the wind" (Isaiah 7:2). For Judah's enemies had made an alliance among themselves to overthrow the Davidic dynasty. Such an eventuality would seem to abrogate the promise of God (2 Samuel 7:8-16). God sends Isaiah and his child, Shear-jashub, to console Ahaz. Even though Judah's enemies are powerful, God will keep the divine promise. God gives a sign of the divine trustworthiness. A young woman ('almah) shall bear a son and shall name him Immanuel ("God with us").

Matthew understands the prophet to include Jesus in the realm of the promise of Isaiah. Matthew cites Isaiah 7:14 from the Septuagint, which translates the Hebrew 'almah by the Greek parthenos (virgin).

Matthew's church is uncertain, much as Judah in the time of Isaiah. The Matthean community is in tension with Judaism. It suffers from broken pastoral relationships within its community (for example, Matt. 5:21-26; 18:10-35). And the church is trying to sort out its relationship to the larger culture. For Matthew, the birth of Jesus Christ functions as a sign of God's continuing presence with the community much as Isaiah spoke of the birth of the child during the reign of Ahaz.

Beyond interpreting texts from the first Testament predictively, the church made use of such prophecy in the mouth of Jesus and in reference to its own life. For instance, in the Synoptic Gospels, Jesus predicts his own death and resurrection three times (Mark 8:31; 9:30-32; 10:33-34 and parallels). He predicts the destruction of the temple and the apocalypse (Mark 13:1-27 and parallels). In Luke, Jesus anticipates the Gentile mission and antagonism between the church and some elements in the synagogue (Luke 4:16-30). These events occur in Acts. Most scholars of the origins of Christianity regard these as instances of "prophecy after the fact." The early Christian community seems to have put such prophetic prediction into the mouth of Jesus. Jesus thus appears to have divine foreknowledge and to interpret the experience of the church.

Predictive prophecy that has been fulfilled, including prophecy after the fact, helps establish the community's confidence that God can be trusted in the present and in the future. Further, predictive prophecy that is fulfilled has the effect of bolstering the church's confidence in the sacred Scriptures of Judaism and in Jesus. And it provides a basis for confidence in events that are predicted but are as yet unfulfilled (for example, Isaiah's vision of the wolf living with the lamb). Indeed, the most dramatic predictive prophecies of the early church are applied not to the first coming of Jesus but to the second (for example, Mark 13:24-27; 1 Thess. 4:13-5:10; 2 Pet. 3:1-18). When Jesus is long delayed, why should the church continue in eschatological hope? In part, because God has proven faithful in the past, as evidenced by the prophecies that came true.

When preaching from a text in the Second Testament that interprets a text from the First in a predictive way, the preacher may want to do three things. (1) The preacher can help the congregation realize that the text in the First Testament had a life of its own long before the church. Today's church can often be instructed by that text without reference to the later testament. A preacher could take this approach to Isaiah 7:14 in the context of Judah. (2) But, the preacher can point to ways in which the passage from the older testament illumined the experience of the later church. Does the preacher notice similarities of function between the use of the predictive text in the First and Second Testaments? What are the similarities between the setting of Isaiah 7:14 in the worlds of Judah and Matthew? Does the birth of Jesus function as a sign for today's church? (3) The preacher may want to emphasize that the promises of God through the First Testament are still good for the Jewish community. The church's experience of these promises does not invalidate them for Judaism. Indeed, the church can appreciate the text on two levels: in its own literary setting in the older testament and as a lens through which to understand its experience of Christ.

3. *References in the Second Testament that criticize Jewish scripture, people, practices, or institutions.* Several early Christian texts appear to

criticize Jewish people, practices, and institutions. The most vivid exemplifications are found in the Gospels, Acts, and in Hebrews.

On the one hand, the church emerged from Judaism. As we have seen, the church used the texts and categories of Judaism to help interpret its experience. Many early Christians were Jewish and could rightly be called Christian Jews. On the other hand, some in the church criticized aspects of Jewish belief and practice.

How did this situation come about? The specific answer to this question is a matter of scholarly discussion.[17] However, we can give a general response that would embrace the judgments of most scholars. Tensions developed among Jews who did not identify with the church and Christian Jews and Gentile Christians (particularly after the fall of Jerusalem in 70 C.E.). These tensions developed even while some Christian Jews remained within the synagogue. The most important tensions, apparently, had to do with accepting Gentiles into the church without asking them to adopt detailed Jewish customs and beliefs. As the church developed its own identity and life, it came to interpret a number of ideas along different axes than its Jewish parent. The church justified its beliefs and practices by both interpreting itself in the language and images of Judaism and by distancing itself from aspects of Judaism that it no longer regarded as normative. Through the centuries, the church has sometimes magnified these impulses by interpreting references to Jews and Judaism in the Second Testament as "images of everything bad in religion."[18]

This ambivalence is especially prominent in the Fourth Gospel. It is impossible to understand the revelation of God in Jesus without a knowledge of Judaism. Virtually all the major terms that interpret Jesus echo Jewish literature. For example: word, bread of life, water of life, light of the world, shepherd, and vine. Yet, the Jesus of the Fourth Gospel also criticizes Jewish leaders and many Jewish practices. And the author of this Gospel uses "the Jews" to represent many in the world who resist the saving revelation of God in Jesus. At several points, John seeks to demonstrate that the revelation of God through Jesus is superior to the revelation encased in prior Jewish tradition.

For instance, in John 6, a crowd wants to know how to gain eternal life. Jesus replies that they can attain it by believing in the one whom

God has sent, i.e., by joining in the Christian community (6:28-29). The Jews then ask what sign Jesus will give them so that they can have the assurance to believe. After all, Moses gave a sign: manna from heaven (6:30-31). According to John, Jesus himself is now the sign. "I am the bread of life" (6:35). The will of God is that all believe in Jesus and thereby gain eternal life. But unfortunately, the Jews do not believe. Only those who believe will be raised on the last day (6:36-40).

John makes a devastating critique of Jewish tradition. "Your ancestors ate the manna in the wilderness, and they died" (6:49). The solemn words "and they died" are in striking contrast to "I am the living bread that came down from heaven. Whoever eats of this bread will live forever; and the bread that I will give for the life of the world is my flesh" (6:51). The Jewish people, apart from Jesus, face death.

The Jewish crowd, of course, wants to know how Jesus can give them his flesh to eat (6:52). Jesus explains that when he speaks of his flesh he is speaking of the Lord's Supper. Those who partake of the Lord's Supper (i.e., Christians) will live forever whereas those who partake of the manna of Moses will die (6:53-59).

At points, the Second Testament seeks to show that the church (and not the Jews of the first century) is the community that practices the intention of the First Testament. In Mark 2:23-27, the Pharisees fail to grasp the true meaning of their own tradition of Sabbath observance. The Markan Jesus instructs them, "The sabbath was made for humankind, and not humankind for the sabbath." Jesus is the true interpreter of the Jewish tradition. Henceforth, the church should pay attention to him and not to other interpreters of Judaism (e.g., the Pharisees).

We hasten to add that preachers need to be careful not to find disparagement of Judaism where it is not. For instance, many preachers assume that Paul viewed the Torah as teaching the Jews to practice works righteousness. As we noted in chapter 1, details of scholarly analysis vary. But most contemporary scholars believe that Paul regarded Torah positively, even if he did not think it was applicable to Gentile Christians. Thus, one ought not to depict Paul as disparaging Torah or Judaism as such.

Expanding from the case of Paul, we posit a question that a preacher might ask of any text in the Second Testament that appears to present the First Testament or Jewish people and customs in a negative light. Does this text really present Judaism negatively or does it only seem to do so?

A preacher might do at least five things when confronted with a sacred text from the hand of the early church that appears to diminish Jewish texts, people, practices, or institutions.

(1) The preacher can help the congregation understand whether the Second Testament actually diminishes Judaism or whether it only appears to do so because of the church's inherited perceptions.

(2) The preacher can help the congregation understand the situation in the first century C.E. in which these texts came to expression. While this situation is understandable (if regrettable) it is not normative for today's church.

(3) The preacher can resist the inclination to ask the congregation to identify with Jewish characters or practices when they appear in a diminished way in a text in the Second Testament. One of the most common principles of hermeneutics is to get the congregation to identify with a character in the text and to hear the word of the text from the perspective of that character. For example, in Acts 3:1-10, a lame person is healed outside the Beautiful Gate. Peter explains what has happened (3:11-26). In response, Jewish leaders arrest Peter and John. The Jewish leaders release the two apostles without punishment only because the leaders fear the crowd (4:1-22). Peter and John then meet with the other apostles and the place shakes—a sign that God is with them.

A preacher may tend to urge the congregation to identify with the Jewish leaders and to ask, "How are we like the Jewish people in the story? How do we reject God's healing work and workers?" This, however, reinforces a negative stereotype of the Jewish people. Of course, Christians in our day *do* reject God's healing work and workers. But the preacher can make the point that religious leaders today hinder God's work without painting the point with anti-Jewish language. If the circumstances in the congregation are appropriate, the preacher might otherwise ask the community to identify with the man who was healed. "How does God's healing grace come to us?" Indeed, God can heal the church of its anti-Jewish prejudice.

(4) When dealing with a text that downplays or invalidates aspects of Jewish practice, the preacher might help the congregation realize that it is legitimate for the church not to follow Jewish practice but that the church can do so without debunking Jews or Judaism.

(5) The preacher can help the congregation affirm that God's covenantal relationship with the Jewish people is still in force. Indeed, Christians can rejoice in the continuing witness of the Jewish people to the God of love, grace, mercy, and justice.

When the Testaments Come Together in a Lectionary

The lectionary most widely used in North America is the Revised Common Lectionary (RCL).[19] While we focus principally on how the First and Second Testaments are related in this table of readings, much of our discussion can be adapted to other lectionaries. And many of our comments in the preceding section apply to the relationship of the lessons in the lectionary. The lectionary, however, does have its own logic that calls for specialized remarks.

The lectionary supports the Christian year. The Christian year is designed to help the congregation remember (or discover) several formative themes of the Christian faith: God manifests the divine purposes in Christ (Advent, Christmas, Epiphany Day). God demonstrates divine love and power in the life, death, resurrection, and ascension of Jesus and in bestowing the Spirit on the church (Lent, Easter, Pentecost Day). God leads the church in growth in discipleship and witness (Ordinary Time). God reveals the eschatological fulfillment of all of God's promises (Advent).

The scripture texts in the lectionary are chosen to illumine these themes. Strictly speaking, one does not preach the lectionary. One preaches the Christian year using the assigned passages as lenses through which to consider the emphases of the day or season.

The lectionary appoints four readings for each Sunday and for most holy days: a Psalm (for use in the liturgy), and a selection each from a Gospel, a letter, and from a book of the First Testament (other than a Psalm or from Acts). The readings are organized into three patterns of one year each: Year A centers on Matthew; Year B centers on Mark; Year C centers on Luke. The Fourth Gospel is sprinkled throughout the two major cycles (Advent-Epiphany and Lent-Pentecost).

The reading from the Gospel guides the emphasis for the day (insofar as a day has an emphasis). From the first Sunday of Advent through Trinity Sunday, the other readings are intended to coordinate with the Gospel reading. In Ordinary time after Pentecost, the RCL provides two options for the reading from the First Testament (and the preacher must choose which one to use). One set of readings coordinates the passage from the Hebrew Bible with the Gospel. The other pattern disengages the First Testament from the Second and presents semicontinuous readings from the Hebrew Bible. In Year A, the readings cover the ancestral stories of the Pentateuch; in Year B, some of the historical books and Wisdom literature; in Year C, the prophets.

The lectionary is rightly praised.[20] It leads the preacher and congregation to a broader exposure to the Scripture than would ordinarily be the case when the preacher is freely selecting texts for the service. It confronts preacher and members with difficult passages that most would happily avoid. The lectionary brings the First Testament into the purview of pastor and community.

But, the First Testament is still disadvantaged in most of today's lectionaries. The Christian year and the lectionary are Christocentric. The Gospel reading determines the emphasis for the day. Thus, the sacred Scriptures of Israel are typically in the role of supporting Christology. The Hebrew Bible is seldom heard in its own voice.

In most services of worship, the Gospel is given pride of place in the reading of the Scriptures. The Gospel reading is often draped in more elaborate liturgy than the reading from the First Testament.

The sheer number of readings further diminishes the importance of the First Testament in the lectionary. The RCL contains about 435 readings from the last twenty-seven books of the Bible but only about 270 from the first thirty-nine books (not including Psalms). This is in inverse proportion to the actual length of each part of the Bible.

These factors downplay the importance of the Old Testament. Of course, the pastor can always elect to preach only from the passage from the First Testament (or from the psalm). But even then, the overall liturgical context diminishes the First Testament. Unfortunately, the Gospel reading often contains polemics against Jewish people, beliefs, practices, and institutions. The most prominent reading of sacred literature in the service of worship can thereby directly undermine the excerpt from the First Testament.

In the Sundays following Easter, the First Testament disappears altogether from the RCL. This symbolically cuts the taproot between the Jewish heritage and the resurrection.

Not surprisingly, some important material from the Hebrew Bible is not well represented in the lectionary. For instance, passages dealing with creation (certainly a significant concern for a world moving ever closer to ecocide) are infrequent. A pastor might create an emphasis on creation that extends over several weeks by building on the texts and themes found in our discussion of creation in chapter 2.

The congregation never hears the sweep of the narrative that begins with Genesis 1 and concludes with Daniel. The semicontinuous readings of the Hebrew Bible in the summer and the fall do help the church get a sense of pieces of the saga. But the Christian community never hears the whole in the setting of worship. Since Christians today seldom encounter the Bible outside the sanctuary, few people have opportunity to develop a narrative framework within which to place people, places, and events from the ancestral texts. And more, the waxing and waning of the story of Israel creates an emotional and intellectual fabric that is presumed for the reading of the Second Testament. Without continuous reading, this fabric may not be fully incorporated into Christian consciousness.

This is prologue to the problem that is most frequent for the weekly lectionary homilist: the connection of the First Testament to the Second in the lessons for a given Sunday. The preacher's first responsibility is to determine the relationship between the two testaments in the readings. The preacher must then identify the text(s) on which to preach and decide whether to comment directly on the relationship between the texts from the two testaments in the sermon.

Some ministers mistakenly think that they should bring all three texts into the sermon each week. But, a single text often requires so much interpretation that it is sufficient for a single sermon.[21] To bring more than one text into the sermon can complicate the message and confuse the listener. And if the preacher treats more than one text in a sermon on a Sunday on which the texts are not really connected, the preacher may mislead the congregation into thinking that the texts are related. However, when the relationship among the testaments is genuinely illuminating, the preacher may find it helpful to bring lections from both testaments into the sermon.

The RCL posits three types of relationships between texts from the First and Second Testaments: (1) parallel texts, (2) contrasting texts, and (3) typology.[22] Each of these yields a different approach in the sermon.

1. *Parallelism.* In parallelism, aspects of the reading from the Hebrew Bible are parallel to aspects of the text(s) from the hand of the earliest church. For instance, on the Third Sunday in Lent in Year C, the three texts all call for repentance. In Isaiah 55:1-9, God invites the people to "Incline your ear and come to me." Paul uses the example of the fate of the Israelites in the wilderness to admonish the Corinthians to avoid idolatry and other evils (1 Cor. 10:1-13). The Lucan Jesus tells the stories of the Galileans who were killed by Pilate and of others who were killed when a tower fell on them. He concludes, " . . . unless you repent, you will all perish, as they did" (Luke 13:1-9). The preacher could show the continuities between the lessons from the two testaments.

2. *Contrast.* In the mode of contrast, the lesson(s) from the Second Testament contrasts with the First Testament lesson. Ordinarily, the contrast is between superior Christianity and inferior Judaism.

Some contrasts are direct. For example, on the last Sunday after the Epiphany, Year C, Exodus 34:29-35 describes Moses descending from Mount Sinai with a veiled face. The Israelites could not bear to look upon his radiance. On the other hand, 2 Corinthians 3:12–4:2 claims that when Moses is read, the Jewish people still have a veil over their minds. By contrast, Christ removes the veil.

Other contrasts are more subtle. For instance, on the Fourth Sunday of Lent, Year A, Samuel anoints David as king of Israel in 1 Samuel 16:1-13. But at the climax of the story of the man born blind in John 9:1-41, the text charges that the Jewish leaders are blind. The dominion of David is inferior to the dominion of Christ.

Contrast can appear even when the lectionary does not prescribe a reading from the sacred texts of Judaism. On the Fifth Sunday of Easter in Year A, Acts 7:55-60 recounts the stoning of Stephen. The Jewish killers are enraged and grind their teeth. By contrast the martyr is filled with the Holy Spirit.

In cases of negative contrast, the preacher can help the congregation understand the contrast and why such thinking emerged in the church. When the text contrasts Judaism and Christianity, the sermon might call attention to the anti-Jewish effects of such polar ways of thinking in the relationships between Jewish people and Christians. The pastor can also encourage the congregation to evaluate the contrast in the light of the criteria of appropriateness to the gospel, intelligibility, and moral plausibility. The preacher could further help the community discern how texts from the first part of the Bible can speak positively to the Christian community without being filtered through the lens of contrast. The Christian community can have its own distinctive identity without disparaging the Jewish community.

The lectionary does present a few cases of contrast when the First Testament corrects the Second or its traditional interpretation. For instance, in Year A, Epiphany 6 and 7, Christians often naively interpret Matthew 5:21-48 as a series of antitheses in which Jesus sets himself over and against a rigid, narrow legalism ("You have heard that it was said to those of ancient times . . . but I say to you."). However, the presence of Psalm 119:1-8, 33-40 in the lections for those days reminds the preacher that the law was not envisioned in the Jewish community as rigid and legalistic. In this light, scholars today speak less of antitheses in the Sermon on the Mount and more of Jesus as an interpreter in the interpretive tradition of Israel who seeks to draw out the contemporary implications of the ancient text.

3. *Typology.* The RCL also posits the passage from the First Testament as a type that is fulfilled in the Second. For example, on the Second Sunday of Advent, Year C, Malachi 3:1-4 predicts a messenger who will prepare the way for the coming of God. Luke 3:1-6 implicitly identifies John the Baptist as this messenger. In such instances, the

preacher might show how Malachi had a message for his own day and how his words also provide an interpretive framework for Luke to explicate the ministry of John. For Luke, John functioned in his day much like the messenger functioned for Malachi.

We are repeatedly impressed by the genuine interrelatedness of texts from the two parts of the Bible on many days in the RCL. However, some selections appear to be quite arbitrary and without obvious connection (even on days when the preacher expects the readings to be connected).

When the relationship between the two testaments is arbitrary, the preacher has two options. For one, she or he can call this arbitrariness to the attention of the congregation so that the congregation does not get the impression that an organic affinity exists between the texts. For another, the preacher may select another reading from one testament that better illumines the other readings. For instance, on the Fifth Sunday of Easter, Year A, the epistle is 1 Peter 2:1-10, which climaxes with the affirmation that the church is a royal priesthood, a holy nation. This language is rooted in Exodus 19. The preacher might therefore omit one of the other readings and substitute Exodus 19. Or, again, on the Third Sunday after Epiphany (Year C), Luke 4:14-20 (Jesus' inaugural sermon at Nazareth) is better complemented by Isaiah 61 ("The spirit of the Lord God is upon me") than by the story of the reading of the law in Nehemiah 8.

The preacher might take up the suggestion of James A. Sanders to create a lectionary that centers on the story of the Hebrew Bible.[23] The lections could begin with the primeval history and go thence through the story of the Hebrew people and their unfolding life. The emphases might include the promises to Abraham and Sarah, the Exodus, the wanderings, the conquest, the rise of the monarchy, the prophets, the divided nation, the Exile, the restoration, and the Maccabean revolt. The table of readings could integrate wisdom passages and differing viewpoints (e.g., the books of Samuel, Kings, and Chronicles). If used, readings from the Second Testament could be chosen because they show how themes from the First Testament shape the faith and practice of the church.

Since the First Testament is constitutive of Christian identity, it is important that it come into the minds and hearts of the congregation. Since Christians have sometimes neglected and abused the First Testament and the people it represents, it is important for the church to rectify itself. Occasions when the testaments come together provide the preacher with natural opportunities to help the congregation reflect on these matters.

In addition, preachers need conscientiously to preach from the First Testament. As a starting point, we recommend that ministers review their preaching texts for the past year. At a minimum, preachers ought to focus on a passage from the First Testament at least once a month. And pastors ought regularly to deal with how the Second Testament draws directly and indirectly on the First.

CHAPTER SEVEN

FIVE KINDS OF SERMONS

In the five sermons that follow, we illustrate the interpretive program developed in this book. These are not the only ways in which sermons could be developed from the particular biblical texts. Not only do the texts themselves offer multiple possibilities for preaching, but particular preachers in particular contexts discern particular emphases that seem to them particularly fitting for particular occasions. We offer these because they represent the themes of *Holy Root, Holy Branches.*

The first sermon is a straightforward appropriation of an obviously paradigmatic text of the kind we illustrated in chapter 4. This is probably the hermeneutical pattern that will be most frequent when the preacher turns to a text from the Hebrew Scriptures. The second sermon deals with an aspect of Jewish tradition (levirate marriage) that, on the surface level, does not appear to offer much of positive value to today's church. The sermon is based on a text that falls into the category of those discussed in the first part of chapter 5, "Material That Appears to Be Antiquarian or of Interest Primarily to the Jewish Community." The third sermon encounters a text (Ecclesiastes) that manifests theological difficulties along the lines discussed in the second part of chapter 5, "Material That Is Theologically Inappropriate, Unintelligible, or Immoral." The fourth sermon focuses on a passage from the Second Testament (the martyrdom of Stephen) that refers directly to a passage from the First. This sermon also raises the difficult problem of how to deal with passages that have an anti-Jewish element. The fifth sermon brings together texts from each testament that occur together in a lectionary but between which there is no direct literary relationship. The last two sermons were developed in the frameworks articulated in chapter 6.

FIVE KINDS OF SERMONS

Sermon One
"The Surprise of Deliverance"
John Holbert
Exodus 1:1–2:10

This sermon illustrates straightforward movement from a paradigmatic text to the sermon. The sermon is based on the exegesis of the text in chapter 4. The sermon is itself a single narrative.[1]

There was always something peculiar about the Israelites. Oh, they looked and talked and acted and worshiped in peculiar ways; that goes without saying. But among the vast multitude of pharaoh's slaves, they stood out somehow.

They certainly caught the eye of the old pharaoh, "the king of Egypt," as they liked to call him, something no Egyptian would ever dream of saying. One day, in the middle of the usual boring staff meeting in the palace, during another discussion of the splendor of pharaoh's proposed tomb, he suddenly blurted out, "We have to do something about those Israelites!" It was the only subject that could take his mind off his expectation of a blissful eternity. "They just keep multiplying! They are like rabbits! We just have to stop them!" The silence was deafening. No one dared to offer a suggestion before he did. And, of course, he had a plan. He always had a plan.

"Let's see. How long do the men work in the brick-maker's huts? Sixteen hours? Hardly long enough I'd say." He said all this with his vilest smirk. "Increase it to twenty hours," he shouted, and he hooted with kingly laughter. The whole room joined him; they always laughed loudly at the royal jokes. Well, they were not quite fools, were they? But nobody in the room quite got the point of the plan; or if they did, they waited wisely until the old boy explained it to them.

"Don't you see? If we work them hard enough, the last thing on their minds when they return home will be multiplication, if you get what I mean." He chortled an obscene little chortle. They all got it, and chortled appreciatively. "Well, what are you waiting for?" The building masters bolted from the room, each trying to be the first to abuse his Israelite workers even more.

153

In a narrative sermon it is important to establish the tone of the sermon as quickly as possible. In our brief analysis of this biblical text in chapter 4, we indicated that the tone was humorous, playfully making fun of Pharaoh and establishing the Israelites as in every way superior to the Egyptians. Thus, we want to allow that humor to arise in our telling of the story.

A second important concern for the beginning of a narrative sermon is to signal, however subtly, what the focus of the telling will be. That is why we began with an immediate reference to the "peculiarity" of the Israelites. The sermon will strive to show that that peculiarity is in fact the presence and power of their God whose unalterable will is to deliver them from slavery.

Several months passed. Pharaoh, and his wisest courtiers, expected the plan to work. It was shrewd and devilishly clever. But when the slavery census lists were handed to pharaoh, he exploded with rage. "By Isis, those rabbits are still at it in a big way! I cannot believe my eyes—a 43 percent increase this past month alone. I'll show them. If twenty hours a day won't do it, how about twenty-two?" With that he collapsed, red-faced and gasping, on his pile of leopard skins.

But the extension of Plan A was no better. Each month's figures continued to rise, and the mystery of the multiplying slaves deepened along with the growing dread of them among the Egyptians.

But Pharaoh was not pharaoh for nothing, even if it was little more than an accident of birth. In a surprising move, he demanded that two lowly Israelite midwives be brought to the divine throne room. No one could guess what Plan B was to be, but the great court listened carefully as their king-god shouted orders at the midwives whose names were Shiphrah and Puah—but, of course, great Pharaoh would hardly deign to stain his tongue with such heathen names. "When you two *women*—and I use the term loosely in your case—(he waited for the expected burst of laughter) come to those filthy places where your kind give birth, if it is a male child, kill him on the spot. But if it is female, you can let her live." All this he said with the slyest of grins.

Some in the room were shocked. Not at the call for murder; it was, after all, only slaves being discussed. No, the plan itself seemed seriously flawed. Was it not *women* who gave birth? Would it not be far wiser and much more effective to kill the girls—no girls, no multiplying? But the room was silent. Pharaoh had spoken. Shiphrah and Puah left, their eyes set in determination.

It is important now to move the story along. There is always danger in a narrative sermon of overdescribing, of painting the background to excess. If the focus is on the surprising deliverance of God, it is crucial to establish the sharp differences between the power of Pharaoh and the midwives and to begin to suggest that Pharaoh is not as shrewd as he thinks he is. It will soon become obvious that Pharaoh is not struggling with lowly Israelites on their own but is engaged in combat with a God far greater than he. But one of the beauties of the story is that the real combat is disguised with a domestic scene.

Six months passed, and by the figures on the royal scrolls, it became obvious to Pharaoh that his Israelite messengers of death had not been carrying out their assigned murderous task. In fury, he hailed them back into the throne room. "Why have you done this? Why have you let all those little boys live?" He had by now completely lost the divine cool. The midwives answered sweetly and politely, without a hint of hesitation. "Well, your majesty, you should know that Hebrew women are not at all like Egyptian women. You see, they are so full of life that by the time we arrive at the place of birth, they are already back to work, lugging their newborns with them! We just cannot get there fast enough! Sorry; we did our best."

Several of Pharaoh's courtiers opened their mouths to protest this attack on the fine women of Egypt, uttered by these filthy foreigners, and to urge Pharaoh to reject out of hand their lies about fleet-footed Israelite slaves. But the sound stopped in their throats when they heard Pharaoh bellow, "Throw every male born in Egypt into the sacred Nile but let every girl live!" In horror, the court emptied, Pharaoh collapsed in a dead faint. He had demanded that every male baby be drowned, whether Israelite or not, but he still had not figured out that killing the girls would be far better. The king-god of Egypt was clearly not as clever as he assumed; in fact, it might be said that the old boy was several mud-bricks short of a load.

The absurdity of the scene with the midwives needs emphasis, especially Pharaoh's murderous plan, their refusal to complete the plan, their outra-

geous responses to his demands for an explanation, and his quite insane Plan C that includes wholesale male genocide. If the Hebrew text is read, as opposed to the Septuagint, Pharaoh's demand is that all male babies, both Israelite and Egyptian, be drowned. Pharaoh the shrewd has become Pharaoh the foolish fanatic. He has been outsmarted by the midwives, a defeat that foreshadows a much greater defeat as the story unfolds.

Guess what? Pharaoh's dastardly plan to have all the male babies thrown into the Nile worked. An Israelite male baby *was* thrown into the Nile, but a death by drowning was hardly the purpose. This baby's mother, seeing that her child was healthy, plotted to keep him with her and would not expose him to the evil edict of the mad Pharaoh. But babies do grow, and their lungs become strong. The poor woman must give him over to fate or rather to the God of her people. She devised a desperate plan. She built a tiny ark, a vessel patterned on the ark of that long-ago sea voyager Noah. Just to be sure of the little boat's safety, she daubed it all around with bitumen and pitch, exactly as Noah did his ark. With a quiet prayer, she launched the ark onto the Nile, expecting never to see her boy again. But the boy's sister walked through the reeds at the river's bank, watching the fate of the ark.

Pharaoh's daughter, along with her large company of serving women, went down to the river for their daily bath. As she bathed, her eye fell on the ark that floated calmly on the river. She asked one of her maids to bring it to her. She opened the roof of the ark and took a long look at the child. The child was crying lustily. There was a silence among the women. The baby's cries were the only sound on the river.

They all knew the command of the Pharaoh. Several of the maids moved to overturn the ark and stifle the cries of the baby forever. But Pharaoh's daughter "took pity on him." Though the baby was clearly a Hebrew, she forced her maids back away from the ark.

At that same moment, the baby's sister rushed out of the reeds and daringly prostrated herself before the divine woman. "Shall I go and get a Hebrew nursemaid for you?" She asked. "Yes," said the daughter of the Pharaoh, and the girl rushed back to her mother. "My brother is safe, and you will never guess where!" she laughed, as she dragged her mother down to the Nile. Both woman and girl now prostrated themselves before the daughter of Pharaoh, and waited for her instructions.

"Take this child and nurse him for me," she commanded, "and I will pay you well for it." The mother could barely contain a loud guffaw. The child she had thought to have lost forever was now back in her arms! Not only that. She had been commanded by the daughter of Pharaoh herself to nurse her own child and to be paid for it in the bargain! When she and her daughter and her restored son had gotten out of earshot, she laughed uproariously. Even the baby chuckled with joy.

The story is told so well in the Bible that the preacher need only follow its plot carefully. We emphasize two aspects. First, the congregation needs to know that the baby's vessel is indeed an ark, using the same word found in Genesis. This emphasis nicely connects that story with this one, suggesting that the God of creation is also the God of deliverance.

Second, the delightful part of the story where the baby's own mother ends up nursing the child and gets paid for it, is emphasized as an important element of the humor of the tale and of the surprising action of deliverance once again. Such an action again foreshadows the great deliverance that this small story prefigures.

Pharaoh's daughter named her adopted baby Moses, a word that sounds something like the Hebrew word "to draw out." She pulled him out of the water, so it sounded appropriate. But every Egyptian knew that in the Egyptian language, the word Moses means "son of." They remembered several ancient pharaohs with the name, Tutmoses, "Son of Tut," for example. But whatever his name meant, this Moses turned out to have an astonishing destiny. God used him, quite literally, to deliver the people from their Egyptian slavery. But most of you already know that part of the story. It's the one made famous by Cecil B. DeMille and Charlton Heston.

But, this smaller story needs to be remembered, too. You see, there is only one adult male mentioned in the whole thing, and he is murderously insane. The delivered, the helpless baby Moses, is himself delivered by five women. It really was a bad mistake for Pharaoh to let all those girls live. They could grow up to be deliverers much like

Shiphrah and Puah, like Moses' sister and mother, even like, believe it or not, Pharaoh's own daughter.

There really is something peculiar about these Israelites. And what is peculiar is their God, a God who is in the business of surprising deliverance. You just don't know where, or how, or with whom, this God is going about the business of deliverance. But one thing you can bet the bank on: God's business *is* deliverance. Just get ready. You might be surprised.

Ending a narrative sermon is always the most difficult part. It needs to carry the focus of the sermon without bashing the listener over the head with it. Since the theme of this telling of the story is God's surprising deliverance, it was important to get those words into the ending so that the congregation could hear them again. And it was important to focus on the five women's deliverance of Moses, the part of the plot that best illustrates the surprise of God's deliverance.

It might be useful for you to go back to chapter 4 and re-read our analysis of Exodus 1:1–2:10, looking for those ideas that made their way into the narrative sermon. Of course, our analysis there is very brief and only scratched the surface of the material. Nevertheless, we think that this narrative sermon illustrates at least one facet of the paradigm of divine deliverance. Of course, this is only one of many ways that one could narrate that story and only one emphasis that could be chosen to narrate it. If you have not tried a narration like this one, you may find that a congregation will welcome a story they may not have heard before. Furthermore, you may find that this kind of preaching is just good fun.

Sermon Two
"A Future for Levirate Marriage"
Ronald Allen
Deuteronomy 25:5-10

This text portrays a custom, levirate marriage, that was common in ancient Israel and its neighbors but is no longer practiced. It does not appear to offer much positive value to the church. Using the hermeneutic articulated in chapter 2, the sermon finds that the text can be instructive to the contemporary community. The preacher did not comment on the uses of the text in the Second Testament (Mark 12:18-27 and parallels) because the text from Deuteronomy makes an important point on its own. The Gospel themes would complicate and frustrate the focus of this particular sermon. Another sermon might deal with this text in the context of the discussion about resurrection in Mark 12:18-27 (and parallels).

You're on a trip and your route has taken you off the interstate highway and onto a narrow blacktop state road. You see an old gas station converted to another use. "Antiques," the sign reads. You pull over and walk among things of yesteryear. A chifforobe. (Do your children even know the word chifforobe?) A wood-burning stove. Kerosene lamps. Everything has the stale smell of being closed up for too long.

The antique store is fascinating. You may buy something because it will add to the decor of your family room or because it makes you nostalgic. But few of these things are genuinely useful.

I imagine many of us respond to our reading from Deuteronomy regarding levirate marriage in much the same way. The title comes from the Latin word, *levir*. That word means a husband's brother. If the husband should die without a son, the passage directs the husband's brother to marry the widow. And the passage contains a legal grievance procedure for the widow if her brother-in-law should neglect to do so. She is to pull the sandal off his foot and spit in his face. Hardly a model of conflict resolution by today's standards.

When I first read this passage, I found it like stopping at an antique store. Fascinating, but not very helpful as I look for guidance into what God has to say to a world in which nearly as many marriages end in divorce as in death. What does this law have to do with the single life or with people who live together without marriage? More and more people—women and men—regard the patriarchal worldview that lies behind this text as not only antique but pernicious. Does levirate practice apply to same-gender marriages? Our passage presumes that polygamy is legal. But people who practice polygamy today go to jail. Would Deuteronomy have us go to jail for levirate marriage? This passage seems to smell like an antique store.

The preacher does not move too quickly to the positive values that can result from this text. It is important to bring to the surface of the sermon puzzlements that are likely to be on the minds of the congregation. This not only helps the listeners pay attention to the cultural differences between themselves and the biblical world, but it helps them realize that the preacher is on their wavelength. And when such puzzles are identified, the congregation is likely to set them aside and follow the movement of the sermon. If the puzzles go unidentified, the congregation may keep playing with the pieces in their minds ("But what about . . .polygamy?") and not give full attention to the sermon.

But as I studied the passage, I began to sense instructive connections between the ancient world and our own. In a manner of speaking, I began to see a future for levirate marriage. Well, not exactly for levirate marriage as such, but for values, attitudes, and practices that are similar to levirate marriage.

The sermon tries to alert the hearers to the interpretive axis on which the sermon is going to unwind. This encourages them to invest themselves in the sermon but to do so while listening on both a surface and a deeper level.

The brother-in-law and the widow are to conceive a child in order to preserve the dead man's name. Who cares about preserving a dead man's name? But the name was important to the ancients. The name was ancient shorthand for children, possessions, land, and immortality. In antiquity, the ancients believed that after a person died, that person's legacy lived through those who bore the name. Those who bore the name would receive the land, the possessions, and the animals of the deceased. These were more than creature comforts; these made it possible to live. You had to have shelter from the elements, a place to grow food, and a way to make clothing, or you became a beggar. And, as unfair as it may seem to us, the name was passed from male to male.

In the world of Deuteronomy, a woman was secure only when she was properly related to a man. When young, she was her father's daughter. At the age of marriage, she became a wife. Much of her identity came through her association with her husband. She achieved her potential as a wife when she bore a son to carry on the name. In recent years, we have come to see exceptions to these customs (for example, the loyalty of Ruth to Naomi and the leadership of the judge

Deborah). Sensitive interpreters have opened our eyes to the negative aspects of such views and practices. But this was the way most women lived in Israel.

A woman who was not in relationship with a man was on her own for survival. In Bible times, they did not have social security. When you grew old, you depended on your children to take care of you. A childless widow had no one to care for her. Without property, without source of food or clothing, she might be dependent on gleaning the leftover crops from the fields and on the handouts of others. It was a vulnerable life.

The congregation needs some basic information about the practice of levirate marriage. This is given simply and directly. The motif of justice is in the background (see our discussion of justice in chapter 4).

How would you feel if you had to slip into the cornfield behind the combine and pick up the ears that it had missed in order to find food for you and your family? How would you like it if the farmer and the farmer's family drove by and saw you? When I was growing up, my mother worked for the county welfare department. She would take my old clothes to the children of some of her clients. Every once in a while, I would see children in the hallways at school wearing my old clothes. I was always glad for them to have my clothing, but I felt awkward when I saw them. I sometimes thought, "I know something about you that no one else knows. I won't say anything to anyone, but I know it." I do not know how they felt. But they seldom talked to me. And they never looked me in the eye. Vulnerable.

These brief stories in the sermon attempt to help the congregation get an empathetic feel for the situation of the widow.

The law of levirate marriage was designed to protect some of the most vulnerable in the community. It provided a home, a place, security, and identity. It gave a practical expression to God's will for all in the community to have fullness of life. God loves each and every member of the covenant community and God wills for each and every one to have the maximum opportunity for life.

We see the seriousness of this concern in the last part of the text. If the surviving brother-in-law refuses to marry the widow, she can go to the gate and present her case to the elders. In the world of the Bible, the gate is the place where the elders, the leaders, of the community meet in order to hear complaints about injustice. The gate is kin to our courtroom and the elders function much like our legal system.

The widow explains her situation to the elders. She has no son. Her brother-in-law has refused to perform his responsibility. The elders summon him and remind him of his role. If he persists in refusing, the widow is to go to him, pull off his sandal, spit in his face, and say, "This is what is done to the man who does not build up his brother's house." Why does she take off his sandal? Because in Israel, the sandal was a symbol of responsibility. In particular, it was a symbol of accepting responsibility for the land. It was the custom in those days to ratify a land transaction by walking around the land (Deut. 1:36). So, when the widow removes the sandal of the brother-in-law, the act is a public declaration that he is irresponsible. The act is especially humiliating both because it took place in public and because it was performed by a woman. A woman—normally weak and vulnerable—is the agent of justice.

This grievance procedure is important in its own right. But it is important for a larger reason, too. It gives permission to protest abuse. Not only that, but it suggests that the community is to provide mechanisms whereby abuse can be named and resolved.

But, why would a man refuse to perform the levirate responsibility? Here we need to be cautious. I have two sisters-in-law. They are both intelligent, strong, beautiful, and delightful. I love them. But marry them? Really, I can't imagine it. I do not love them in the same way that one loves a spouse. However, the people of Deuteronomy's day did not marry for romantic love. Marriage was more of an arranged affair. To be sure, husbands and wives could be tender and loving, but the ancient man would not likely be reluctant to marry a woman because he did not find her romantically attractive.

So why would a brother-in-law refuse? If he married the widow, and if they had a son, then the child would legally be the offspring of the dead brother. The child would then inherit the brother's estate and property. If there were no son, then, the surviving brother might inherit the property of the dead brother. Why not marry the widow?

Selfishness. Looking out for numero uno. Our era has no monopoly on greed.

Our text, then, has a double provision. It provides for the childless widow. And it also provides for the greedy brother-in-law. If he fulfills his responsibility, he is saved from the interior rot that comes with greed and from the exterior humiliation that comes when his irresponsibility is the headline on the evening news.

But what of today? If God does not want me to marry my sisters-in-law, what is the future of levirate marriage?

The sermon now moves to the deeper values of the text for today's community.

Many today are in situations similar to that of the widow: vulnerable, facing an uncertain future, in a crisis of identity. As a matter of fact, some of you widows are very much like the widows of antiquity. Alone, on fixed incomes, overlooked by your former friends whose spouses are still living, and wondering where you will go when your bodies fail. And younger women, too. Girls molested by fathers and brothers. Women in the workplace earning twenty-five percent less than men for doing the same job. Sexual harassment is often a part of their job expectation. Women abused by husbands and boyfriends. Women raped, then left with intense shame and silence. Vulnerability is an equal opportunity employer. Some of you men are caught similarly. A young man in high school holds his bladder all day long so he will not have to go into the restroom where the gangs lie in wait. A man works thirty years on an assembly line. He does everything the company asks him to do. He is fifty-seven years old. Then one day, management decides to automate and downsize. Now, he's standing in the unemployment line.

The text is specifically about justice for women. The preacher tries to preserve this emphasis by citing analogies primarily from the experience of women. However, the passage speaks in behalf of all who are vulnerable. Hence, the sermon allows specific points of contact for men.

If you are such a person, this text has a word. God is for you. God wants you to have a life of peace and security, just as God wanted peace and security for the widows of Israel. And God intends for this world to have practical help for you.

In ancient Israel, levirate marriage was one way God's will for love and justice came to practical expression. Today, I believe, God's concern is expressed whenever we assume appropriate responsibilities with one another. Just as levirate marriage enacted God's love in the days of Deuteronomy, we mediate divine love through acts of caring in our daily relationships and in the ways we order our communities. And, in the process, we are released from preoccupation with greed and self-centeredness.

Elizabeth, about eighty years old, was diagnosed with terminal cancer. Her husband, a physically exhausted man, took her home bedfast and helpless. A volunteer woman named Lynn came to provide respite care.

Elizabeth's house was rundown. During one visit a rat ran out from under a heater. Elizabeth was incontinent and the results were evident in soiled laundry stacked around the house and even on the carpet. Elizabeth was unresponsive much of the time.

But, week after week, Lynn came. She washed Elizabeth and did her nails. She brought pictures and music. She talked with Elizabeth about the older woman's fears. Lynn baked and found other people to cycle into the caring network.

At the end, Elizabeth had to go to a nursing home. While she was there, her husband fell and knocked himself unconscious. He laid at home for three days, before he was found and hospitalized. In the peculiar way that such things sometimes happen, no one told Elizabeth why he stopped coming to see her. She thought he had died. During those three days, Elizabeth went into a profound depression. She gave up. She felt that she would die utterly alone.

When Lynn heard what had happened, she abandoned her plans and went to the husband (in the hospital) and Elizabeth (in the nursing home). Lynn told Elizabeth that her husband was too weak to talk on the phone. But he was alive. Elizabeth was not alone.

That night Elizabeth died in peace.

Elizabeth's pastor said later, "During the funeral preparations, the extended family and [the husband] mentioned to me several times, how present and wonderful Lynn continued to be to them in this time of grief. Everywhere I went, she [Lynn] had been, offering comfort and help and most importantly, a truly loving friendship."[2]

In one way, that is a long way from Deuteronomy 25 and levirate marriage. But in another way, it isn't far at all.

> The concluding illustration shows how the deeper values of the text can be embodied. In this case, the person who performs the levirate-like act is not a spouse but a friend. In terms of dynamic analogy, Elizabeth is in a situation like that of the widow in our text. Lynn is analogous to the brother-in-law. We hope this encourages the congregation to reflect on levirate-like possibilities across the span of life relationships.

Sermon Three
"Is This All There Is?"
Ronald Allen
Ecclesiastes 1:1-3, 12-24; 2:18-23; 6:10-12

In this sermon, the preacher deeply appreciates aspects of Ecclesiastes but seeks to challenge other aspects and to offer an alternative theological interpretation of matters central to the text. The sermon attempts to establish sympathetic identification between the text and the congregation. The sermon then moves to challenge the text.

"Is this all there is to life?" That is the question of the woman sitting behind her desk. She had grown up in physical and psychological abuse. She married too soon to a man who was emotionally distant except for unpredictable, violent outbursts. The divorce was bitter.

After the divorce, years ago, the job she had as a waitress did not pay much. She and the children had lived in a cramped apartment while she struggled in school. They were always on top of each other—fighting, yelling, constant threats, and tension. Even though she was present, she often felt absent as she sat at the formica-top kitchen table trying to study.

A better job meant more space, but the emotional scars were deep. And she had to bring home work at night. Forms to fill out. One after another. All alike.

Today, she was sitting at her desk when she got the call from her supervisor. "Come to my office, please." The workforce is being reduced. The last to come are the first to go.

She goes back to her desk. She thinks of her life. She sees that pile of forms. "Is this all there is to life?"

We do not all experience the same degree of futility. But I imagine that sooner or later, most of us feel like our lives, or some parts of them, are pointless. If so, you are not alone. Other people in this sanctuary raise such questions. I ask these questions. So does Ecclesiastes: "What do mortals get from all the toil and strain with which they toil under the sun?" (2:22).

The beginning of the sermon attempts to establish identification between the listeners and sermon as a prelude to the point of view of Ecclesiastes that is being emphasized in the sermon.

Ecclesiastes' answer to that question is negative, pessimistic, even cynical. "Vanity of vanities! All is vanity" (1:2). The Hebrew word that we translate vanity *(hebel)* is often rendered "vapor." Life is like a vapor. Here one minute and gone the next. And what is left? Like steam from the spout of the teakettle. Gone.

The writer of Ecclesiastes has searched for wisdom, for the knowledge of God, and the meaning of life. The sage has looked at life in all its phases: birth, work, the accumulation of possessions, fame, the good, the bad, the ugly, and even death. "I saw all the deeds that are done under the sun; and see, all is vanity and chasing after wind" (1:14).

Ecclesiastes concludes that even some of the sacred teachings of Israel are a vapor. According to one strain of the tradition, the good should prosper and the evil suffer. But Ecclesiastes notices that the reverse is sometimes true (8:14). In that culture, old age was supposed to be the time of supreme value. But Ecclesiastes regards old age as the "days of trouble." Indeed, " . . . the pitcher is broken at the fountain, and the wheel broken at the cistern, and the dust returns to the earth as it was . . . " (12:6-7). Old age: a broken pitcher. Ecclesiastes admonishes, "Remember your creator in the days of your youth" (12:1) because when you get old, you won't be able to. You might not want to. Is that all there is?

Life is a vapor. The writer of Ecclesiastes cannot understand *why* this is so. The sage cannot unravel the meaning of existence. It is hidden (7:23-8:9).

And even if we could know the purpose of it all, what difference would it make? "Whatever has come to be has already been named . . ." (6:10). God has predetermined all that shall be. You remember that poem that seems so lovely, "For everything there is a season, . . . a time to be born, and a time to die . . . " (3:1-2). Well, sad to say, that poem is a statement of determinism. God has already decided when you will be born and when you will die and everything that happens in between. And the double tragedy is that you cannot work around God's decision because you don't know what it is. So what's the point?

The preacher voices questions and problems that continue to plague human consciousness. The preacher hopes that the listeners hear their own perplexities in the text and in the sermon. These are not rhetorical questions, but questions that cut to the bone of human meaning. In the material that follows, the sermon lifts up aspects of the text that are genuinely and directly helpful to today's congregation. The fact that a biblical writer would openly raise such questions and doubts can help the congregation have the courage to do the same.

Yes, sometimes I wonder why Ecclesiastes is in the Bible. But I also know people who feel about life much the way the writer of Ecclesiastes does. Some of these people are in this sanctuary right now. To them, this ancient sage is a soul friend. Because Ecclesiastes is in the Bible, they—and we—can realize that we have no question that is too hard to voice. We need not hide our feelings of frustration and futility from God or from our congregation. The book of Ecclesiastes, after all, is in the Bible where everyone can read it. The pages are not glued together and there is no warning from the theological surgeon general that says it may be hazardous to your religious health. We can talk as straight to God and to one another as the Bible itself—without fear of censorship or recrimination.

But is Ecclesiastes right? Is life just a meaningless vapor? I am convinced that the ultimate answer is no. To be sure, along the way, Ecclesiastes offers some very valuable perspectives on God and life. But in the end, our ancient soul friend has missed a crucial point.

The preacher clearly indicates his or her perspective on the text. It is both good news and bad. In the next paragraphs, the preacher continues with sympathetic identification by naming qualities of the text that are appropriate for today's community.

At one level, Ecclesiastes is right to say that our knowledge of God is limited. However, God does not do things to confuse us. But we are finite. We have limits on how much of God and life we can take in. God is fuller, greater, and more overflowing than we can grasp. Even if life were completely transparent, we could not understand it completely because our internal software is just not big enough to process it all.

At another level, Ecclesiastes is right to say that life does not always unfold according to some of our traditional religious teachings. Some texts (not all) in the Bible promise that the faithful will prosper and the wicked will suffer. But, at least in material terms, we know it does not always work out that way. The tornado does not stop at every house to check on the faithfulness or unfaithfulness of the inhabitants before determining the degree of damage to inflict. Even in the realm of moral behavior, we all know the cheat who made it big and the honest, frugal person who is always on the page next to chapter 11. Life cannot be reduced to neat slogans.

At still another level, Ecclesiastes helps us name the ambiguities of our existence for what they are: ambiguities whose meaning is not always clear. For instance, in marriage or friendship, can you always draw a clean line between supporting and suffocating? When faced with an important decision, is it always crystal clear which choice is of God and which is not? Can one always think in such polar terms? Should a person choose one good vocation, or another? Should a sixteen year old (or a thirty-two year old) abort or not?

Ecclesiastes helps us name the ambiguities of life. Sometimes we simply have to make the best choices we can in the light of the best data that we have at the moment. We make our choices and live with the ambiguities, but always aware that God is bigger than our choices. And our choices do not completely limit what God can do.

Now, the preacher is ready to challenge the text. It is important to be respectful of the text but to let points of disagreement come to clarity.

But there are also points at which Ecclesiastes is not so helpful. In fact, there are points at which Ecclesiastes is misleading and even pernicious.

According to this sage, our experiences are determined in advanced by God. "Whatever has come to be has already been named . . ." (6:10). Today, we hear this viewpoint at funerals. My uncle died not long ago. Many people comforted the family with words like these. "Well, it was his time to go."

But, if God has life mapped out, what is the point of human freedom? We would simply be automatons going through the motions. All your struggles—a cruel charade. The outcome would already be known to everyone in heaven but you. The nights you laid awake wondering whether you were making the best decisions for your teenage daughter or son. The knot in the pit of your stomach as you prepared to confront your boss. The agony of trying to help your parents figure out whether or not this is the time to leave their lifelong home and move into the nursing home. If the outcome is already known, what is the point? What about our joys and achievements? Pleasant enough, but we cannot take too much satisfaction in them. After all, our lives were just printing the program already set on the divine disk.

Fortunately, Ecclesiastes' view of God is not the only one in the Jewish and Christian houses. Others of Ecclesiastes' day—including some of the other sages—saw God differently. According to the Proverbs, for instance, God has left clues in the world that reveal divine intentions to us. "Wisdom cries out in the street; in the squares she raises her voice" (Prov. 1:20). When we pay close attention to life, we can discern wisdom. I think it is fair to say that most of the biblical writers saw God as omnipresent and omniactive, but not as the writer of a completely predetermined script. God wants good for all, but circumstances sometimes conspire to prevent the good that God can give. A hymn cries out to God, "Pure, unbounded love thou art."[3] In different circumstances, love may take different faces, but it is still love.

The preacher tries to make it clear that his objection to the text is not idiosyncratic. He is part of a community of interpreters in the Hebrew

Scriptures themselves who do not find the views of Ecclesiastes to be adequate. Likely, many listeners will find their own responses to the book of Ecclesiastes supported by this community.

Based on this way of thinking, and on my own experience of life, I believe that God is always present and always participating with us in life. God is always with us as we make our life decisions, but God does not make them for us.

When we make good choices, God rejoices and tries to help us intensify the good. And when we make bad choices, God works with us to minimize the damage and to make the best of them. Life is a kind of partnership with God. Even though God is a very Senior Partner, God does not, cannot, make our choices for us. But God is always with us, trying to help us realize the maximum good in every situation. Sometimes, that maximum is nothing more than the knowledge of God's presence, but that can mean a lot.

A person is being eaten alive by cancer. God did not send the disease. Unilaterally, God may not be able to end the disease in the blink of an eye. But God wants the dying person and the family to be aware of the divine presence and love. If the patient blames God, God does not stop willing good for that patient. But the victim's choice restricts his or her availability to the divine presence. If the victim acknowledges God's presence and love, it is easier for God to manifest that love to the patient. The patient is more likely to name it and embrace it. The knowledge of God's presence may not end the disease or the pain, but it is a comfort.

Ecclesiastes despairs because life is a vapor that vanishes in meaninglessness. Our experiences do not matter because everyone dies.

The basic purpose of preaching is to show how good news from God renews the listening community. The last part of the sermon tries to be explicit about the good news of the theological point of view that is proposed as an alternative to Ecclesiastes.

I respond in three ways. First, what we do makes a difference to ourselves. It makes a difference to my perception of the depth and quality of my life to know that I am trying to be aligned with God and with God's purposes for the world.

I enter the study, and discover that one of our children has been playing on the computer and has erased a chapter from a book that I am writing. It makes a difference to my own self-perception as to whether I explode like a grenade or whether I try to approach the incident from the standpoint of a six year old who needs guidance into proper behavior in the study.

Second, our lives make a difference to other people and to the world. How I respond to the child who erased my chapter makes a difference to that child. Yes, someday I will die. But the good—and the bad—in my relationship with our child will live through that child and through others who are touched as that child becomes an adult, and perhaps, has children.

Third, our lives make a difference to God. God is ever present. God feels our every feeling. God registers our every thought. God is with us in every action. This means that everything we do has a direct effect upon God. Therefore, everything we do has meaning to God.

Sometimes God laughs with us. Sometimes God weeps with us. But at all times, God is with us and God is for us.

You occasionally hear someone talk about "meaningless suffering." By this, they usually mean that the suffering does nothing to help either the person suffering or anyone else. Children caught in war. A person in the prime of life maimed by an accident. A homeless person freezing to death in a downtown park. True, such suffering may not benefit those who are caught in its vice. It may even be cruel. But it is not meaningless, because all suffering means something to God. It may not be good. It may be tragic. But it is significant because God feels it and takes it into the divine life where it is cradled in God's heart forever.

"Is this all there is to life?" That's what the woman asks as she sits in her windowless office wondering what will happen next. How I wish she could know that is not what God wants for her. How I wish she could know that God is with her, aching with her emptiness. How I wish she could know in that very moment, and in every moment in the future, God is doing everything that God can do to help her.

Such knowledge would not spontaneously remake her past or repair her relationship with her children or get her a new and better job. But it might help her. It might not get her a bright new world. But it would be a lot better for her than pessimism, cynicism, and despair.

"Is this all there is to life?" No, it is not. With God, there is always more.

Sermon Four
"To Be a Pilgrim"
John Holbert
Acts 7

Deal w/ @ bottom pg. 141
issue

This sermon illustrates preaching on a text from the Second Testament that draws on texts from the First Testament. In order to understand Acts 7, one must understand the passages from the older testament that Stephen cites.

However, Acts 7 has a decidedly anti-Jewish polemic. Stephen claims that the Jewish people (at least the ones stoning him) are a stiff-necked people who have failed to understand their own tradition and have killed its best exemplification, Christ. As we have noted earlier, recent scholarship is inclined to understand this polemic in the framework of the prophets. Stephen speaks prophetically, like an Amos or a Jeremiah; Stephen critiques other Jewish people on the basis of their own tradition. However, this perspective does not change the fact that Stephen was a Christian Jew critiquing non-Christian Jewish people. Later generations of Christians have tended to read the text as a Christian repudiation of Judaism.

The two authors of this book have slightly different points of view on how to handle this. The preacher, John Holbert, is sensitive to the problem. But he believes that he can then ask the congregation to identify with the Jewish people in the text so that the congregation comes to understand its own stiff-neckedness and its own need to become a pilgrim people. Today's congregation becomes analogous to the Jewish people who stoned Stephen. Ronald Allen, on the other hand, believes that this use of the text subtly leaves an anti-Jewish image in the mind of the listener. He would prefer for the sermon to be more explicitly critical of the anti-Jewish themes of the text. He would say that if the preacher is called to help the congregation identify its stiff-neckedness, that call is better articulated on its own and without making an analogy with Jewish people in a text.

We include this sermon, and we make a public note of these two different points of view, in order to encourage the reader to think about and discuss these differences. Which side of the discussion do you find more persuasive? Or do you have a fresher alternative?

Nothing makes me madder than someone who thinks they know my subject better than I do. I have spent long years studying and thinking and praying about things biblical, and when some newcomer comes along who claims to know it better—well, I would rather fight than listen! I am especially uncomfortable when this person is a new convert, "on fire" with zeal and relentless energy. Secretly, I might envy the zeal, but publicly I am ready for debate. Do you feel that way about things you hold dear?

That is how those Jewish people must have felt when Stephen stood before them and claimed to know what their own texts said far better than they did. I can't blame them, can you? Put yourself in the position of a faithful Jew and listen to the speech of Stephen.

At the beginning of a sermon on a Second Testament text that heavily uses the First Testament, it is important to set the boundaries of the discussion. We want to help the congregation begin to understand the position of the Jewish people as they listen to Stephen's speech, a speech designed to explain to them their own tradition in a way quite foreign to their understanding. As we noted in chapter 6, we must be especially careful with these sorts of texts that appear to diminish Jewish texts, people, practices, or institutions. In the case of this text, it has quite obviously arisen in a time when the early church was in the process of distinguishing itself sharply from its Jewish heritage. In such a process it is inevitable that the newer tradition may, in its urgent desire to separate itself, caricature its predecessor. This is both understandable and regrettable. Still, it must be shown that such a response in and of itself is not normative for today's church. Also, it is possible that beneath the apparent diminution of Judaism lies a deeper intention in the speech of Stephen. One of the sermon's goals is to demonstrate how this is so.

"Brothers and sisters, God called Abraham, our ancestor, to leave the familiarity of his Mesopotamian home and said to him to go to a land that God would show him. He first moved to the northern town of Haran, and then, after the death of his father, he moved to this very land."

The Jewish people would surely have welcomed this opening. It recalled the famous verses of Genesis 12, those lines that underlay God's choice of Israel and God's gift of the land. Stephen placed himself among them as a descendant of this same Abraham.

Stephen goes on to emphasize an arresting point about this land that God has given. God "did not give him any of it as a heritage, not even a foot's length." No instead, God promised it as a heritage to him and his descendants. Stephen here wants his hearers to remember that the land itself is not the significant part of God's transaction with Abraham. What should be uppermost in the mind of those who remember the story is the promise of God to Abraham's descendants. Do not rely on the physical land as the surety of God's promise, says Stephen. Rely on the promise itself, which may take ever new forms in the future of God.

As we move through the speech, the preacher indicates what we think is the central claim of the deeper intention of the speech: as God called Israel to be a pilgrim people from its very beginning, so God still calls all who would respond to God to be pilgrims in the world. Thus, though Stephen is separating Christianity from Judaism on the surface of the speech, he is at the same time emphasizing one of the central claims about our response to God enshrined in both traditions. The contemporary church needs to hear and embrace the latter claim.

Stephen then turns his history lesson to the family of Jacob and Joseph. After a very brief summary of the long story, which covers some fourteen chapters of Genesis, he concludes with the unusual emphasis concerning the final burial place of the ancestral family. Jacob died in Egypt, he says, but "their bodies were brought back to Shechem and laid in the tomb that Abraham had bought for a sum of silver from the sons of Hamor in Shechem." Though this is certainly a recognized part of the Jewish tradition, the fact is that at the time of this speech, Shechem lay in Samaritan territory. Stephen's Jewish hearers would not have welcomed the reminder that one of their most ancient sacred sites now was in the hated place of the Samaritans. Such a statement would surely drive the audience to a fight.

But the deeper concern is this: God is not limited by national boundaries but calls us all to look beyond them as we see that the whole world is the provenance of God.

The history according to Stephen moves on. He sees in the life of Moses, the liberator of Israel, a statement of God's use of the outsider, the rejected one, to effect the divine will. Moses was "abandoned" as an infant, adopted by the hated Egyptians, rejected for doing the good deed of saving an Israelite from abuse, and driven into a foreign land for fear of his life. But the greatest surprise in the story, says Stephen, is that "this Moses whom they rejected" God had sent as "ruler and liberator." But even after he freed them from slavery in Egypt, "our ancestors were unwilling to obey him; instead, they pushed him aside, and in their hearts they turned back to Egypt."

You may have noticed something extraordinary in this speech, something notable by its absence. Stephen does not mention Jesus a single time! Though it seems quite clear that Stephen is creating a portrait of Moses that is in many specific ways parallel to the life of Jesus, he does not draw the parallel explicitly. Why not? It may just be a rhetorical nicety, a clever device to draw the hearers in, to allow them to draw the right conclusions on their own.

But there is more. Once again, the speech urges us to look beyond the unexpected, to see in the outcast and rejected the hand of God. Moses, says Stephen, is a pilgrim who moved outside the norms of his day to effect the liberation of Israel. In what ways must the contemporary church and its members move outside of the expected norms in order to witness the work of God and to participate in it?

The preacher continues to emphasize the theme of pilgrimage while showing something of the surface meaning of the speech. He is trying hard to balance the sharp Jewish rejection of the speech with the deeper intention of the call of God to become pilgrims.

Stephen now accuses the ancestors of Israel, and by implication his contemporary hearers, with idolatry. He begins with the obvious reference to the golden calf in Exodus but moves quickly to quote both Jeremiah and Amos who accused their hearers of idol worship as well. With this part of the history, he announces that the worshiping practices of his hearers are just as idolatrous.

In a rising crescendo of accusations, Stephen concludes with a shocking assault. "You stiff-necked people (just like the long-ago Egyptians), uncircumcised in heart and ears, you are forever opposing the Holy Spirit, just as your ancestors used to do. Which of the prophets did your ancestors not persecute?" "You are the ones that received the law as ordained by angels, and yet you have not kept it." And with that, they grabbed Stephen, took him outside the city and stoned him to death. He died as Jesus died, with forgiveness of his murderers on his lips.

Was Stephen only talking to the Jewish people of his own time? Or are we listening in on the conversation, not as bystanders, but as active participants? Just who were these Jewish people who were listening to Stephen? They were the faithful religious ones of their day, striving to work out in their own lives the will of God who had chosen them and called them to be "a light to the nations." They knew their history; they studied it regularly and as faithfully as they knew how.

And who are we who are listening to Stephen? We are the faithful religious ones of our day, striving to work out in our lives the will of the God who has chosen us. We know our history, more or less; and we study it occasionally. But what do we hear in it?

Has the history of God become a divine seal of approval for ways of living that we have decided for ourselves? Is God really only a United Methodist? "Come forth to be my pilgrim people," says God.

Has this history become a way to affirm the way we worship, the way we sing, the way we pray? Does "real" worship of God have to conform to my way of doing it? "Come forth to be my pilgrim people," says God.

Has our history become a way to separate ourselves from other Christians, from other religions, from the nonreligious? Do we read the history to say that we are better? Have we become little more than a shrinking clique, casting stones at all those who exist outside our version of the true faith? "Come forth to be my pilgrim people," says God.

This history has a terrible way of hardening, of solidifying in our memories until it becomes little more than a pale reflection of its true, challenging self. You see, even those who would be like Stephen need to hear God say, "Come forth to be my pilgrim people." Those persons who are convinced enough about something to give their very lives for it can be the most dangerous, uncaring, and unlistening people of all. Leave your comfortable and absolute assurances, your easy certainties, and your pleasant platitudes. Come forth to be my pilgrim people!

We think it is crucial at the end of a sermon like this to be as clear as we can about the precise point of our reading as it peers through the surface layer of the text. There can be no denying that the speech of Stephen is an early church polemic against the Judaism of its time, and that Stephen, as the church's first martyr, is portrayed as a great hero of the emerging faith. Our sermon tries to see underneath those obvious polemics, polemics that are based on a denial of God's universal love and that we judge not to be normative for the contemporary church. We attempt to discover the deeper intention of the text, which proves to be crucial for today's church.

These sorts of texts are extremely difficult to handle in fully appropriate ways. Acts 7 and many texts like it from the Second Testament are a painful part of our Christian tradition and need to be addressed by the preacher with awareness of the complex issues involved.

Sermon Five
"The Fire that Separates and Supports"
Ronald Allen
Jeremiah 23:23-29; Luke 12:9-56

This sermon is based on two texts from Proper 15, Year C, the Revised Common Lectionary. While the two texts are brought together in the lectionary, Luke's Gospel does not directly cite or allude to the text from Jeremiah. However, Jeremiah 23:23-29 illumines our understanding of Luke 12:49-56. This sermon illustrates how the First Testament can often enrich our understanding of the Second even when the two are not directly related. In the language of chapter 6, these passages are in a parallel relationship; aspects of the reading from Jeremiah are similar to those in the reading from Luke.

I find Jesus' words disturbing. "I came to bring fire to the earth. . . . Do you think that I have come to bring peace to the earth? No, I tell you, but rather division!" This will divide households. Father against son, son against father, mother against daughter, daughter against mother, and in-laws against in-laws.

This does not sound like the Jesus of the old favorite hymn, " . . . and the joys we share as we tarry there, none other has ever known."[4] This does not sound like the Jesus who said, "Blessed are the peacemakers." In today's passage, Jesus' sentiments seem far removed from the emphasis on mutuality and community that are so much a part of theology in our day.

As a parent of five children, I am not sure that I want our children to know that these verses are even in the Bible. And in a day when family life in North America is under such great stress, I am hard-pressed to imagine how Jesus' words can be good news for families.

What Christian sense can we make of these sayings? Does the Jesus of Luke really want to divide the human family even more than we are already divided? Does Jesus want to make our personal worlds into little Bosnias?

The text from Luke sounds remarkably strange in our middle-class North American ethos. The opening of the sermon acknowledges this strangeness and tries to help the listeners articulate some of the feelings and questions that arise when many of them hear this passage.

We get help from the context of the passage in the Gospel of Luke. At the beginning of chapter 12, a crowd has gathered around Jesus. He sets up his portable flip chart and pulls out his felt-tipped pen and teaches. The subject is the full coming of the rule of God.

On the one hand, Jesus assures them that God's good pleasure is to give them the divine rule in its fullness. For Luke, this rule is a great time of community when all relationships are the way God wants them to be. Jew with Gentile in common service to the one God. Poverty ended; abundance for all. The blessings of the Holy Spirit omnipresent. The ideal social order is in place with more than liberty and justice for all. They do not earn it. It is a gift from God. And Jesus demonstrates it in his ministry.

On the other hand, the coming of this new day creates a crisis. People have to decide: do I join with God's renewal of the world or do I turn against it?

The preacher has tried to sketch dimensions of the Lukan worldview that are essential to understanding the passage. This congregation needs to understand that this worldview contains promise (the coming of the reign of God) and crisis (saying yes can bring about difficulty).

Jesus is saying to those who say yes to God's invitation that they will encounter obstacles in their relationships with those who say no. When you say yes to God, inevitably you say no to some familiar patterns of thinking and behavior. And some people will not understand your change. They may turn against you. Even the people closest to you—such as your father and your mother, your daughter or your son, or your closest friends.

This sometimes happens when an alcoholic sobers up or when a drug user goes for treatment. The old drinking buddies get huffy. A reformed drug user once said that when she returned to speak with her former companions, they spit on her.

In a junior high school, the in-group liked to make jokes at the expense of students of other races and social groups. One member of the in-group had a troubled conscience about this. "I knew it wasn't right, so one day I said so." She had to find a new circle of friends.

These simple, everyday incidents are designed to help the congregation feel the separation that sometimes results from saying yes to God's reign manifest through Jesus.

Evidently, this happened in the early church. Some families split apart when one member identified with the renewal taking place through Jesus. Can you imagine how painful this would be? To feel rejected by your own flesh and blood?

Luke tries to help his community understand this phenomenon by putting this saying into the Gospel. Jesus predicts what will later happen in the church. This helps give the early church the confidence to accept the divisiveness that accompanies their saying yes to God.

If we were talking about this reality today, we might put it differently. We might not have Jesus say, "I came to bring division." We might say, "Jesus did not come in order to separate you from the people nearest you. However, you need to understand that if you say yes to God, that will sometimes result in a painful separation between you and your family and friends."

The preacher has just drawn on the hermeneutic of reading the text in both its surface and deeper dimensions. In the section that follows, the preacher connects the deeper dimensions of the text to the ministry of Jeremiah. A hermeneutic of solidarity enables the congregation to understand that Jesus and the church are in continuity with the paradigm of Jeremiah and Israel.

Jeremiah helps us remember that such separations were not new with Jesus or the church. In Jeremiah's day, many people had turned away from God. They had abandoned the covenant and they had abandoned God's teaching. The wealthy were exploiting the poor. The people were worshiping false Gods. False prophets had arisen in the land. But through Jeremiah, God says, " . . . let the one who has my word speak my word faithfully. . . . Is not my word like fire . . . and like a hammer that breaks a rock in pieces?"

Frequently in the First Testament, fire accompanies the separation of those who say yes to God from those who say no. God's Word is that kind of fire: it creates a crisis in which you say yes or no. This is the sense in which Jesus uses the same image. "I came to bring fire to the earth."

Jesus is not a pyromaniac. But God's fire inevitably brings us to a decision. Do we say yes or do we say no? And sometimes a community splits apart like a rock that cracks under a hammer.

God does not want that. God never wants acrimony between people. But sometimes divisions result when one says yes to God. In the process, you say no to some other values and behaviors. The people who are committed to those values sometimes react to you with hostility.

That happened to Jeremiah. He preached the word faithfully. But he became the target of an assassination plot (Jer. 11:18–12:6). They put him in stocks (20:1-6) and brought him to trial (26:7–19). They falsely accused him of deserting his people. They detained him (37:11-15). During the Exile, Jeremiah suffered because of saying yes to witness to God (37:1–44:30).

So, Jesus is not saying something new. He is talking in terms as old as the Hebrew Bible. He is not trying to drive people apart. He is trying to help them understand what might happen when they say yes to God.

The sermon now turns to a positive consideration of how to respond when the fire of the gospel results in difficult separations in life. The sermon tries to show how biblical ideas and images are of direct help.

But how do you respond when someone you love turns you off or even turns against you? Many of us instinctively respond in kind. If we get turned off, we turn the other person off. If someone gets angry at us, we become angry with them. And sometimes we react the most strongly to people who are the closest to us. Perhaps we feel the pain of their disappointment more deeply than we feel the pain of those whom we hardly know.

During the Vietnam protests, one of my friends at seminary who was very active in the protest movement received a bitter letter from her father who had fought in the front lines in the Second World War. The father wrote at length about his intense disappointment in his daughter's values and behavior. How could she turn against the nation for which he had risked his life? How could she undermine the young people who were risking their lives in Vietnam? She said that when she first read the letter, she felt a deep sense of rejection. She was hurt and she wanted to hurt him in return. And she intended to use the high moral ground of the correctness of her cause as the basis of her response. "Righteous anger" we called it in those days.

But she remembered Jeremiah. "We call him the weeping prophet because he wept with anguish over the situation of his people. I do not believe he spoke in anger. I believe he spoke in tears." And she was taking a course in the interpretation of the Gospels where she encountered Jesus' words, "But I say to you that listen, Love your enemies, do good to those who hate you, bless those who curse you, pray for those who abuse you" (Luke 6:27-28).

So she wrote her father a long and sensitive letter. She tried to describe her own feelings. She tried to describe how she imagined he must be feeling. She explained that she was trying to be true to the best of her convictions just as she understood that he was being true to the best of his. She did not want the differences between them to turn into a whirlpool of mutual anger and recrimination. More painful exchanges followed, but they continued to communicate. And eventually, she said, they achieved a new plane of honesty and mutual respect. "Even though he cannot support my efforts, we understand each other in a way that we did not before."

Unfortunately, there is no guarantee that doing good to those who harass you will resolve the tension in a relationship. Sometimes bad feelings continue for years. But I know that I feel better about myself and about other people when I know that I have done all that I can to act in behalf of keeping the relationship together. I cannot be responsible for how other people respond. But I can be responsible for blessing those who curse me. This may not create a new social world. But it can help my small part of the world from degenerating into a continuous personal Bosnia.

But what keeps you going? In the midst of the risks and hassles, what gives you the strength to keep going? Remember that on the day of Pentecost God sent the Holy Spirit to fill the church. God is omnipresent. And do you recall the symbol of the coming of the Spirit? Yes. Fire. Tongues of fire rested over each believer. Fire, the symbol of that which separates, is also the symbol of that which supports.

If you are like me, the painful experiences of life often seem much more potent, much more lasting, than the positive experiences. Pain seems deep and long lasting. Joy, so often, seems ephemeral, easily punctured. Sometimes I need assurance that the good news is as real as the bad. I do not know that Luke means to use the symbol of fire in this way. But the fact that the same symbol is used for separation and support helps me feel that the reality of God's presence is at least as great as the frustration and pain that comes with separation.

Oh, there's a risk in saying yes to God. But the risk can be worth it. A few months ago, I went with a group of colleagues and trustees on a study trip to India. We visited a rural health care center started by two Christian physicians. That part of India has practically no medical care in the villages. One of the purposes of this center is to train local people in basic health care. A village selects one of their residents to be trained to provide basic health care in the village.

We rode on a bus to a very remote village. They introduced us to the local health care worker, a wiry short older woman with a wrinkled face. She looked like hundreds of other poor women we had seen that day. As you know, the caste system in India is still strong, especially in remote areas. This woman is an untouchable. The name says it all.

Her village nominated her to receive the training to become their health care provider. But can you imagine the risk? Would her own family think that she had violated her place in society and turn away? What if she took the training but the upper castes would not allow her to work with them? Would she become completely isolated?

But the day we visited, she knelt on the ground, and she opened the medical kit and piece by piece showed us its contents. Through a translator, she explained how she used each piece. She handled each piece of equipment and each medicine as if it were precious. Then she stood and spoke with fire in her eyes. The translator told us that before she took the training, almost half the infants in that village died before the age of two. But not one, not one, has died since she came back from the training ten years ago. I wish that such fire could be kindled in all of God's people.

As we were leaving, the translator explained that before she took the training, in her language, her name was Katara, which means "garbage." But now she is called Lakshmi, which means "health, wealth, good fortune." She took the risk. It led to a new life.

In all the risks that you take for God, remember this: the God of fire is with you. That support bears you up in all separation.

The sermon ends quickly. Preachers sometimes tend to overwork the end of a story or the end of a sermon. If a story is well told, and if the preacher trusts the story and the listeners, then the preacher can give the congregation delicate directions in which to think about the story but trust them to fill out the story and connect it to their own experience. This, not so incidentally, is a model for storytelling that is frequent in the Hebrew Scriptures.

ANNOTATED BIBLIOGRAPHY

This bibliography lists (and slightly annotates) representative works which pursue issues on the subject of Christian preaching from the First Testament, on the relationship between the testaments and on the relationship between Judaism and Christianity. The bibliography is representative and not exhaustive. Further materials may be found in the standard bibliographical resources (especially *Old Testament Abstracts, New Testament Abstracts* and *Homiletic*). Several journals regularly carry articles on preaching from the First Testament, for example, *Interpretation, Journal for Preachers.*

Achtemeier, Elizabeth. *Preaching from the Old Testament.* Louisville: Westminster/John Knox Press, 1989. Primarily using form and rhetorical criticism, devotes chapters to narrative, law, prophets, psalms, and wisdom. See also her earlier book *The Old Testament and the Proclamation of the Gospel.* Philadelphia: The Westminster Press, 1973.

Allen, Ronald J. *Contemporary Biblical Interpretation for Preaching.* Valley Forge: Judson Press, 1984. Survey of historical-critical methods with focus on their use in preaching.

Anderson, Bernhard, editor. *The Old Testament and Christian Faith.* New York: Harper and Brothers, 1963. Thirteen essays by leading midcentury scholars, e.g., Bultmann, Cullmann, Wright.

Barr, James. *Old and New in Interpretation.* London: SCM Press, 1966. Seminal focus on history, revelation, relationship of two testaments, typology, and allegory. These themes permeate Barr's extensive corpus.

Barrois, Georges. *The Face of Christ in the Old Testament.* Crestwood, N.Y.: St. Vladimir's Seminary Press, 1974. Orthodox view of Old Testament and its relationship to Christian faith.

Barton, John. *Reading the Old Testament.* Philadelphia: The Westminster Press, 1984. Readable introduction to methods of interpretation.

Bright, John. *The Authority of the Old Testament.* Grand Rapids: Baker Book House, 1975 (originally published 1967). Discusses authority of First Testament; considerable attention to preaching. Classic.

Brueggemann, Walter. *Finally Comes the Poet.* Minneapolis: Fortress Press, 1989 and *The Prophetic Imagination.* Philadelphia: Fortress Press, 1978. Highly influential works characterized by imaginative biblical readings done in the service of contemporary witness.

Boadt, Lawrence, Helga Croner, and Leon Klenecki, editors. *Biblical Studies: Meeting Ground of Jews and Christians.* New York: Paulist Press, 1980. Essays comparing and contrasting Jewish and Christian approaches to interpretation of Scripture.

Brooks, Roger and John Collins, editors. *Hebrew Bible or Old Testament?* Notre Dame: University of Notre Dame Press, 1990. Methodological and theological explorations.

Carson, D. A. and H. G. M. Williamson, editors. *It Is Written.* Cambridge: Cambridge University Press, 1988. Essays on scripture citing scripture in First and Second Testaments and Second Temple texts.

Charlesworth, James and Walter Weaver, editors. *The Old and the New Testaments.* Valley Forge: Trinity Press International, 1993. Relationship of so-called intertestamental literature to the Bible.

Childs, Brevard. *Biblical Theology of the Old and New Testaments.* Minneapolis: Fortress Press, 1992. Latest in succession of provocative treatments of issues pertinent to this book.

Dodd, C. H. *According to the Scriptures.* New York: Charles Scribner's Sons, 1953. Argues that the Second Testament uses First in service of defending the faith of the church. A focal work for a generation.

Dunn, James D. G. *The Partings of the Ways.* London: SCM Press and Philadelphia: Trinity Press International, 1991. Sees monotheism, election, covenant, and temple as dividing Christianity and Judaism.

Ellis, E. Earle. *The Old Testament in Early Christianity.* Tübingin: J. C. B. Mohr Verlag, 1991. Survey of basic questions with bibliography.

Evans, Craig and Donald Hagner, editors. *Anti-Semitism and Early Christianity.* Minneapolis: Fortress Press, 1993. Considers polemics between Christians and Jews within framework of prophetic critique.

Fackre, Gabriel. "Perspectives on the Place of Israel in the Christian Faith," *Andover Newton Review,* vol. 1, no. 1 (1990), pp. 7-17. Identifies thirteen perspectives.

Fasching, Darrell, editor. *The Jewish People in Christian Preaching.* Lewiston: Edwin Mellen Press, 1984. Counsels respect for Judaism in Christian sermons.

Goldingay, John. *Approaches to Old Testament Interpretation: Updated Edition.* Downers Grove: Inter-Varsity Press, 1990. Surveys modes of appropriating the First Testament by the church; idem., *Theological Diversity and the Authority of the Old Testament.* Grand Rapids: Wm. B. Eerdmans Publishing Co., 1987. Wrestles with how to deal with different (and difficult) perspectives in First Testament.

Gowan, Donald. *Reclaiming the Old Testament for the Christian Pulpit.* Atlanta: John Knox Press, 1980. Using form criticism and tradition criticism, focuses on historical texts, sagas, short stories, law, wisdom, and prophets.

Greidanus, Sidney, *The Modern Preacher and the Ancient Text.* Grand Rapids: Wm. B. Eerdmans Publishing Co., 1988. Literary criticism illumines preaching Hebrew narratives and prophecy.

Hayes, John and Carl Holladay. *Biblical Exegesis: A Beginner's Handbook.* Atlanta: John Knox Press, 1982. Primer in exegetical method.

Hayes, Richard. *Echoes of Scripture in the Letters of Paul.* New Haven: Yale University Press, 1989. Creative examination of First Testament's "echoes" in Paul.

Holbert, John C. *Preaching Old Testament.* Nashville: Abingdon Press, 1991. Employs literary criticism as key to preaching on narrative texts. Deals with plot, character, and point of view. Includes sermons.

ANNOTATED BIBLIOGRAPHY

Janzen, Waldemar. *Old Testament Ethics: A Paradigmatic Approach.* Westminster/John Knox Press, 1994. Views Old Testament ethics in terms of paradigms: familial, priestly, wisdom, royal, and prophet. Interprets Jesus as paradigm.

Johnson, Dan G. *Neglected Treasures: Rediscovering the Old Testament.* Wilmore, Ky.: Bristol House, 1989. Brief, positive studies of nine books of First Testament.

Kaiser, Walter. *The Old Testament in Contemporary Preaching.* Grand Rapids: Baker Book House, 1973. Magesterial evangelical treatment.

Klenecki, Leon, editor. *Toward a Theological Encounter: Jewish Understandings of Christianity.* New York: Paulist Press, 1991. Jewish theologians express their understandings of Christianity.

Levenson, Jon D. *The Hebrew Bible, the Old Testament and Historical Criticism.* Louisville: Westminster/John Knox Press, 1993. Major Jewish consideration of issues; highlights differences.

Lindars, Barnabas. *New Testament Apologetic.* Philadelphia: The Westminster Press, 1961. Classic exposition of Dodd's approach.

Lohfink, Norbert. *Great Themes from the Old Testament.* Edinburgh: T & T Clark, 1982. Fascinating development of fifteen themes from First Testament such as pluralism, divine sovereignty, and power in community.

Lowry, Eugene. *Living with the Lectionary.* Nashville: Abingdon Press, 1992. Critical appraisal of Revised Common Lectionary.

McCurley, Foster. *Proclaiming the Promise.* Philadelphia: Fortress Press, 1974. Lutheran. Centers on motif of promise. Includes sermons. McCurley and John Reumann trace the presence of Gospel and Law in both testaments in *The Witness of the Word.* Philadelphia: Fortress Press, 1986.

McKenzie, Steven L. and Stephen R. Haynes, editors. *To Each Its Own Meaning.* Louisville: Westminster/John Knox Press, 1993. Contributors outline and critique methods of biblical interpretation.

Olsen, Dennis. "Preaching the Forgotten Texts of the Old Testament," *Journal for Preachers,* vol. 13, no. 4 (1990), pp. 2-10. Practical advice on preaching overlooked texts.

Rad, Gerhard von. *Biblical Interpretations in Preaching.* Nashville: Abingdon Press, 1977. Sermons by a leading midcentury scholar.

Rothschild, F. A., editor. *Jewish Perspectives on Christianity.* New York: Crossroad Publishing Co., 1990. Studies of how significant Jewish thinkers, e.g., Buber, Baeck, Rosenzweig, have perceived Christianity.

Sanders, James A. *From Sacred Story to Sacred Text.* Philadelphia: Fortress Press, 1987. Develops idea of scripture as paradigm. Many others of Sanders' writings explore similar concerns.

Segal, Alan. *Rebecca's Children.* Cambridge: Harvard University Press, 1986. Views early Christianity and Judaism as quarreling over who is the rightful interpreter of traditions of Israel.

Seitz, Christopher, editor. *Reading and Preaching the Book of Isaiah.* Philadelphia: Fortress Press, 1988. Authors explore community, themes, preaching from Isaiah. Good case study.

Smith, J. Alfred, Sr. *New Treasures from Old.* Elgin: Progressive Baptist National Convention Publishing House, 1987. Reviews scholarship on Hebrew Bible and offers practical advice on preaching.

ANNOTATED BIBLIOGRAPHY

Stuart, Douglas, "Preaching from Old Testament Poetry" in *Newell Lectureships,* edited by Timothy Dwyer. Anderson: Warner Press, 1992. vol. I, pp. 133-206. Introduction to biblical poetry with attention to preaching on psalms and wisdom; idem., *Old Testament Exegesis.* Second Edition. Philadelphia: The Westminster Press, 1982. Thorough introduction to exegetical method.

Stuempfle, Herman. *Preaching Law and Gospel.* Philadelphia: Fortress Press, 1978. Sees Law and Gospel in both parts of Bible.

Trible, Phyllis. *Texts of Terror.* Philadelphia: Fortress Press, 1978. Investigates several texts that raise serious theological questions.

Van Buren, Paul. *A Christian Theology of the People Israel.* New York: The Seabury Press, 3 vols. A Christian approach to Hebrew Bible and Judaism based on principle of solidarity.

Westermann, Claus, editor. *Essays on Old Testament Hermeneutics.* translated by James Luther Mays. Atlanta: John Knox Press, 1963. Fifteen significant essays from midcentury interpreters. Classic.

Williamson, Clark M. *A Guest in the House of Israel.* Louisville: Westminster/John Knox Press, 1993. Christianity's understanding of itself and Judaism from postholocaust perspective; idem., editor, *A Mutual Witness.* St. Louis: Chalice Press, 1992. Essays explore commonalities in the witnesses of Jewish and Christian communities; idem., *Has God Rejected His People?* Nashville: Abingdon Press, 1981.

Wilson, Marvin. *Our Father Abraham.* Grand Rapids: Wm. B. Eerdmans Publishing Co., 1989. Identifies Jewish roots of Christian faith.

Wolff, Hans Walter. *Old Testament and Christian Preaching.* Translated by Margaret Kohl. Philadelphia: Fortress Press, 1986. Sermons by major German scholars of the Hebrew Scriptures.

NOTES

PREFACE

1. Lee Martin McDonald, *The Formation of the Christian Biblical Canon* (Nashville: Abingdon Press, 1988), pp. 180-81.

2. Frances Young, *Virtuoso Theology* (Cleveland: The Pilgrim Press, 1990), p. 76.

3. Donald Juel, "New Testament Reading of the Old: Norm or Nuisance?" *Dialog* 31 (1992), p. 198, argues that Christian interpreters should give greater weight to the LXX [the Septuagint] than to the Hebrew text as the normative version of the First Testament for use in the contemporary church since the LXX was more widely in use in the early church than the Hebrew and Aramaic text. We disagree. But the point is well taken that Christian scholars of the Second Testament do not always pay sufficient attention to the LXX as a part of the matrix of interpretation of the Second Testament.

4. On naming the parts of the Bible see, for example, James A. Sanders, "First Testament and Second," *Biblical Theology Bulletin* 17 (1987), pp. 47-49; Andre Lacocque, "The 'Old Testament' in the Protestant Tradition," in *Biblical Studies: Meeting Ground of Jews and Christians,* ed. Lawrence Boadt, Helga Croner, and Leon Klenicki (Mahwah: Paulist Press, 1980), p. 121; Roland Murphy, "Old Testament, Tanakh and Christian Interpretation," in *Hebrew Bible or Old Testament?* ed. Roger Brooks and John Collins (Notre Dame: University of Notre Dame Press, 1990), pp. 12-13; Lawrence Boadt, *Reading the Old Testament* (New York: Paulist Press, 1984), pp. 19-20; Juel, "New Testament Reading of the Old," p. 183.

5. These are Wisdom of Solomon (sometimes known as Ben Sira or Sirach), Ecclesiasticus, Baruch, Tobit, Judith, Prayer of Manasseh, I and II Macabees, I Esdras, three short additions to Daniel and one to Esther. The Letter of Jeremiah is sometimes listed by itself (and not as part of Baruch) and II Esdras is included in the Latin Vulgate.

1. The Old Testament in the Christian Pulpit

1. Through empirical study of sermons actually preached in local congregations, Joseph E. Faulkener, discovered that in the Christian Church (Disciples of Christ): "Old Testament references are offered as the textual base in 24 percent of the sermons. Of the thirty-nine books in the Old Testament, fifteen are cited at least once, but 52 percent of all the Old Testament citations are from three books: Isaiah, Jeremiah, and the Psalms. An additional 28 percent are from Genesis, Exodus, 1 and 2 Samuel, and 1 Kings." Joseph E. Faulkener, "What Are They Saying? A Content Analysis of 206 Sermons Preached in the Christian Church (Disciples of Christ) during 1988," in *A Case Study of Mainstream Protestantism,* ed. D. Newell Williams (St. Louis: Chalice Press, and Grand Rapids: Wm. B. Eerdmans Publishing Co., 1991), p. 427. We suspect that the percentages are about the same in other Christian denominations.

We further suspect that the use of the Common Lectionary and the Revised Common Lectionary account for the heavy concentration of sermons based only on a handful of Old Testament books. In any event, these statistics illustrate the relative silence of the First Testament in the Christian pulpit and the selected voices from the First Testament that are heard.

2. For overviews of how the relationships between the testaments have been interpreted in Christian history, see James Barr, *Old and New in Interpretation* (London: SCM Press, 1966); John Bright, *The Authority of the Old Testament* (London: SCM Press, 1967); Hans Van Campenhausen, *The Formation of the Christian Bible* (London: Adam and Charles Black, 1972); A. H. J. Gunneweg, *Understanding the Old Testament,* trans. John Bowden (Philadelphia: The Westminster Press, 1978); D. L. Baker, *Two Testaments, One Bible* (Downers Grove: Intervarsity Press, 1977); Brevard Childs, *Biblical Theology of the Old and New Testaments* (Minneapolis: Fortress Press, 1992).

3. We hear virtually all of these approaches, including the distorted ones, in sermons given in our classes and in sermons that we read and hear (and watch) in the media. Many of the objectionable approaches are so deeply embedded in popular Christian piety that we hear them even in the sermons of preachers who embrace the historical-critical and literary-critical methods of interpreting the Bible and who are theologically sophisticated. We hasten to add that distortion is not the norm. But the continued appearance of distortions points to the depth of the problem to which this book is addressed.

4. For discussions of theologians who devalue the First Testament, see Gunneweg, pp. 142-49; Baker, pp. 84-85; Henning Graff Reventlow, *Problems of Old Testament Theology in the Twentieth Century,* trans. John Bowden (Philadelphia: Fortress Press, 1985), pp. 28-43; Joseph Blenkinsopp, "Tanakh and the New Testament: A Christian Perspective," in *Biblical Studies: Meeting Ground of Jews and Christians,* ed. Lawrence Boadt, Helga Croner, and Leon Klenicki (New York: Paulist Press, 1980), pp. 96-109. Although not a real Marcionite, Rudolf Bultmann, one of the most influential biblical scholars of this century, voiced a viewpoint similar to Marcion's. See his "Significance of the Old Testament for the Christian Faith" in *The Old Testament and Christian Faith,* ed. Bernhard W. Anderson (New York: Harper and Brothers, 1963), pp. 8-35, esp. p. 31. In the same volume, Carl Michaelson points to differences between Bultmann and Marcion by arguing that Bultmann did not reject the Hebrew Bible but regarded it as providing nonrevelatory preunderstanding that paved the way for the gospel. See his "Bultmann Against Marcion," pp. 49-63, and see Baker, p. 187.

5. On law and gospel, see Childs, pp. 532-65.

6. For a review of this position, see Baker, pp. 163, 179-81, 402-3.

7. For further discussion of what we will call the deuteronomic paradigm, see chapter 2.

8. J. C. Rylaarsdam, "Exodus," in *The Interpreter's Bible,* ed. George A. Buttrick et al. (Nashville: Abingdon Press, 1954), vol. 1, p. 980, cited in Jacob M. Myers, *Grace and Torah* (Philadelphia: Fortress Press, 1975), p. 16.

9. With unusual clarity, the Reformers saw the appearance of both law and gospel in both testaments. On the development of Luther's understanding of law and gospel, see James S. Preus, *From Shadow to Promise* (Cambridge: Harvard University Press, 1969), pp. 200ff. For a mature contemporary Lutheran view that emphasizes the

dialectic of law and gospel in each testament, see Richard Lischer, *A Theology of Preaching* (Nashville: Abingdon Press, 1981), pp. 46-65 and on Lutheran preaching of these themes see Herman G. Stuempfle, Jr., *Preaching Law and Gospel* (Philadelphia: Fortress Press, 1978). Calvin's views on the law are similar to those of Luther but Calvin more systematically calls attention to the value of the law as a guide for Christian living in the discussion of his third use of the law. See John Calvin, *The Institutes of the Christian Religion*, trans. Ford L. Battles, ed. John T. McNeill (Philadelphia: The Westminster Press, 1950), vol. I, pp. 371-72.

10. For extensive bibliography, see Craig Evans and Donald Hagner, editors, *Anti-Semitism and the New Testament* (Minneapolis: Fortress Press, 1993).

11. For a review of the wide-ranging scholarly discussion on Paul and the Law, see the enumeration of scholars in Brice L. Martin, *Christ and the Law in Paul* (Leiden: E. J. Brill, 1989).

12. The degree and circumstances of this situation are debated by the scholarly community. For a history of scholarly discussion, see James D. G. Dunn, *The Partings of the Ways* (London: SCM Press, and Philadelphia: Trinity Press International, 1991), pp. 1-8. For discussions of specific texts, see Evans and Hagner, as well as George M. Smiga, *Pain and Polemic: Anti-Judaism in the Gospels* (New York: Paulist Press, 1992), and Norman A. Beck, *Mature Christianity in the Twenty-First Century: A Recognition and Repudiation of the Anti-Jewish Polemic in the New Testament,* revised and expanded edition (New York: Crossroad Publishing Co., 1994).

13. This way of approaching the relationship of the two testaments and their religions is similar to that which is sometimes discussed under the rubrics of letter (Old Testament) and spirit (New Testament) (see Gunneweg, pp. 13-14, 22, 146), or earthly (Old Testament) and spiritual (New Testament) (see Baker, pp. 127-32). Childs addresses related concerns under the heading of ethics in the Hebrew Bible (pp. 673-84).

14. On this discussion, see Gunneweg, pp. 166-72.

15. An exceptionally clear expression of this point is Leslie Newbigin, *The Gospel in a Pluralistic Society* (Grand Rapids: Wm. B. Eerdmans Publishing Co., and Geneva: World Council of Churches, 1989), pp. 80-88.

16. On allegorical interpretation of the First Testament, see Baker, pp. 45-48, 112-14, 223, 262-63, and Childs, pp. 13-14.

17. See Frances Young, *Virtuoso Theology* (Cleveland: Pilgrim Press, 1990), pp. 76-78, 84-85, 93-94, 97, 101-3, 120-22, 136-37, esp. 150-154. Stanley Hauerwas, *Unleashing the Scriptures: Freeing the Bible from Captivity in America* (Nashville: Abingdon Press, 1993), argues that allegorical interpretation of the Bible is necessary in order for Christians to account for "the multiple senses of Scripture." "This kind of appeal to allegory is useful as long as one remembers that allegory is not about an individual discerning deeper spiritual meaning—as if the text had such meaning in itself—but rather allegory is the attempt at the renarration of the text for the good ends of the community" (p. 40). We reply that Hauerwas' approach denies the integrity of the text. Furthermore, Hauerwas opens the door for the interpreting community to read the text in the light of nothing more than its own presuppositions and prejudices. Far from "unleashing the Scriptures," Hauerwas's proposal could make the Bible even more docile than it already is. The fastest way to tame the Bible in the church is to hear in the Bible nothing more than confirmation of a community's

preexisting prejudices. This, of course, is not what Hauerwas intends. But we believe Hauerwas's proposal could be taken as authorizing such reductionism. In any event, there should be no necessary conflict between interpreting the Bible critically and interpreting it in and for the community of faith. In the church, critical biblical scholarship is intended to help the community hear the text in its own voice. To be sure, contemporary hermeneuts have argued that texts are multivalent and that interpreters are always biased (at least to a degree) concerning what they hear in texts. Hermeneutics in the last thirty years have made it abundantly clear that it is all but impossible to recover "the" meaning of a passage; all interpretation is biased (a fact that is both positive and negative). However, when these problems are recognized, they seem less potentially dangerous to us than opening the window to allegorical interpretation, even when motivated by "the good ends of a community." A community's self-perception of its "good ends" may be insidious. For our judgment on legitimate allegorial interpretation, see note 20.

18. Three widely influential expressions of typology are Gerhard von Rad, "Typological Interpretation of the Old Testament," trans. John Bright, *Interpretation* 15 (1963), pp. 174-91 (which also appears in *Essays on Old Testament Hermeneutics,* ed.ited by Claus Westermann [Richmond: John Knox Press, 1963], pp. 17-39); Jean Danielou, *From Shadow to Reality* (Westminster, Md.: The Newman Press, 1960), and Leonhard Goppelt, *Typos,* trans. Donald H. Madvig (Grand Rapids: Wm. B. Eerdmans Publishing Co., 1982). For updated discussions see Baker, pp. 239-70; Gunneweg, pp. 209-13; Childs, pp. 13-14; Northrup Frye, *The Great Code* (New York: Harcourt, Brace, Jovanovich Publishers, 1982), pp. 78-138; Brevard Childs, *Biblical Theology of the Old and New Testaments* (Minneapolis: Fortress Press, 1992), pp. 13-14; and John E. Alsup, "Typology," *The Anchor Bible Dictionary,* ed. David Noel Freedman et al. (New York: Doubleday, 1992), pp. 682-85.

19. Barr, *Old and New,* pp. 103-17.

20. As a general principle, we contend that a biblical text may be interpreted allegorically when the text itself (or the document within which the text is found or the assumptions in the community that gave birth to the text) gives a clue that it is to be taken allegorically and orients the reader to the key with which to interpret the allegorical symbols. Ezekiel 17, for instance, contains an allegory (17:1-10) and an interpretation (17:11-21). On distinctions between typology and allegory, see Baker, p. 259.

21. For discussion of this perspective, see Baker, passim.

22. For representative scholarly discussions of this motif, see Walter Zimmerli, "Promise and Fulfillment," trans. James Wharton, *Interpretation* 15 (1963), pp. 310-38 (which also appears in *Essays on Old Testament Hermeneutics,* pp. 89-122); Gurden C. Oxtoby, *Prediction and Fulfillment in the Bible* (Philadelphia: The Westminster Press, 1966); F. F. Bruce, *This Is That: The New Testament Development of Some Old Testament Themes* (Exeter: The Paternoster Press, 1968); idem., *The Time Is Fulfilled* (Grand Rapids: Wm. B. Eerdmans Publishing Co., 1978); Eugene J. Fisher, "Catholic Liturgy: From Theory to Praxis," in *The Jewish Roots of Christian Liturgy,* edited by Eugene J. Fisher (Mahwah: Paulist Press, 1990), pp. 172-174; Gunneweg, pp. 179-89; Bright, pp. 136-40, 192-96, 198-205; Baker, pp. 166, 216, 258 (for distinction between typology and prophecy), 292-94, 344-45, 373-74; Childs, pp. 167-80, 453-56, 476-83, and passim.

23. In chapter 6 we present a way whereby preachers can both honor the historical and literary contexts of Old Testament prophecies of the future and make sense of the Christian writings that use these prophecies to interpret the significance of Christ.

24. For a review of major ways in which the relationships between the two testaments have been understood, see Baker as well as Gerhard Hasel, *Old Testament Theology: Basic Issues in the Current Debate*, 4th ed. (Grand Rapids: Wm. B. Eerdmans Publishing Co., 1991), pp. 172-93. For review of scholarship and a creative theological statement, see Childs, esp. 11-52, 717-27.

25. Readers who cannot affirm this premise may have difficulty with aspects of our book.

26. Clark M. Williamson, *A Guest in the House of Israel* (Louisville: Westminster/John Knox Press, 1993), p. 135.

27. Ibid., pp. 135-36. See similarly Paul Van Buren, *Discerning the Way* (New York: The Seabury Press, 1980), pp. 139ff. Christian theologians envision different schemes of the relationship between the Jewish people and Christians and their sacred writings. For a review see John Pawlikowsky, *Christ in the Light of the Christian-Jewish Dialogue* (New York: Paulist Press, 1982).

28. Schubert Ogden, *The Point of Christology* (New York: Harper & Row Publishers, 1982), pp. 58-59, passim.

29. For examples of Jewish interpretation of the Bible today, see e.g., *The Tora: A Modern Commentary,* ed. W. Gunther Plaut (New York: Union of American Hebrew Congregations, 1981) and *The JPS Torah Commentary,* ed. Nahum M. Sarna (Philadelphia: The Jewish Publication Society: 1989ff). Some scholars think that biblical studies could be an arena in which Jewish people and Christians could meet on common ground, e.g., Lawrence Boadt, Helga Croner and Leon Klenicki, editors, *Biblical Studies* (New York: Paulist Press, 1980). For critical discussion, see Jon Levenson, "Theological Consensus or Historicist Evasion? Jews and Christians in Biblical Studies" in *Hebrew Bible or Old Testament?* ed. Roger Brooks and John Collins (Notre Dame: University of Notre Dame Press, 1990), pp. 109-46 and his *The Hebrew Bible, The Old Testament and Historical Criticism* (Louisville: Westminster/John Knox Press, 1993).

30. Walter Harrelson and Randall M. Falk, *Jews and Christians* (Nashville: Abingdon Press, 1990), p. 69. Emphasis in Harrelson and Falk.

31. Elizabeth Achtemeier, *Preaching from the Old Testament* (Louisville: Westminster/John Knox Press, 1989), p. 56.

32. Without trying to be exhaustive, and recognizing that several of these authors would likely demur from complete endorsement of our viewpoint we list the following as generally representative of this fourth wave: John L. McKenzie, *A Theology of the Old Testament* (New York: Doubleday, 1974); Donald Gowan, *Reclaiming the Old Testament for the Christian Pulpit* (Atlanta: John Knox Press, 1980); Ronald Hals, *Grace and Faith in the Old Testament* (Minneapolis: Augsburg Publishing House, 1980); Terence Fretheim, "The Old Testament in Christian Proclamation," *Word and World* 3 (1983), pp. 223-30; Hemchand Gossai, "The Old Testament: A Christian Heresy Continued?" *Word and World* 8 (1988), pp. 150-57; idem., "The Old Testament Among Christian Theologians," *Bible Review* (1990), pp. 22-26; Rolf Rentdorf, "Toward a Common Jewish-Christian Reading of the Bible" in *Hebrew Bible or Old Testament?* pp. 89-107; Murray Haar, "A Proposal for Christian Use of

the Old Testament: A Hermeneutic of Listening," *Dialog* 31 (1992), pp. 165-70. There are tendencies sympathetic to this stream (but also reservations) in Childs, *Biblical Theology of the Old and New Testaments,* esp. pp. 70-81, 719-27 (who regards the New Testament as fulfilling the Old and the Old as necessary to interpret the New; see p. 722). Elizabeth Achtemeier agrees that the Hebrew Bible can be fully instructive for the church, but she argues that it is best preached in concert with the Second Testament. For example, see her *Preaching from the Old Testament,* pp. 56-58 and her earlier *The Old Testament and the Proclamation of the Gospel* (Philadelphia: The Westminster Press, 1973).

2. The Old Testament as a Paradigm of God's Presence, Purpose, and Power

1. Thomas S. Kuhn, *The Structure of Scientific Revolutions* Second Edition (Chicago: University of Chicago Press, 1970), p. 23.

2. James A. Sanders, *From Sacred Story to Sacred Text* (Philadelphia: Fortress Press, 1987), p. 5.

3. Kuhn, *The Structure of Scientific Revolutions,* p. 23. In a later work, *The Essential Tension* (Chicago: The University of Chicago Press, 1977, pp. 292-319), Kuhn subdivided the category of paradigm into the categories of disciplinary matrix, model, and exemplar. Thomas S. Kuhn, *The Essential Tension* (Chicago: The University of Chicago Press, 1977), pp. 292-319. While we recognize the usefulness of Kuhn's more nuanced language, we retain the single term paradigm because it is already in use among theologians and because it serves our purposes well enough.

4. For example, Van Harvey, *The Historian and the Believer* (New York: Macmillan, 1966), pp. 253-58; Sallie McFague, *Metaphorical Theology* (Philadelphia: Fortress Press, 1982), pp. 103-44, idem. *Models of God* (Philadelphia: Fortress Press, 1987), pp. 29-58. Elisabeth Schüssler-Fiorenza, *Bread Not Stone* (Boston: Beacon Press, 1984), pp. 10-15, makes a distinction between the Bible as archetype and prototype.

5. James Barr, *The Bible in the Modern World* (New York: Harper & Row Publishers, 1973), p. 115. Barr's statement requires some subtle reframing. "The" model was expressed with different nuances in Israel as indicated by the fact we can identify four different trajectories within it.

6. Ibid., pp. 30-34.

7. Sanders, *From Sacred Story to Sacred Text,* p. 5. See also pp. 71-72. Paul D. Hanson, *The People Called* (San Francisco: Harper & Row Publishers, 1986), pp. 527-35, also speaks of the paradigmatic events and of paradigms in the Old Testament. Cf. idem., *The Diversity of Scripture: A Theological Interpretation.* Overtures to Biblical Theology (Philadelphia: Fortress Press, 1982), pp. 12, 66, 78, 115, 125. Waldemar Janzen discusses the following paradigms in his *Old Testament Ethics: A Paradigmatic Approach* (Louisville: Westminster/John Knox, 1994): familial, priestly, wisdom, royal, and Jesus. Walter Brueggemann takes a similar approach toward the Torah of the priest, the counsel of the sage; and the word of the prophet in his *The Creative Word* (Philadelphia: Fortress Press, 1982).

8. Sanders, *From Sacred Story to Sacred Text,* p. 41.

9. Ibid., p. 6.

10. Our description of this paradigm is not a hard conceptual "center" of the theology of the Old Testament in the way that Old Testament scholars sometimes speak of this quest. Our "overarching paradigm" is a general way of understanding God and the world that underlies the different trajectories of the First Testament. On the attempt to find a "center" for the First Testament and the problems related to that attempt, see John Goldingay, *Theological Diversity and the Authority of the Old Testament* (Grand Rapids: Wm. B. Eerdmans Publishing Co., 1987), pp. 1-30, 167-99, and Gerhard Hasel, *Old Testament Theology: Basic Issues in the Current Debate,* 4th ed. (Wm. B. Eerdmans Publishing Co., 1991), pp. 131-79; George W. Coats, "Theology of the Hebrew Bible," in *The Hebrew Bible and Its Modern Interpreters,* ed. Douglas A. Knight and Gene M. Tucker (Philadelphia: Fortress Press and Chico: Scholars Press, 1985), pp. 239-62. Our "overarching paradigm" is conceptually similar to Paul Hanson's "trajectory" (*The Diversity of Scripture,* p. 115, and *The People Called,* p. 9). It is also similar to Walter Harrelson's "core tradition." For example, see his "Life, Faith and the Emergence of Tradition," in *Tradition and Theology in the Old Testament,* ed. Douglas A. Knight (Fortress Press, 1977), pp. 11-30. Harrelson locates his core tradition in the historical emergence of Israel, while we derive our overarching paradigm from more general theological emphases in the canonical form of the First Testament. For Harrelson's summary of themes central to the Hebrew Bible, see his "The Hebrew Bible and Modern Culture," in *The Hebrew Bible and Its Modern Interpreters,* pp. 496-98.

11. The notion of trajectory is adapted from James M. Robinson and Helmut Koester, *Trajectories Through Early Christianity* (Philadelphia: Fortress Press, 1971). The materials that constitute each paradigm are not static but develop as the trajectory encounters fresh circumstances. Speaking differently, Paul Hanson uses the notion of trajectory in connection with the overarching purposes of God in the First Testament. Together, the individual paradigms plot a trajectory (*The People Called,* p. 9; *The Diversity of Scripture,* p. 115).

12. Each of the four trajectories functions paradigmatically. Scholars sometimes divide the First Testament into other categories for purposes of analysis. For example, some authors focus on literary genre (such as narrative and poetry) as an organizing principle for discussion, while others focus on the subject matter (such as law and prophecy) or on categories of books (such as Pentateuch, history, wisdom). We select our four paradigms because, as theological streams of consciousness, they represent relatively distinct theological worldviews that span various types of literature and subject matter. Narrative, for instance is found in all four trajectories. An important interpretive question is, What is the theological use to which a particular narrative is put in its paradigm? These trajectories received their present form relatively late in the life of biblical Israel. The reconstruction of the development of Israel's life and thought has been the mainstay of Old Testament scholarship since the Enlightenment. In recent years, two disciplines have focused on this task in fresh ways: tradition history and canonical criticism. For an introduction to tradition history, see the essays in Knight, *Tradition and Theology in Israel.* For an introduction to canonical criticism, see James A. Sanders, *Torah and Canon* (Philadelphia: Fortress Press, 1972), and Brevard S. Childs, *Introduction to the Old Testament as Scripture* (Fortress Press, 1979).

13. As we note below, the prophetic texts are among the most frequent ones that combine emphases from different trajectories and that go beyond the trajectories.

14. James Sanders repeatedly develops the theme of dynamic analogy. For example, see his "Hermeneutics" in *The Interpreter's Dictionary of the Bible* (Supplementary Volume), ed. by Keith Crim (Nashville: Abingdon Press, 1976), p. 406; *God Has a Story Too* (Philadelphia: Fortress Press, 1979), pp. 20-22; *Canon and Community,* Guides to Biblical Scholarship Series (Philadelphia: Fortress, 1984), p. 71. See also Neill Q. Hamilton, *Jesus for a No-God World* (Philadelphia: The Westminster Press, 1969), pp. 176ff.

15. Where does the preacher find such a principle? As will become evident in chapter 3, we turn to a historic Protestant principle that the gospel itself is the criterion by which to evaluate the content of the scripture. In this context, the term gospel refers not to the literary genres of Matthew, Mark, Luke, and John but to the good news that is at the heart of the content of the Christian faith. For an especially clear and succinct statement of this principle, see Richard R. Osmer, *A Teachable Spirit* (Louisville: Westminster/John Knox Press, 1990), pp. 90-98, 175-81.

16. Gerhard von Rad, *Genesis* (London: SCM Press, 1961), pp. 73-99; see also the essays in *A Walk in the Garden,* ed. by Paul Morris and Deborah Sawyer (Sheffield: JSOT Press, 1992); Martin Luther, *Luther's Commentary on Genesis* (Grand Rapids: Zondervan Press, 1957), pp. 63-88; Nahum Sarna, *Understanding Genesis* (New York: Schocken Books, 1966), pp. 23-27; Howard Wallace, *The Eden Narrative* (Atlanta: Scholar's Press, 1975).

17. Karl Barth, *Church Dogmatics,* trans. by G. T. Thompson and Harold Knight (New York: Charles Scribner's Sons, 1950), vol. 1, pt. 2, pp. 1-2.

18. Janzen identifies these as key paradigms for understanding Old Testament ethics: the familial paradigm as the locus for interpreting law, the priestly and wisdom paradigms, the royal and prophetic paradigms. He also regards Jesus as a paradigm.

19. This first great paradigm of the Deuteronomist finds a clear analogy in the Second Testament where it is also claimed that we respond in love to the love first offered to us from God in Jesus Christ.

20. Of course, the Deuteronomic paradigm cannot be applied in a wooden way to every evil and natural disaster. Today, for instance, a tornado, cannot be interpreted automatically as God's specific judgment upon a community. But aspects of the ecological crisis, as well as many evils in the human community, result from disobedience.

21. The contemporary preacher is likely to be troubled by the apparent contrast between the affirmations of God's love for Israel and the fact that Israel's enemies are often cut down like grass under a lawn mower with a newly sharpened blade. The preacher may also be troubled by aspects of divine judgment on the people of Israel. We consider these and other difficult cases in chapter 5.

22. Janzen, pp. 106-7.

23. For a recent and reliable summary of the many attempts, see Katharine J. Dell, *The Book of Job as Skeptical Literature* (Berlin: Walter de Gruyter, 1991), pp. 57-107.

24. Arguments have been made for wisdom influence for example in Genesis 1-11; 37-50; 2 Samuel 9-20; Esther; and various of the prophets, for example Amos, Habakkuk, Isaiah, Jeremiah, and Hosea. James L. Crenshaw's extremely broad definition of wisdom allows for such suggested influence. See his article, "Wisdom," in *Old Testament Form Criticism,* ed. by John H. Hayes (San Antonio: Trinity University Press, 1974), pp. 255-64.

25. Especially see Gerhard von Rad, *Wisdom in Israel* (Nashville: Abingdon Press, 1972).

26. See especially Robert Davidson, *The Courage to Doubt* (London: SCM Press, 1983) for a fine summary of this in the First Testament.

27. The translation of *hebel* is debated. Some would render it vapor, irony, futility, vain, or transcience.

28. An excellent summary of the vast literature on the subject of the meaning of Job may be found in Dell, *The Book of Job*, pp. 5-56.

29. Eduard Dhorme, *A Commentary on the Book of Job* (London: Thomas Nelson Publishers, 1968), pp. cxii-cli and 584-564; Robert Gordis, *The Book of God and Man* (Chicago: The University of Chicago Press, 1965), pp. 118-35; Leo G. Perdue, *Wisdom in Revolt* (Sheffield: Almond Press, 1991), pp. 196-240; N. H. Tur-Sinai, *The Book of Job* (Jerusalem: Kiryath-Sepher, 1958), pp. 521-88.

30. A useful guide for preaching on the proverbs is Thomas G. Long, *Preaching and the Literary Forms of the Bible* (Philadelphia: Fortress Press, 1989), pp. 53-65.

31. On the development of apocalypticism in the Old Testament, the standard work is still Paul D. Hanson, *The Dawn of Apocalyptic,* rev. ed. (Philadelphia: Fortress Press, 1979).

32. For an introduction to this literature, see John J. Collins, *The Apocalyptic Imagination* (New York: Crossroad Publishing Co., 1984).

33. Ernst Käsemann overstated the case with his emphasis that apocalyptic literature is the mother of Christian theology, but apocalyptic literature is certainly one the most formative elements in much of the literature of the Second Testament. See Käsemann's *New Testament Questions of Today* (London: SCM Press, 1969), esp. pp. 72-108 and 107-38. For a more current assessment of the place of apocalyptic literature in early Christian life and thought, see the bibliography in Adela Yarbro Collins, "Apocalypses and Apocalypticism: Early Christian," *The Anchor Bible Dictionary,* ed. by David Noel Freedman, et al. (New York: Doubleday, 1992), vol. 1, pp. 288-92.

34. Some scholars regard this image as referring to the resurrection of the nation of Israel. For possibilities and ambiguities in interpretation, see John E. Goldingay, *Daniel.* Word Biblical Commentary (Waco: Word Books, 1989), pp. 306-8 and W. Sibley Towner, *Daniel. Interpretation: A Bible Commentary for Teaching and Preaching* (Atlanta: John Knox Press, 1984), pp. 181-82.

35. The most forceful statement of this approach is still Walter Brueggemann, *The Prophetic Imagination* (Philadelphia: Fortress Press, 1978). Janzen discusses the relationship of these offices with sensitivity on pp. 140-76.

36. The deuteronomic paradigm seems to lament the fact of the monarchy (I Sam. 8) but still provides guidance for the proper functioning of the monarchy (e.g., Deut. 17:14-20). The king is much more positively valued in the priestly paradigm as will be seen in our study of Psalm 110 in chapter 3.

37. 2 Chronicles 15:3, for instance, laments that the community was without a teaching priest.

38. On the surface, God's actions sometimes appear to contemporary people to be unloving. But on the deeper level, most of the actions that appear problematic to contemporary people were understood by ancients to testify to God's love, power, and faithfulness. The destruction of the nations, for instance, often witnesses to God's love

for Israel. Even the judgment and disciplining of Israel was ultimately understood to be for Israel's good. However, such actions are not themselves demonstrations of love for all. An even deeper insight is that God ultimately wills to bless *all* people (e.g., Gen. 12:1-3) and that even the nations will be gathered into God's presence (e.g., Isa. 45:14-24). The Hebrew Bible itself thus contains the clue that enlarges its own witness to divine love as being for all.

39. For creative reconstructions (with reviews of scholarship), see John P. Meier, *A Marginal Jew: Rethinking the Historical Jesus* (New York: Doubleday, 1991); E. P. Sanders, *Jesus and Judaism* (Philadelphia: Fortress Press, 1985); and Paula Fredrickson, *From Jesus to Christ* (New Haven: Yale University Press, 1988). For a strong positive christological statement, see Clark M. Williamson, *A Guest in the House of Israel* (Louisville: Westminster/John Knox Press, 1993), pp. 188-201. On the difficulty of recovering the historical Jesus, see Clark M. Williamson and Ronald J. Allen, *Interpreting Difficult Texts* (London: SCM Press and Philadelphia: Trinity Press International, 1989), pp. 31-34.

40. For Waldemar Janzen's development of this notion, see pp. 193-209.

41. The portraits of Jesus in the Gospels (and material emanating from the church through the ages) contain an unfortunate element: antagonism against Jewish people, practices, and institutions. These must be exposed and critiqued as inappropriate to the good news of Jesus Christ. See Williamson and Allen, pp. 1-8, 28-56.

42. Schubert Ogden, *The Point of Christology* (San Francisco: Harper & Row, Publishers, 1982), pp. 58-59, passim.

43. Of course, this is only one way to understand the relationship of Jesus Christ, Judaism, and Gentiles in the first century and in Christian theology. For a crisp overview of thirteen different perspectives on this issue, see Gabriel Fackre, "Perspectives on the Place of Israel in the Christian Faith," *Andover Newton Review,* vol. 1, no. 2 (1990), pp. 7-17. Other helpful reviews are John T. Pawlikowski, *Christ in the Light of the Jewish-Christian Dialogue* (New York: Paulist Press, 1982), pp. 8-35 and Eugene J. Fisher, "Covenant Theology and Jewish-Christian Dialogue," *American Journal of Theology and Philosophy* 9 (1988), pp. 5-40.

3. Twelve Steps to the Sermon on the Old Testament

1. For a bibliography of books that present other approaches to exegetical and hermeneutical method, see Ronald J. Allen, *Preaching the Topical Sermon* (Louisville: Westminster/John Knox Press, 1992), pp. 146-47.

2. This chapter is not a comprehensive guide to exegesis of the First Testament. We highlight selected aspects of exegesis as they pertain to our focus. For further discussion of critical approaches, see the appropriate books in the annotated bibliography that deal specifically with exegesis of the First Testament, especially those by Achtemeier, Barton, Goldingay, Gowan, Greidanus, Holbert, Kaiser, Long, McCurley, McKenzie, Rhoads, and Rogerson.

3. The exegesis of this Psalm is widely debated. For representative studies with attention to the history of scholarship, see Leslie C. Allen, *Psalms 101–150.* Word Biblical Commentary (Waco: Word Books, 1983), pp. 83-87 and H. J. Kraus, *Psalms 60–150,* trans. Hilton C. Oswald (Minneapolis: Augsburg Press, 1989), pp. 343-55.

4. Gordon H. Matties, *Ezekiel 18 and the Rhetoric of Moral Discourse.* SBL Dissertation Series 126 (Atlanta: Scholars Press, 1990), pp. 11-21. This illustrates again the importance of considering texts on their own merits and not trying to force them unnaturally into a trajectory.

5. On the close relationship of form and meaning in texts and sermons, see John C. Holbert, *Preaching Old Testament* (Nashville: Abingdon Press, 1991); Don M. Wardlaw, ed., *Preaching Biblically* (Philadelphia: The Westminster Press, 1983); Sidney Greidanus, *The Modern Preacher and the Ancient Text* (Grand Rapids: Wm. B. Eerdmans Publishing Co., 1988); and Thomas G. Long, *Preaching and the Literary Forms of the Bible* (Philadelphia: Fortress Press, 1989).

6. For a fresh translation of the Psalms and practical help for their use, see John Holbert, S. T. Kimbrough, Jr., and Carlton R. Young, *Psalms for Praise and Worship* (Nashville: Abingdon Press, 1992).

7. Paul D. Hanson, *Dynamic Transcendence* (Philadelphia: Fortress Press, 1978), p. 74.

8. Ibid., pp. 74-75.

9. Charles Wesley, "Love Divine, All Loves Excelling," in *The United Methodist Hymnal* (Nashville: The United Methodist Publishing House, 1989), no. 384.

10. Alexander Campbell, *The Christian System* (Cincinnati: Standard Publishing House, 1901) pp. 4-5. Here, the term complacent means "unwarranted." Campbell's statement is the climax of his principles for biblical interpretation. The heart of the gospel is that God is love (pp. 90-91).

11. To be candid, not all theological communities will regard these as the essential issues or questions around which to center a conversation with a text. But each community will wrestle with such issues from the standpoint of its presiding theological vision and will ask, "Does the text offer today's community a vision of God and world that the community can embrace in the light of the community's deepest convictions about God and the community's best knowledge of the ways in which the world works? Contrariwise, does the text challenge these assumptions in ways that ought to be taken seriously?"

12. On these criteria, see Schubert Ogden, *The Point of Christology* (San Francisco: Harper & Row Publishers, 1982), pp. 89-96; David Tracy, *Blessed Rage for Order* (New York: The Seabury Press, 1975), pp. 71-81; Ronald J. Allen and Clark M. Williamson, *A Credible and Timely Word* (St. Louis: Chalice Press, 1992), pp. 71-120. David Watson, *God Does Not Foreclose: The Universal Promise of Salvation* (Nashville: Abingdon Press, 1990), contends that God's promise of salvation is universal but cautions that the Christianity community should avoid the trap of relativity, that is, of saying that universal love is the common denominator of all religions. We do not know enough about other religions to say whether or not universal love is common to all. The theological assumption of this first criterion is based on God's love as revealed through Israel and Jesus Christ.

13. John Goldingay offers eight models by which interpreters can affirm some viewpoints and criticize others in his *Theological Diversity and the Authority of the Old Testament* (Grand Rapids: Wm. B. Eerdmans Publishing Co., 1987), pp. 97-166.

14. For a critique of the notion of intelligibility, see Stanley Hauerwas and William Willimon, *Resident Aliens* (Nashville: Abingdon Press, 1989), pp. 19-24.

15. Howard Snyder, *EarthCurrents* (Nashville: Abingdon Press, 1995), identifies eight different wordview paradigms in philosophical and theological circles around the globe today.

16. Of course, one enters into a story (or some other kind of text) precisely by suspending disbelief, as pointed out by James Crenshaw, *Samson: A Secret Betrayed, A Vow Ignored* (Atlanta: John Knox Press, 1977), pp. 21-22. But when one emerges from the text, one must decide what is true (and how it is true) and what is not.

17. Hauerwas and Willimon particularly stress this point, p. 24.

18. For positive possibilities for preaching from such texts, see chapter 5.

19. For a fuller discussion of these matters, and bibliography, see chapter 6.

20. This is sometimes a delicate matter since three languages (Hebrew, Aramaic, and Greek) are involved. The Hebrew and Aramaic of the Old Testament are translated into Greek in the Septuagint and in the New Testament. The standard guide to following these movements is still Edwin Hatch and Henry Redpath, *A Concordance to the Septuagint* (Grand Rapids: Baker Book House, 1987, o.p. 1897). Pastors who do not read the biblical languages can still pay attention to how the Hebrew and Aramaic Old Testament makes its way in the New by using an English concordance that correlates the English translation with the ancient languages.

21. The most comprehensive study of Psalm 110 in the Second Testament is still David M. Hay, *Glory at the Right Hand.* Society of Biblical Literature Monograph Series 18 (Nashville: Abingdon Press, 1973); cf. Donald Juel, *Messianic Exegesis* (Minneapolis: Fortress Press, 1989), pp. 135-50.

22. Of course, Psalm 110 is not about general human institutions. The monarch played a special role in Israel: to represent the divine will in ordering human affairs. Thus, the exercise of monarchy is ideally a model for other institutions.

23. See Holbert, Greidanus, Long, and David G. Buttrick, *Homiletic* (Fortress Press, 1987), pp. 333-64.

4. Texts and Themes from the Old Testament

1. The term "theme" is not from the language of technical biblical scholarship. We use the word informally to speak of a motif, a reality, an idea, an image, a practice, a mode of thought, a value, or an expression found in several texts in the Hebrew Scriptures. When tracing a theme, the preacher must take care to honor the individuality of particular trajectories and texts. See Ronald J. Allen, "Preaching on a Theme from the Bible," *Pulpit Digest,* vol. 75, no. 526 (1994), pp. 78-86. The number of themes found in the First Testament is seemingly almost endless. However, a thematic investigation must be more than a word-study. It must take into account the literary, historical, and theological contexts of the material under study. Long ago James Barr debunked the word-study approach in *The Semantics of Biblical Language* (Oxford: Oxford University Press, 1961). For a fascinating development of the thematic approach, see Norbert Lohfink, *Great Themes from the Old Testament,* trans. Ronald Walls (Edinburgh: T & T Clark, 1982).

2. The easiest ways to locate themes (and the passages that illumine them) are to use a concordance or a Bible dictionary.

3. Genesis 1 is from the hands of the priestly writers in its present form; and it exhibits, *par excellence,* priestly theology. But its underlying conviction (that a sovereign God initiated the form of the world as we know it) is shared by the other trajectories (e.g., Deut. 32:6; Prov. 8:22; and Isa. 66:2).

4. For a helpful discussion of the traditions that underlie this text, see Brevard Childs, *Exodus* (Philadelphia: The Westminster Press, 1974), pp. 218-24.

5. Such a series could also incorporate texts from other trajectories to compare and contrast the priestly views with the views from other trajectories.

6. See John C. Holbert, " 'Deliverance Belongs to Yahweh': Satire in the Book of Jonah," *Journal for the Study of the Old Testament* 21 (1981), pp. 59-81 for a convenient summary of the major options.

7. James A. Sanders, *God Has a Story, Too* (Philadelphia: Fortress Press, 1974).

8. John C. Holbert, *Preaching Old Testament* (Nashville: Abingdon Press, 1991).

5. Texts That Apparently Offer Little or Nothing to the Christian Pulpit

1. See Lillian Passmore Sanderson, *Female Genital Mutilation: A Bibliography* (London: The Anti-Slavery Society for the Protection of Human Rights, 1986).

2. For a survey of theories concerning the origin of circumcision, see Julian Morgenstern, *Rites of Birth, Marriage and Death and Kindred Occasions Among the Semites* (Cincinnati: Hebrew Union College Press, 1966), pp. 48-80.

3. Scholarly discussion on circumcision in the Second Testament is immense. As examples of the need to honor the complexities of the early Christian witnesses, see Raymond E. Brown, "Not Jewish Christianity and Gentile Christianity but Types of Jewish/Gentile Christianity," *Catholic Biblical Quarterly* 43 (1983), pp. 74-79 and Paula Fredricksen, "Judaism, the Circumcision of Gentiles and Apocalyptic Hope: Another Look at Galatians 1 and 2," *Journal of Theological Studies* 42 (1991), pp. 532-64.

4. This discussion continues into the present. Some contemporary Jewish people (notably in the Reform and Reconstructionist Movements) do not insist on maintaining traditional dietary habits. See, for example, *American Reform Response,* ed. Walter Jacob (New York: Central Conference of American Rabbis, 5743 [1983]), pp. 128-31.

5. For a succinct overview of theories, see John Hartley, *Leviticus.* Word Biblical Commentary (Dallas: Word Books, 1992), pp. 142-46.

6. Ronald E. Clements, *God's Chosen People* (Valley Forge: Judson Press, 1968), p. 33.

7. Mary Douglas, *Purity and Danger* (New York: Praeger Publishers, 1966), p. 55.

8. Patrick D. Miller, Jr., *Deuteronomy.* Interpretation: A Bible Commentary for Preaching and Teaching (Louisville: John Knox Press, 1990), p. 162.

9. Douglas, p. 57.

10. For example, see Menachem Haran, *Temples and Temple Service in Ancient Israel* (Winona Lake: Eisenbrauns, 1985), p. 256.

11. For example, see Richard J. Clifford, *The Cosmic Mountain in Canaan and the Old Testament* (Cambridge: Harvard University Press, 1972), pp. 171-81.

12. Jon D. Levenson, *Sinai and Zion* (New York: Winston Press, 1985), p. 175.

13. The Jewish people did not universally endorse the temple. Within the Hebrew Bible, for example, the Rekabites (Jeremiah 35) did not recognize the validity of the temple. Some scholars think that Third Isaiah was a trenchant critic of the temple. For example, Paul D. Hanson, *The Dawn of Apocalyptic* (Philadelphia: Fortress Press, 1975), pp. 177-79; compare pp. 245-47. Note also the critical view of Walter Brueggemann, *1 Kings*. Knox Preaching Guides (Atlanta: John Knox Press, 1982), pp. 23-32.

14. Gary Anderson notes that the rebuilding of the temple not only lifts the curse from the land but reestablishes a mechanism to collect and redistribute grain, the latter being necessary for prosperity. Gary A. Anderson, *Sacrifices and Offerings in Ancient Israel: Studies in their Social and Political Importance* (Atlanta: Scholars' Press, 1987), pp. 91-126.

15. For a survey of scholarly discussion and attitudes towards the temple in the Second Testament, see James D. G. Dunn, *The Partings of the Ways* (London: SCM Press and Philadelphia: Trinity Press International, 1991), pp. 33-97.

16. For an orientation to sacrificial theory, see Hartley, pp. lxvii-lxxiii.

17. For a brief overview of theories on the origin of sacrifice, see Josph Henninger, "Sacrifice," *The Encyclopedia of Religion,* ed. by Mircea Eliade (New York: Macmillan, 1987), vol. 12, pp. 550-54.

18. Donald E. Gowan, *Reclaiming the Old Testament for the Christian Pulpit* (Atlanta: John Knox Press, 1980), p. 96.

19. Our formulation describes the work of blood sacrifice in a very simple way. Recent years have seen more detailed reflections on blood sacrifice and cultic violence. For a representative discussion, see René Girard, *Violence and the Sacred* (Baltimore: Johns Hopkins University Press, 1977); Robert Hammerton-Kelly, *Sacred Violence: Paul's Hermeneutic of the Cross* (Minneapolis: Fortress Press, 1992).

20. For a survey of interpretations on the relationship between the sacrifice and God, see Hartley, pp. 63-66, 257-77.

21. Gowan, p. 98.

22. Victor Turner, *The Forest of Symbols* (Ithaca: Cornell University Press, 1967), pp. 29-39.

23. For examples, see Roland de Vaux, *Ancient Israel,* trans. John McHug (New York: McGraw-Hill Book Co., 1965), pp. 454-56 and Gary Anderson, "Sacrifice and Sacrificial Offerings (OT)," *The Anchor Bible Dictionary,* ed. David Noel Freedman, et al. (Garden City, N.Y.: Doubleday, 1992), vol. 5, pp. 881-82.

24. Scholarly literature on this subject is vast. For a traditional summary of positions in the period of the Second Temple (with judicious discussion of scholarship), see Earl Richard, *Jesus: One and Many* (Wilmington: Michael Glazier Press, 1988). For an interesting typology see Arland Hultgren, Jr., *Christ and His Benefits* (Philadelphia: Fortress Press, 1987). Still a staple is Gustaf Aulen, *Christus Victor* (New York: Macmillan, 1969). For a survey of approaches to Christology, see John Macquarrie, *Jesus Christ in Modern Thought* (Philadelphia: Trinity Press International, 1990). For a feminist statement, see Rita Nakashima Brock, *Journeys by Heart* (New York: Crossroad Publishing Co., 1988), esp. pp. 90-100.

25. Waldemar Janzen, *Old Testament Ethics: A Paradigmatic Approach* (Louisville, Westminster/John Knox Press, 1994), pp. 107-8.

26. For a discussion of purposes of holy war, see the bibliography in Gerhard von Rad, *Holy War in Ancient Israel,* trans. Marva Dawn (Grand Rapids: Wm. B. Eerdmans Publishing Co., 1991), pp. 135-66.

27. Texts in the Wisdom literature also manifest an act-consequence ethic in which an action results in judgment (for example Prov. 5:1-23; 6:20-35). But the prophets typically presume the deuteronomic or priestly paradigms.

28. A few of the prophets regard the situation of their day as so dire that it is beyond the possibility of repentance. Note our discussion of Micah 6 in chapter 4. But even when it is too late for repentance to avert national calamity, God promises to preserve a remnant (e.g., Mic. 4:6-7; Zeph. 2:5-7; Jer. 23:1-4).

29. Bernhard W. Anderson, *Understanding the Old Testament* 4th ed. (Englewood Cliffs: Prentice-Hall, 1986), p. 402.

30. According to process theology, God is not able unilaterally to effect changes in situation but offers for each situation a higher possible aim that those in the situation can reject, adapt, or accept. A community may make bad choices that point to destruction. However, all along the way, God continually offers the community the possibility of choices that can lead to its renewal. God does not abandon or withdraw. For a popular presentation of God's modes of activity from the standpoint of process thought, see Robert Brizee, *Where in the World is God?* (Nashville: The Upper Room, 1987). Other theological viewpoints understand these matters differently.

31. George Mendenhall, *The Tenth Generation* (Baltimore: Johns Hopkins University Press, 1973), pp. 69-104. See further, Walter Brueggemann, *Praying the Psalms* (Winona, Minn.: St. Mary's Press, 1982), pp. 67-79.

32. James A. Sanders, "Enemy," *The Interpreter's Dictionary of the Bible,* ed. George A. Buttrick, et al. (Nashville: Abingdon Press, 1964), vol. 2, p. 101.

33. Carroll Stuhlmueller, *Psalms 1* (Wilmington, Del.: Michael Glazier Publishing Co., 1983), p. 313; *Psalms 2* (Michael Glazier Publishing Co., 1983), p. 190.

6. When the Testaments Come Together

1. Henry M. Shires. *Finding the Old Testament in the New* (Philadelphia: The Westminster Press, 1974), p. 15.

2. A list of major New Testament citations and allusions to the literature of Second Temple Judaism (the Apocrypha and the Pseudepigrapha) is found in *The Text of the New Testament,* ed. Kurt Aland and Barbara Aland (Grand Rapids: Wm. B. Eerdmans Publishing Co., 1979), pp. 769-75 and adapted in Lee Martin McDonald, *The Formation of the Christian Biblical Canon* (Nashville: Abingdon Press, 1988), pp. 172-77.

3. For a bibliography on this discussion, see, for example, E. Earle Ellis, *The Old Testament in Early Christianity* (Tuebingen: J. C. B. Mohr, 1991).

4. C. H. Dodd, *According to the Scriptures* (New York: Charles Scribner's Sons, 1953), p. 126. The most influential development of Dodd's thesis is Barnabas Lindars, *New Testament Apologetic* (Philadelphia: The Westminster Press, 1961).

5. For examples of this shifting perspective, see Donald Juel, *Messianic Exegesis* (Minneapolis: Fortress Press, 1988) and Richard B. Hays, *Echoes of Scripture in the Letters of Paul* (New Haven: Yale University Press, 1989).

6. Christopher Stanley, *Paul and the Language of Scripture* (Cambridge: Cambridge University Press, 1992), p. 29.

7. For examples of positions in this discussion, see I. Howard Marshall, "An Assessment of Recent Developments" in *It Is Written,* ed. D. A. Carson and H. G. M. Williamson (Cambridge: Cambridge University Press, 1988), pp. 7-9.

8. The early church also employed interpretive and literary techniques from Hellenism.

9. For more elaborate typologies of the relationship between the testaments, see Marshall, p. 10; James Barr, *Old and New in Interpretation* (London: SCM Press, 1966); Foster R. McCurley, *Proclaiming the Promise* (Philadelphia: Fortress Press, 1974), pp. 15-18; S. W. Mayo, *The Relevance of the Old Testament for the Christian Faith* (Lanham: University Press of America, 1982).

10. Hays, p. 16.

11. Ibid., pp. 18-21, 23-24. Hays delineates seven criteria for determining the presence of echoes, pp. 29-32.

12. Phyllis Trible, *God and the Rhetoric of Sexuality* (Philadelphia: Fortress Press, 1978), pp. 105-15.

13. Dodd, p. 127.

14. For a discussion of typology, see chapter 1.

15. See further J. J. M. Roberts, "A Christian Perspective on Prophetic Prediction," *Interpretation* 33 (1979), pp. 241-53.

16. Richard Longenecker, *Biblical Exegesis in the Apostolic Period* (Wm. B. Eerdmans Publishing Co., 1975), pp. 93-95, notices four exegetical presuppositions that help explain the early church's use of Old Testament texts: corporate solidarity, correspondence in history, eschatological fulfillment, and messianic presence.

17. For reviews of this discussion, see James D. G. Dunn, *The Partings of the Ways* (London: SCM Press and Philadelphia: Trinity Press International, 1991), pp. 1-18, and Craig Evans and Donald Hagner, eds., *Anti-Semitism and Early Christianity* (Minneapolis: Fortress Press, 1993); Norman A. Beck, *Mature Christianity in the Twenty-First Century: A Recognition and Repudiation of the Anti-Jewish Polemic in the New Testament,* revised and expanded edition (New York: Crossroad Publishing Co., 1994); George M. Smiga, *Pain and Polemic in the Gospels* (New York: Paulist Press, 1992).

18. Clark M. Williamson and Ronald J. Allen, *Interpreting Difficult Texts* (London: SCM Press and Philadelphia: Trinity Press International, 1991), p. 2.

19. The Consultation on Common Texts, *The Revised Common Lectionary* (Nashville: Abingdon Press, 1992).

20. For comprehensive examination of the lectionary see Eugene L. Lowry, *Living with the Lectionary* (Nashville: Abingdon Press, 1992), and Shelly Cochran, *Liturgical Hermeneutics* (unpublished Ph.D. Dissertation, Drew University, 1990).

21. If the sermon centers on only one text, the other lections are often read aloud but not interpreted. Some of the passages that are only read aloud may raise serious questions in the listeners. If so, the lector may want to offer brief interpretive comments at the time of the reading, which develop the ancient and contemporary significance of the reading.

22. *The Revised Common Lectionary,* p. 12.

23. James A. Sanders, "Canon and Calendar: An Alternative Lectionary Proposal," in *Social Themes of the Christian Year,* edited by Dieter Hessel (Philadelphia: The Geneva Press, 1983), pp. 257-63.

7. Five Kinds of Sermons

1. On this type of narrative preaching, see John C. Holbert, *Preaching Old Testament* (Nashville: Abingdon Press, 1991).

2. Sue McDougal, "A Story of Respite" in *Saints and Neighbors,* ed. Britton Johnston and Sally Johnson (Chicago: Center for Church and Community Ministries, 1991), pp. 67-70.

3. Charles Wesley, "Love Divine, All Loves Excelling" in *The United Methodist Hymnal,* no. 384 (Nashville: The United Methodist Publishing House, 1989).

4. C. Austin Miles, "I Come to the Garden Alone," in *The Hymnal for Worship and Celebration* (Waco: Word Music, 1986), p. 425.

SUBJECT INDEX

INDEX

dietary laws, 44-46, 60-61, 110-14

differences between Judaism and Christianity, 60-61

disobedience, 38-43, 125-28

echoes of OT and other Jewish writings in NT, 75-77, 132-41

Eden, 37, 64, 139

emotion released by biblical symbol, 116-17

ethnic Israel (vs. universal church), 21-22

exegetical method, 63-84

experience as theological source, 52-53

experience of text in its literary genre, 70-71

external/internal dichotomy, 20-21

feminine, wisdom as, 52

"Fire that Separates and Supports, The" (sermon), 177-83)

First Testament
alluded to by Second, 135-45
as designation for OT, 12-13
correcting Second in lectionary, 149

form for sermon, 82-84

four trajectories in OT, survey of, 38-58

"Future for Levirate Marriage, A" (sermon) 158-65

genre of text as clue to sermon, 82-84

gentiles, 19, 21, 26, 29-30, 60, 106, 110, 142

God
creator, 86-87
integrity of, 100-101
of Israel and of Jesus Christ, 29-31
judgment upon Israel, 125-28
judgment upon nations, 125-28
not responsible for actively inflicting destruction 125-26
power of, 88-90
redeemer, 87-88
as sovereign of universe, 36-38

gospel
as criterion for evaluating texts, 72-74, 121-31

and law, 17-20
summary of, 29, 71

Greek Bible, as designation for NT, 13

Hebrew Bible, as designation for OT, 12-13

Hebrew Scriptures, as designation for, OT, 12-13

hermeneutics, 34-36, passim

hesed (steadfast love), 85-95, 106, 121

historical context, determination of, 68

holiness
in deuteronomic trajectory, 107-109
way of (Priestly trajectory), 43-47

hope, radical (apocalyptic trajectory), 53-58

idolatry 112-13

imperative, relationship to indicative, 39-40, 80-81

imprecations, 74-75, 128-131

inappropriateness to gospel, (criterion of) 72-73, 118-30

indicative
importance of, in preaching, 80-81
precedes imperative 39-40, 80-81

interpretation of OT by NT, 75, 132-51

Israel, deliverance of 95-99

"Is This All There Is?" (sermon), 165-72

Jerusalem, temple of 114-17

Jesus Christ
coming again (second coming, parousia) 10, 26-27, 53-56, 59, 140-41
commandment to love in continuity with Israel, 40
and First Testament, 33-34, 58-59, 61-62, 106, 132-51
as fulfillment of promises to Abraham and Sarah, 26, 77
and God of Israel, 10, 16, 26, 29-30, 33-34, 40, 58, 61-62, 90, 95, 99, 134
as interpreter of traditions of Israel, 20-21, 142, 149, 177-83

206

INDEX

INDEX

texts
  offering little or nothing to the Christian pulpit, 107-31
  depicting the brutal treatment without censure, 123-24
  witness (vision) of, 35, 71
themes in OT, defined and illustrated 85-106
theological method, 72-75, 102-103
thinking analogically, 34-36, 80-81
"To Be a Pilgrim" (sermon), 172-83
torah, 13, 18, 143
trajectories, 38-58
tsadaqah (justice), 100
two testaments and the contemporary church, 58-61
typology, 24-26, 31, 98, 133, 139-40, 148, 149-50

unconditional love of God, 29-30, 109-10, 120, 121, 122
unintelligibility (criterion of), 71-74, 121-31
universal church (in contrast to ethnic Israel), 21-22

universal sovereignty of God, 36-38
use of OT by NT, 132-51

vengeance, 128-31
vicious portrayals of divine activity, 123-28
violence in NT, 121
vision (witness) of text, 70-71

way of holiness (priestly trajectory), 43-47
Wisdom, 47-53
witness (vision) of a text, 34-35
  deeper, 35, 48, 55, 62, 70-71, 73, 77, 78, 99, 106, 107, 110, 114, 160, 163, 181
  surface, 35, 55, 65, 70-71, 73, 98, 106, 107, 110, 113, 126, 151
Wonderful World of the First Testament, 28
works righteousness, 39, 98-100, 107-108, 117, 143

Zion, 114-17

209

SCRIPTURE INDEX

INDEX